EMPOWERING YOUR CHILD TO FLY

A Family's Guide to Early Childhood Inclusion

JANI KOZLOWSKI, MA

Copyright

Published by Gryphon House, Inc.
P. O. Box 10, Lewisville, NC 27023
800.638.0928; 877.638.7576 [fax]

Visit us on the web at www.gryphonhouse.com.

Library of Congress Control Number: 2023945472

Bulk Purchase

Gryphon House books are available for special premiums and sales promotions as well as for fund-raising use. Special editions or book excerpts also can be created to specifications. For details, call 800.638.0928.

Disclaimer

Gryphon House, Inc., cannot be held responsible for damage, mishap, or injury incurred during the use of or because of activities in this book. Appropriate and reasonable caution and adult supervision of children involved in activities and corresponding to the age and capability of each child involved are recommended at all times. Do not leave children unattended at any time. Observe safety and caution at all times.

This book is not intended to give legal advice. All legal opinions contained herein are from the personal research and experience of the author and are intended as educational material. Seek the advice of a qualified legal advisor before making legal decisions.

TABLE OF CONTENTS

Preface

In 2022, I fulfilled a lifelong dream to write a book about early childhood inclusion and my personal and professional experiences.

I am an early childhood educator with a disability.

I am the daughter of a parent with a disability.

I am the mother of a son with a disability.

That book is called *Every Child Can Fly: An Early Childhood Educator's Guide to Inclusion.*

It's filled with stories from my own experiences in life as a mother, as a pre-K teacher in the classroom, and through my work as a speaker and technical assistance provider for early intervention, early childhood special-education programs, Head Start and child-care programs, and state-level early childhood leaders.

Because of these personal and professional perspectives, I decided to write that book to support early childhood educators to feel confident and competent in serving all children, including children with disabilities or suspected delays. When I wrote *Every Child Can Fly*, I didn't let my husband read it until after it had gone to print. I didn't want to question myself, worry that I revealed too much or too little, or get his story of our parenting journey mixed up with mine. So ultimately, he read the book in its entirety after it was a done deal. One thing that really resonated with me was that he said how helpful the book would have been during the time that we were "in the thick of it" ourselves as parents of a child with a disability.

I stepped out of my comfort zone when writing that book, because in it I shared that I was born with a rare orthopedic impairment called *Spondylometaphyseal dysplasia* or SMD. It is a form of dwarfism, and I stand at four feet six inches tall. I am a "little person," which is the preferred term for many people in the United States who have the medical condition of dwarfism. SMD is a relatively "tall" form of dwarfism. Many little people have shorter arms and legs, but my arms and legs are proportional to the rest of my body. People typically regard me as just a petite lady, albeit a *very* petite lady. In addition to being a little person, I have significant curvature in my spine and have dealt with pain in my joints throughout my life. Many months of my childhood were spent in recovery mode from more than twenty orthopedic surgeries. I had a few surgeries that included recovery in something called a spica cast, which is a cast that starts right under the armpits and goes all the way down to the toes. In seventh grade, and again during my senior year of high school, I had a type of surgery called a spinal fusion. Due to the curvature in my spine, the doctors had to "fuse" vertebrae together so my spinal cord would be protected. As a result, I spent several months of my senior year wearing a medical device called a halo as I recovered.

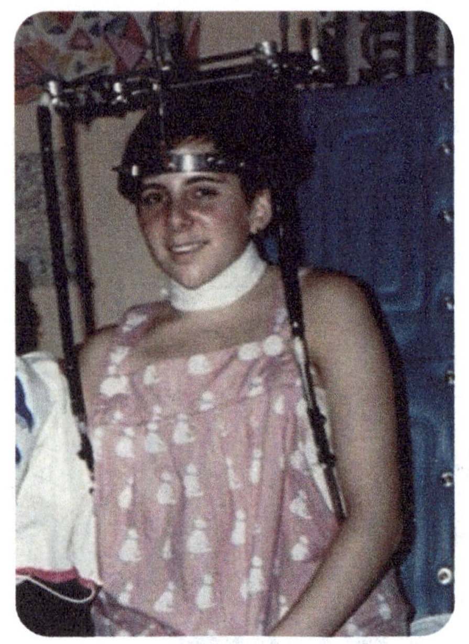

In college, I had my first hip-replacement surgery and used crutches for a time as I walked around on campus. I refused to use a handicap sign in my car because I didn't want people to think that I was "handicapped." I struggled a great deal to be seen the same as everyone else, as most children do. These experiences shaped me as a person, and I am proud of the fact that I have been able to overcome many challenges. Over time, I have even learned strategies for coping with the stares. Being a little person with a big smile is very powerful. My size makes people look at me, and my smile disarms them. They mostly smile back. Children almost always smile back.

As an adult, I now have artificial joint replacements in my hips, knees, and ankles. My legs are bionic. My spine is fused from the base of my skull to the middle of my back. I cannot turn my head from side to side or up and down. I use my torso to turn my head. Sometimes I feel as though my skeletal system is a jigsaw puzzle with pieces that don't quite fit together. I'm kinda funky on the inside, in ways that you would know only from looking at an X-ray.

SMD is a condition that I have, but it is not who I am. It has been significant in my life, however, because of all of the surgeries and because it affects my height and my joints and my spine. I have had some very difficult experiences living as a little person in this world, mainly because I look different from everybody else. Even though I have achieved a great deal of success in my life as an early childhood professional, as a wife, and as a mother, the truth is that people still stare at me in the grocery store. Out in public, people judge me by my size and my disability.

I inherited SMD from my father, so he was also a little person and had difficulty walking. My mother would pull us around in a little red wagon on long walks.

My dad dealt with many of the same struggles as I have and overcame many challenges. My father was born and grew up in Buenos Aires, Argentina. In the Latin culture, it is especially difficult to be a short-statured man, but my father didn't let his height affect his dreams. He was a motivated student and successfully graduated from medical school.

When my parents decided to have a child, they went to many doctors to find out if there was a chance that my father's condition could be passed down to his offspring. They were told not to worry, that my dad's condition was not genetically inherited. Years before in Argentina, he had been told that his condition was called rickets, which is caused by a lack of vitamin D in childhood. Even though my father was a doctor himself, he was terrified of having surgery and didn't really follow up on his own health care or even ask that much about it. My mother became pregnant without concern. At first all was well, although I was born prematurely and weighed only three pounds, three ounces at birth. I had to be in the intensive care unit for quite some time before my parents could bring me home, but other than that they didn't think that there would be any issues. For a time, that was true.

As a child, I viewed disability through the lens of how other people reacted to my father when they first met him and how he responded to those reactions. His strategy was basically not to take himself too seriously. My father was a psychiatrist and jokingly called himself "The Shrink." He even had a personalized license plate on his car that read SHRINK, and he loved it that people laughed every time he got out of the car. Like me, he rejected the notion of the label of *handicapped* and taught me how to disarm awkwardness through a smile or joke. He taught me not to worry so much about the stares because they were just human nature. He said that the world is like a field of blue flowers, and when a pink flower appears in the field, what do you do? You look at it!

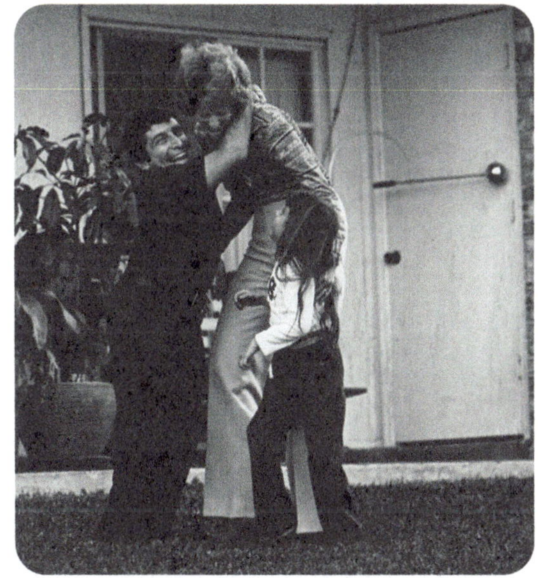

My parents doted on me. I was a princess to my father and mother. Both of my parents showered me with love and attention, for which I will be forever grateful. I always felt cherished.

It was only over time that my parents learned that I have the same skeletal issues as my father. As a result, my father learned the truth of his own condition through the process of finding out how best to care for his child. And through it all, my mother cared for both of us. My father dealt with a great deal of guilt throughout his life because he felt responsible for my disability.

I often think of the Smokey Robinson song "The Tears of a Clown" when I think of my him. He presented a happy and secure exterior, but I wonder if that was a mask for his true feelings. Were there tears when no one was around? My father had a large personality, which may have been to compensate for his small stature. It's hard to know exactly how he felt because my father died many years ago. My mother was there for me through it all. She remarried and found happiness with my stepfather and is a doting granny to my son.

My dad had a lot of demons. His work was listening to other people's problems. He lived with a lot of physical pain. People always stared, and he lived with the effort of trying to make it seem that everything was okay. I think that my dad also could not stand to see the struggles that I experienced. My mother once told me that before a surgery, my dad would say, "This is all my fault." I remember going into the operating room once and telling the doctor to please tell my dad that it's not his fault. Now as an adult, I can imagine the immense guilt and pain that it must have brought him. As a mother myself, I can't even fathom how difficult that must have been. For some parents, guilt is the biggest feeling they have when they learn that their child has a disability.

Our son, Ricky, was born in Ukraine, and we adopted him when he was seventeen months old. Ricky overcame many obstacles from those early months of deprivation in the orphanage, and later he dealt with attention deficit hyperactivity disorder (ADHD). ADHD is marked by inattention (difficulty with maintaining focus), impulsivity (acting hastily), and being overly active. He received special education services throughout his school years, and Ricky is a successful young adult today. I learned a great deal from him throughout his childhood and continue to learn from him. He is resilience personified! The experience of raising a child with a disability taught me about the importance of maintaining high expectations for children, even when we want to protect them from frustration or disappointment. Ricky is an amazing person, and I am a very proud mama. But those struggles during his childhood were difficult for our family.

Ultimately, my husband did read my first book, and afterwards he said, "Jan, you have to adapt this for families. They need this information too." This seemed like an exciting opportunity. How can I take the information from *Every Child Can Fly,* a book for early childhood educators, and reframe it to share with families? Thinking about this reminded me of a story I told at the beginning of the first book about Valentine's Day. It went something like this:

> ***When I was in preschool, I had been out of school for a couple of months for a surgery and my recovery. The recovery involved a spica cast, and I was unable to walk, stand, or even sit up in a chair.***
>
> ***Being away from school for multiple weeks seemed like a really long time to me as a child. My teacher reached out and asked whether my mother might be able to bring me to school to celebrate Valentine's Day with the class. My mom thought it was a great idea because she knew how much I missed my friends and how much I loved Valentine's Day. I loved the candy hearts and cupcakes with pink frosting. I loved the little foldable cards***

sealed with a sticker or lollipop. I loved the mailboxes that we used to make. We would trade valentines with everyone in the class, and everyone decorated a mailbox for their cards. I loved it all.

I remember feeling nervous about going into the classroom after what felt like such a long time. Because of the spica cast, my mother had to carry me around everywhere. As you might imagine, I worried about what would happen when my friends saw me in my body cast. Would they stare at me? Would they even remember me? But my mother felt that it was important for me to reconnect with my friends at school. She and my teacher assured me that it would be fine. And you know what? It was fine. It was better than fine, because not only did I have my own Valentine's Day mailbox, but everyone had made me a valentine. While this is not really a story of the common definition of inclusion, it is a story about a time when I felt included. It is a story about membership. It is a story about belonging. It is a story about supporting a child to build friendships and connect with her peers.

Now that I've had time to reflect (and tell that story a gazillion times in presentations), I see the point of the story a little bit differently. Think about this story from a child's perspective. Or shall I say, think about it from a *self-conscious* child's perspective. Sure, I loved Valentine's Day, but did I really love it so much that I wanted to be in the spotlight in front of my friends, wearing a full-length body cast? To be carried into the classroom by my *mother?* As a kid, what I wanted more than anything was just to fit in. To be just like everyone else. I didn't like being different, and certainly not *special.* I hated the stares. I hated when I overheard other children ask their parents, "What's wrong with her?" So, I'm pretty sure that the thought of returning to school mid-recovery was daunting to me at best.

But the story cannot be understood without thinking about it from my mother's perspective too. She wanted me to see my friends. She wanted me to have some fun. She wanted me to feel that sense of belonging and love. But I know my mother, and one of the best gifts she ever gave me was the gift of determination. She knew that if I were going to be successful in this world, or even just okay in this world, I would need some fierce determination.

I was going to need some serious grit and resilience. I was going to need to be the kind of child who faced her fears and even became friends with feeling uncomfortable. My mom knew that I needed to learn how to be the kind of child who went to the party wearing a smile and carrying thirty little pink cards adorned with lollipops. While writing this book, I asked my mom to share some of her thoughts and memories from that time. What advice would she give to parents who are "in the thick of it?" She said, "Don't do anything for your child that he or she can do for themselves. Encourage independence, celebrate the successes, and look forward to the next milestone." Very solid advice!

When I became a mother myself and then learned that my child also has a disability, I found myself up against quite a paradox. My own mother's gift of determination was always on my mind when I parented our son. Yet, I struggled with a strong Mama Bear tendency. My nature is to nurture. More than anything when my son was younger, I wanted to protect Ricky from pain. I didn't want him to feel uncomfortable, and when he expressed fear, my instinct was to figure out how to remove the fearful thing.

I'm not proud of this tendency I had as a parent. Fortunately, my husband was more of the "gift of determination" type of parent, and always held the highest expectations of Ricky. My husband had the confidence in our son that he would be able to figure things out for himself. Rick knew that Ricky could be uncomfortable or fearful in a situation and find his own inner resources to plow right through. Our son received the underlying message of this parenting approach as "You are capable. You are competent. You can do hard things. I believe in you."

Rick was also more likely to be the one challenging Ricky to solve problems rather than just giving him the answer. He would suggest that Ricky think about the options or possible solutions, and I typically would sit there and stew because I could tell that the problem solving was making Ricky uncomfortable. Figuring out solutions is hard work!

This Mama Bear tendency continues for me to this day. For example, I'm more inclined to cook something for Ricky rather than teach him how to cook the meal. I'm more likely to do his laundry for him than to force him to do it himself. There are pros and cons to both of our inclinations. Ricky never questions whether his Mom will be there with nurturing, love, attention, and care. Those are constants in his life. My husband is certainly nurturing and caring in his own way, but he also is more likely to make Ricky do his own laundry or cook his own food. Pretty reasonable expectations for a young adult, don't you think? We have found that the collaboration between the two of us that comes from our different styles of parenting is beneficial and supportive. Neither Rick nor I am the "perfect" parent. We have our strengths and blind spots when it comes to parenting. One important consideration, however, is that a child can benefit from all the different approaches through collaboration with other adults in their life. These collaborations can happen through parent-to-parent relationships as well as relationships with other important adults, such as family members, friends, educators, and other professionals.

Through the perspectives I hold, and through the strategies I have learned from others, I hope to share with you both the practical and the personal: practical strategies for navigating the early intervention and early childhood special education systems, along with my own personal stories as a mother and wife, as a daughter, and as an educator. Supporting children with disabilities and their families is a passion for me. I have dedicated my professional career to early childhood education, and I care deeply about young children of all abilities. I know that you are reading this book because there is a child in your life whom you love dearly who may have just been born or recently diagnosed or may have started doing or saying things that worry you. The early years are a critical period of child development. Children develop rapidly during the first five years of life, and for children with disabilities the early experiences in our education system can be consequential. I hope this book will give you some answers to your questions and ideas as to how to navigate the complicated systems of early intervention and early childhood special education. This can be an uncertain time for parents and families, and I hope that this book will ease some of your worries.

One thing that I remind myself of during times of uncertainty is that the need for acceptance and belonging is universal. Each of us is unique. We are each living in a body that we did not choose. We all face challenges. We each bring something to give to this world, and we all are important partners in ensuring the success of the next generation. Children depend on us to get it right. They depend on us to know that we are all worthy of love, happiness, and the opportunity to achieve our greatest potential.

Acknowledgments

This book would not have been possible without the help of a group of families who agreed to let me interview them so that I could share their stories and photos throughout these pages. Family stories bring the content to life, and I am forever grateful that they have shared their stories with me and with the readers! My heart overflows with gratitude and love for these spectacular humans.

Andie Amosson
Olivier and Hilda Bernier
Arielle Branch
Judy David
Kristin Jones
Jaclyn Joseph
Terri Leyton
Amanda Lovette
Jacquece Moore-Law
Leah Mullen
Patricia Reedy
Ben Riepe
Eileen Spahl
Latisha Stuckey
Paulina Vargas

This book has been a labor of love involving my immediate and extended family, friends, and colleagues. I would like to thank all the people who supported me along the way.

My dear husband, Rick, thank you for supporting me with love, words of encouragement, and endless acts of picking up the slack around the house when I was, as you say, "in the zone."

My adored (and adorable!) son, Ricky, thank you for giving me the gift of motherhood and for the greatest gift of all, the chance to be your mother. You are the inspiration for this book and the reason behind my passion for this work!

My mother, Eileen, and stepfather, George, thank you for patiently listening to every detail with so much love and support as I negotiated my way through the writing process.

My friends near and far, colleagues current and past, too many to name, who encouraged me, shared stories from their own experiences to use in this book.

My colleagues and friends who agreed to review all or a portion of this manuscript. Your comments and suggestions were so valuable.

My editor, Stephanie Roselli, for her guidance and patience as I asked for too many extensions and hoped for too many photos to be included in this book. She is an editing master.

You all inspire me daily. Thank you for helping to make this book come to life, and for sharing in my joyous passion for inclusion for young children and their families. We are a mighty fleet!

Introduction

"Inclusion is not a 'place' but a culture that we create when practices are based on rights, inclusive belonging, and contribution."

—PATRICIA HAMPSHIRE AND PATRICK MALLORY (2021)

While writing *Every Child Can Fly: An Early Childhood Educator's Guide to Inclusion,* I spent lots of time thinking about families and the relationships between families and educators. What are the most important components in the family-educator relationship? What makes for a successful partnership? Those questions then led me to think specifically about the family in this whole dynamic. What would have helped me the most during that challenging time when we were "in the thick of it" with our own young child?

This book is an attempt to answer that question. Although almost as soon as I began to write this book, I wondered: How can I answer those questions for families when my experience was only just that, *my* experience? The experience of one mom is not anywhere near the experience of every parent and family—and our experience is unique to boot! As I shared earlier, we became parents through adoption, so I do not have the experience of giving birth or of parenting a child younger

than seventeen months of age. In addition, Rick and I are a white, middle-class, English-speaking, U.S.–citizen, heterosexual couple and have the lens that those characteristics allow. Our viewpoints, therefore, are limited—a single story. Experiences of children and families are varied and diverse. As Nigerian writer Chimamanda Adichie says, "The single story creates stereotypes, and the problem with stereotypes is not that they are untrue, but that they are incomplete. They make one story become the only story" (Adichie, 2016). Adichie reflects that stories matter, but also that many stories matter. I believe that all experiences of children with disabilities and their families matter, so it was critical to include other family perspectives in the creation of this book.

Ultimately, fifteen families agreed to be interviewed. Their stories are woven throughout these pages and the reflections they shared with me also informed decisions about the kind of content to include. Even still, not every viewpoint is represented here. We know that all families are different and unique. You may be in this role as a single parent, grandparent, sibling, stepparent, foster parent, or as a related or unrelated auntie or uncle. I believe that family members, guardians, and friends of the family often serve the same important role as our traditional notion of the parent. Therefore, I have elected to use the terms *parent* and *family member* interchangeably throughout these pages. Whether a parent is biological, adoptive, assigned, or chosen, the function of the role remains the same and should be respected as such.

I believe that families can learn some of the most important lessons from other families, so you'll find family stories, photos, quotes, and lessons learned throughout this book. The stories I was fortunate to capture reveal a fierce love for children. A common thread throughout our stories is the passion we feel for lifting this young child high to the sky in the hope that the world will one day benefit from the amazing gifts the child will contribute.

These were the prompts and questions I used in my family interviews:

1. Tell me about your child.
2. If you could describe your child in three words, what would they be?
3. What are your child's greatest strengths? How do they use those strengths to help them reach their goals?
4. What has been a great success that your child achieved?
5. What were/are your hopes and dreams for your child? Did you have a vision for them early on? How did that develop?
6. What were/are your fears and worries?
7. Tell me about an important memory from your parenting experience.
8. What is your happiest memory? When did you feel the proudest?

9. When was a time that you felt the most grief or sadness? How did you cope?
10. If you could do it all over again, what would you do differently?
11. If you could share one lesson you learned from your parenting experience with other parents going through it right now, what would it be?

To say that I learned a lot from the interviews is the understatement of the year! My worldview of early childhood shifted over the course of these conversations, and I have been in the early childhood education field for more than thirty years.

MY STORY

My work in the field started when I worked as a preschool teacher for a diverse and spirited group of four-year-olds. Actually, I started out in the field when I worked as a nanny all through college. Yes, I was Jani the Nanny. The energy that young children bring to the world has always inspired me. Being around children makes me happy! Even as a child myself, I had always wanted to be a teacher. For a time, I was just a little intimidated by children who are taller than me, so teaching preschool fit the bill. Each child came to my classroom with unique strengths and abilities that unfolded before my eyes throughout our time together.

That journey led me to support Head Start teachers as an education and disability services manager, and later to provide support through workshops and technical assistance to Head Start programs across the country. I taught at a community college, and later I designed child-care quality initiatives and drafted policy as an administrator in the North Carolina Division of Child Development and Early Education. Then, I supported other child-care leaders to do the same. About ten years ago, I started working at the national level, providing technical assistance for leaders through projects funded by the federal Office of Head Start and Office of Child Care within the Department of Health and Human Services, Administration for Children and Families. Now I serve as a technical-assistance specialist for the Early Childhood Technical Assistance (ECTA) Center at the Frank Porter Graham Child Development Institute at the University of North Carolina at Chapel Hill. Through my work at ECTA, I provide support to the state's early intervention and early childhood special education leaders working to support children with disabilities and their families.

My perspective on the work changed radically when I became a mother. Suddenly, the need for inclusive early childhood services became urgent to me because I experienced firsthand the way that *exclusion* can impact a child. For children aged three to five in the United States, the special-education system, more often than not, places children with disabilities in segregated classrooms. Rather than placing children with disabilities in classrooms with their peers without disabilities, they are often put into classrooms where every child has a disability.

This is not a realistic approach. As a person with a disability myself, I work alongside people with and without disabilities. In my community, I spend my free time around people with and without disabilities. We are fortunate that our world is a place of diverse abilities, races, ethnicities, gender identities, sexualities, and everything else that makes us unique individuals. Our world is inclusive, and our community spaces, schools, child-care programs, Head Start centers, and all other early childhood education programs should be too.

> The school Theodore goes to has a hub for kids with different kinds of disabilities. There are plenty of kids in the school with wheelchairs and walkers in the mainstream classes. He's just growing up as part of the group; there's real integration.
>
> **—LEAH MULLEN, PARENT**

BARRIERS TO INCLUSION

Unfortunately, young children with disabilities face many barriers to being included in all facets of life in their community. Rausch, Joseph, and Steed (2019) highlighted some of the research related to exclusion of children with disabilities from community spaces such as parks and playgrounds (Burke, 2012) and from early care and education environments (Barton and Smith, 2015a, 2015b). The researchers point to social barriers created by the lack of accessibility in community playgrounds (Ripat and Becker, 2012) and the subtle messages children with disabilities and their families receive that lead them to feel that they just do not belong in these community spaces where children without disabilities learn and play (Prellwitz and Skär, 2007). As you might imagine, this type of social exclusion is harmful to children and families and can have long-term impacts on their ability to participate in learning opportunities and engage with others (Stegelin, 2018).

Numerous studies have explored the barriers to inclusion in early childhood education settings. These barriers include a lack of funding or other resources for providing individualized supports and a lack of professional-development opportunities for early childhood educators and administrators (Rausch, Joseph, and Steed, 2019; Weglarz-Ward, Santos, and Timmer, 2019). The fragmented nature of the broader early childhood education system in the United States itself is also cited as a barrier to inclusion (Siller et al., 2021). However, researchers have consistently found that the most frequently reported barriers to inclusion are the attitudes and beliefs held by educators, administrators, system leaders, and policymakers. Inclusion tends to exist in the ivory tower—though not in practice—because our thinking has not been challenged about what it means to be an educator for each and every child, regardless of ability. We must work together to create a system in which inclusion is the norm rather than the exception.

We know that children do not need to be "ready" before they can be included with their peers. Rather the program, whether home-based, center-based, or a family child care, should be ready for the children. Delaying inclusion until a time when you think the child is old enough, advanced enough, or anything else "enough" flies in the face of the goal and purpose of inclusion, which is to ensure that children with disabilities have supported opportunities to grow, learn, and thrive alongside their peers.

> June's school has high-quality, inclusive classrooms. They have lots of supports in place, so she can navigate the routine pretty independently. And it's been really neat to watch her thrive when given the space and the support to reach the high expectations.
>
> **—JACKIE JOSEPH, PARENT**

SOME THOUGHTS ON TERMINOLOGY

Words matter. Language is a powerful influence on the perceptions we have of the world around us. We need to be careful with our words. As parents, we want our children to have a sense of belonging. We want our children to feel welcomed in our childcare programs, our family childcare homes, our Head Start and prekindergarten programs, our schools, and in our world. This starts with the words we use.

Is it really okay to label a child who is still in the process of growing and developing? This question is an ongoing struggle for me. As a result, I choose to focus on the practice of inclusion of all children, rather than on any specific label. But, like it or not, we need the labels now. Without the labels in our current system of education, the need for services and supports would be overlooked, and the funding would be lost as well. I often wonder if the labels that help us to justify the supports and services for a child actually do more harm than good overall. It is true that labels do serve a purpose. In addition to their use in demonstrating a need for access to services, labels are also a communication tool among service providers, a way to specify a group of people for advocacy purposes and a way to categorize effective teaching practices. However, labels also can promote a negative self-identity, create stigmas, lead to overgeneralization, and limit expectations that a family may have for their child.

DISABILITY

What is *disability* anyway? It's basically a term that humans created to sort people into the categories of "abled" and "disabled." This assumes that the person with a disability has no ability at all, which of course is completely untrue. We all need help in some aspect of our lives. The term and concept of *disability* is entirely dreamed up by society, and when you look at the notion more closely, well, it kind of falls apart.

There is a continuum of ability in every aspect of human existence. Do you have a disability because you are not a writer? Is my friend disabled because she can't play basketball like Michael Jordan? Of course not! There is diversity in what human beings are capable of doing. We have strengths in some areas of our lives and challenges in others—every single one of us! The term *disability* itself is used to refer to a specific inability to do something that society expects all human beings to be able to do, such as walking upright on two legs, communicating with words rather than with hand gestures, or even thinking and learning in a certain way.

> Emilio's persistence leads him to solve problems and almost make accommodations for himself. When he can't figure out something, he might find a completely different way to approach the situation than I would ever think of.
>
> **—OLIVIER BERNIER, PARENT**

Ultimately, disability is a concept that humans created as shorthand for people who act, behave, interact, or accomplish things in ways that are different from most other people. The thing is, doing something in a different way doesn't have to imply that it is the wrong way to do it. In most cases, the ability to act, behave, interact, or accomplish in different or unique ways is celebrated.

Disability assumes that the individual is unable to navigate the world in an acceptable way, when in fact she simply navigates the world in a different way. All disability categories are subjective. Even types of disability that we would think are straightforward turn out to be much hazier when you zoom in on them. For example, the difference between what is considered poor eyesight and what is considered blindness is a relatively arbitrary distinction. Often, the ability (or disability) is dependent on external factors. For example, my husband is unable to hear out of one ear. In a crowded restaurant, he would likely be considered deaf. In a quiet setting, one on one, his ability to hear is mostly unimpaired. Children with attention issues can often focus intently when they engage in an activity that interests them. Disability is never as fixed or obvious as some might think.

The definitions of disabilities within the medical field change continually, as science evolves over time. For example, as researcher Subini Annamma and colleagues (2013) note, in 1973 the American Association of Mental Deficiency changed the definition of *intellectual impairment* from an intelligence quotient (IQ) score of 85 to an IQ score of 70, and thereby determined that a whole group of people were suddenly "cured" from the label! Even though the term *disability* is subjective, we often use the word in a way that implies certainty.

Some writers have drawn attention to these issues around the word *disability* by using the term *dis/ability.* In writing this book, I have chosen to stay with the conventional spelling of the term, acknowledging the many limitations. As a society, we have the ability to serve as a disrupter of the way that our culture defines *disability.* Through our work together, we can advocate for the learning environments, the practices, the culture, and the community so each child finds the path to navigate the world in their own unique way.

A diagnosis is not the absolute. It's not the most accurate depiction of your child's ability or capability. It's not a prison sentence, nor the end of your dream for your happy, healthy family. Consider it as a new beginning. Your hopes, your dreams will still be realized. Your vision will still come to fruition.

—LATISHA R. STUCKEY, PARENT

SPECIAL

Given where we are in the evolution of terms in education systems, which words should we choose to use? Most people with disabilities, including me, prefer to use the term *disability* rather than *special needs,* because *special* implies that we have needs that are different than others. We don't have "special" needs; we have human needs. When we regard children as having special needs, it isn't a far jump to believe that they will then need to be segregated from others in "special" environments and "special" classes. **Special education is a service, not a place.** Children do not need a special place just because they need certain services or supports.

The language of special needs also implies that children with disabilities need "special" educators. Let me be clear here: I love and respect the special-education profession and special-education professionals. I have learned so much from these professionals who have devoted their lives to that particular field of study. We all need experts who understand and can teach others to implement the supports, strategies, and evidence-based teaching practices designed specifically for children with disabilities. However, if you were to ask the progressive leaders in the special-education field today, they would tell you that the ultimate goal of special education is to help children find success in the general-education classroom as much as possible, through accommodations, services, and other necessary supports.

In this book, I will highlight strategies that are key to supporting children with disabilities at home, in the community, and in inclusive programs, but my friend, there are many more strategies out there. Early intervention providers, therapists, and special educators will teach you something new every time they share their wisdom. My concern is that the term *special educator* implies that children with disabilities must only receive education and supports from someone with some sort of magic intellectual pixie dust. This is just not so. Family members, parents, child-care and Head Start teachers, and others can learn the strategies necessary to support a child, regardless of the nature or severity of the child's disability.

PEOPLE- OR IDENTITY-FIRST LANGUAGE

The use of people-first language is an approach that recognizes the person before the disability and uses accurate, strengths-based language to describe qualities, characteristics, and actions in a respectful way (Snow, 2016). When we describe a child with a disability, it is recommended that we use people-first language; for example, refer to a child who has autism as a "child with autism" rather than as an "autistic child." This acknowledges the fact that autism is something the child has, but it is not who the child is. She may have autism, but she is much more than that! Autism is just one of the features about the child, and people-first language recognizes that fact.

Language is very personal, and people with disabilities and those who support them are a diverse group with diverse perspectives. In fact, some people with disabilities have chosen to embrace the labels and, rather than using people-first language, they advocate for what is called identity-first language, such as "autistic child." This perspective arises from the idea that disability is a natural part of the human condition and is nothing to be ashamed of, that "disabled people" should be proud of that identity.

I know it's confusing. My advice for which language to use when you are speaking with an adult with a disability? Ask the person what they would prefer. Individuals have different preferences. I am a strong believer in people-first language. The thought of calling a child an "autistic child" rather than a "child with autism" makes me feel uncomfortable. While I certainly agree that there is no reason to be ashamed of disability, I stand with the people-first language approach for young children. Until a child is old enough to make those decisions, I think that it is important to use people-first language to reflect the fact that children with disabilities are children first. Like all children, they have many strengths, and disability is what they have and not who they are. In fact, disability may very well be a temporary situation and not a lifelong part of their identity. In any case, our society is just not there yet in terms of letting go of the negative stereotype that exists around disability. As Erin Barton, an associate professor of special education at Vanderbilt University, notes, "Children with disabilities do not need to be repaired or fixed. Just like all children, they need support to succeed" (Barton, n.d.). All children are special, and all children need some form of individualization to thrive and succeed. Children with disabilities are children, first and foremost. Families, specialists, and educators can work together with combined expertise, sharing our lessons learned on behalf of the children we love.

> It's the same with all the families that I know, that's their dream, right? I mean that they want their children to be included. They want them to be themselves. They want them to be in our society without seeing the diagnosis.
>
> **—PAULINA VARGAS, PARENT**

My hope is that as inclusion becomes the norm in approach and practice, the shift in language and the shift away from the use of labels will follow.

This book is intended for parents and family members who seek to understand how best to support their child, whom they love with all of their hearts. My hope is that this book will demystify the early intervention and early childhood special education systems and will also help you to navigate *all* of our early childhood systems, including child care, Head Start, and prekindergarten programs. Children with disabilities can and should be served in the same programs and spaces where children without disabilities are served. This is the heart of inclusion.

HOW THIS BOOK IS ORGANIZED

If you are looking for a guide that tells you all about specific conditions such as Down syndrome, cerebral palsy, autism, or ADHD, you won't find that here (but I will include some links in appendix C, so check those out if you're interested). The good news is that you really don't need to be an expert in any specific disability to be an expert in supporting the important child in your life. Every type of disability includes tremendous variations from person to person in how it presents to the world, so there would never be a way to learn everything.

A mother whom I met recently shared that finding out about all of the variability within her daughter's condition turned out to be one of her greatest lessons. She found that the name of the disability didn't matter all that much. She said, "When I learned that cerebral palsy is really just a term to describe a difference in muscle tone, it opened up all of the possibilities in the world for my child. Who cares that she has cerebral palsy? We just need to make sure that she gets the physical therapy that she needs to strengthen her muscles!"

In this guide, I focus on the systems and services available to support your child. Learn about your role as an advocate for the important child in your life and how you can use advocacy to promote inclusion for your child in early childhood education, and ultimately in school and life in general. The journey you are now on is complex, and I want to help you make sense of all of the options available to you, your child, and your family.

I start in chapter 1 with information about what to do when a concern arises about your child's development. I explain the steps to take and offer information to help you understand screening, evaluation, and assessment within the early childhood context, and I share necessary resources. Chapter 2 dives into your important role as an advocate for your child. To be an effective advocate, you need to understand the systems of support that are available to your child, strategies to identify their strengths, and ideas for considering a future vision for your child. Chapter 3 focuses on early intervention and services for infants and toddlers, and chapter 4 focuses on early childhood special education services for children ages three through five. This information is critical for understanding how these systems work on behalf of your child and family, from referral to service delivery. Chapters 5 through 8 provide a deeper dive into how you can work with your team of specialists and educators to support your child in reaching their goals. We consider how to create learning spaces at home, embed learning through everyday routines, teach friendship and problem-solving skills, and work on your child's learning and development goals. The final chapter addresses how to do all of this while staying healthy and strong, with a sense of balance throughout our lives.

> You can read all the information and listen to all the "experts" and advice from people who have gone before you, but in the end, you just do what feels right for your child and your family. You are the expert of your child. Nobody knows your kiddo better than you.
>
> **—TERRI LEYTON, PARENT**

In addition to family stories and quotes, each chapter also concludes with highlighted resources and an activity, so you can use the book like a journal or workbook to capture your thoughts and relate the content to your own parenting journey.

In appendix A, I share a glossary of terms, because the worlds of early intervention and early childhood special education are full of jargon and acronyms. In appendix B, I explain the Individuals with Disabilities Education Act (IDEA), the Americans with Disabilities Act (ADA), and other relevant legislation. Appendix C offers a collection of online resources for when you want to dig deeper and learn more.

This guide is intended to be used as a way to learn new information as well as a kind of workbook to help with organization and reflection. You will find lots of practical tips and strategies throughout these pages. While I was writing this book, you, the parent or family member, were always on my mind. Again and again, I thought, "What would have been helpful to me when I was navigating this world as Ricky's mom?" This book represents a collection of answers to that question, and I hope you will find answers to your questions as well.

CHAPTER 1

I Have a Concern about My Child's Development. Now What?

Iggy would have tantrums. Some of them would last for two hours. I saw this because I was at home with him. But my husband never saw it, because he was at work. Then, when he would come home, he would say, "This is the sweetest kid." It took a while for my husband to understand that this was happening. It was so frustrating for me.

—ANDIE AMOSSON, PARENT

When my son, Ricky, entered child care for the first time, his teacher, Miss Amy, noticed that he didn't behave the same way as the other children in her class. "He darts from one activity to another," she observed. "He doesn't stay in any center for very long, and so he doesn't seem to be connecting with the other children." She showed me Ricky's art projects and the snowman that consisted of one cotton ball glued to the page. "I guess he's a minimalist when it comes to crafts," Miss Amy said. She wondered if he might benefit from early childhood special-education services. As a parent, I wasn't quite ready to hear this information, even though we had received support from an early intervention service provider when Ricky was younger. Then, we worked with an early intervention specialist at home, and the provider even worked with his teachers at child care. But when Miss Amy shared her observations, it felt like a much bigger deal. I did have to acknowledge the fact that she had seen many children pass through her classroom over the years and likely would recognize when a child's behavior appeared different from other children's.

Early childhood educators and home visitors spend time with lots of different young children, and they are often the first to notice a potential delay in development. You are a partner with your child's teacher, home visitor, or caregiver and have the opportunity to talk with them about your child's development in an ongoing way. Ricky benefited from Miss Amy's keen observation and willingness to share her observations with me. She knew that when developmental concerns are caught early, children benefit.

ALL ABOUT EARLY CHILDHOOD SERVICES

Early childhood is often considered to be the period from birth through age five. The National Association for the Education of Young Children (NAEYC) considers the early childhood period to span from birth through age eight (NAEYC, 2020a). Federal legislation related to children with disabilities considers the early childhood period to be from birth through age five (20 USC 1400, 2004; 42 USC 9801, 2007). In addition to providing supports for families' busy lives, early childhood programs also promote positive outcomes for children. Programs such as Head Start, child care, early intervention, and home visiting have been found to serve as protective factors from negative outcomes (Chacon and Reschke, 2021). What follows are short descriptions of key types of early childhood programs and services, what they offer, and how you can find out about how they operate in your state.

> I've been working with children for a very long time, all ages. I know developmental stages and milestones, and I realized that my daughter wasn't reaching those. The children's development service agency (CDSA) came out, and they did an evaluation. The doctor also noticed that her head growth was not in the normal range. Then, at a year, when her head was still in the less-than-1-percent range, he made another referral to CDSA and also a referral to neurology. And that's what started us on our journey.
>
> **—AMANDA LOVETTE, PARENT**

EARLY CHILDHOOD EDUCATION

NAEYC is a national membership organization for early childhood professionals. NAEYC defines the early childhood educator as "an individual who cares for and promotes the learning, development, and well-being of children birth through age 8 in all early childhood education settings, while meeting the qualifications of the profession and having mastery of its specialized knowledge, skills, and competencies" (NAEYC, 2020b). *Child care* is the term widely used to describe early learning and care provided by an adult other than a parent. Child care is sometimes called "day care," but the early childhood field strongly prefers the term *child care* or *early care and education* instead. These are umbrella terms that include education and care provided in child-care centers, family child-care homes, Head Start and Early Head Start, state-funded prekindergarten programs, school-age child-care programs, child-care options for military families, and informal in-home child care. *Informal in-home child care* is care provided in the child's or caregiver's home by a person who is a relative, friend, neighbor, babysitter, or nanny. Sometimes called "family, friend, and neighbor" care, informal in-home child care is not usually regulated by states.

If possible, young children who attend child care should attend *licensed* early childhood education programs, which means programs that are regulated by state government agencies. Child-care licensing is a process in which states set minimum health and safety requirements that programs must meet to operate legally. States are required by federal law to set and enforce child-care licensing requirements to keep children safe and healthy. In addition, licensed child-care programs are required to be monitored to make sure they continue to meet the health and safety standards. Because each state sets its own standards, you'll need to do some research to find out your state's specific requirements. But most states require that the teacher or caregiver receive important safety training (such as CPR and first aid), and the teacher or caregiver may have college coursework in early childhood education as well.

> Kelsey started going to a developmental daycare center when she was around two. I remember when my mother-in-law visited a few months later. She told my husband that she originally thought it was a mistake not to keep her home, but she saw the big difference in Kelsey after being more independent and around other children.
>
> **—TERRI LEYTON, PARENT**

As you can tell, there are lots of options! A good place to start is the federal Office of Child Care (https://www.childcare.gov). There, you'll find a link to search for child-care options and information about the health, safety, and quality standards for child care in your state. Additional child-care options are available for military families and can be found here: https://militarychildcare.com

HEAD START AND EARLY HEAD START

Head Start refers to federally funded preschool programs that primarily serve three- and four-year-old children. Early Head Start programs serve infants, toddlers, and pregnant women. Services are delivered nationwide through 1,600 agencies that provide early learning programs, as well as supports for health and family well-being (42 USC 9801, 2007). Parents are considered key partners in Head Start, and 10 percent of the funded enrollment must include children with disabilities. There are income requirements to be eligible for Head Start, but some of these may be waived for a child who has a disability or suspected delay (Office of Head Start, Administration for Children and Families, Department of Health and Human Services, 2016). Each program sets enrollment priorities, so check with your local program for details. Find information about the programs in your area and how to apply at https://eclkc.ohs.acf.hhs.gov/how-apply.

STATE PREKINDERGARTEN PROGRAMS

Depending on where you live, state prekindergarten (pre-K) programs are known by many different names such as public preschool, pre-K, junior kindergarten, state-funded preschool, or state-funded prekindergarten. These programs are not available in every state because they are dependent on state funding. They operate through local school districts and/or in partnership with nonprofit organizations, Head Start, child-care, or other programs. These programs are often free or low-cost for families who qualify. Pre-K programs typically serve children from age three to age five and focus on kindergarten preparation. Services may be limited to a portion of the day and may be closed during the summer months. To find prekindergarten programs near you and to learn about the resources in your state, go to https://childcare.gov and select your state.

HOME VISITING

Your state may also offer home visiting as a support for expectant parents and families of children from birth to age five. Trained home visitors provide services and supports in your home, which may feel most comfortable. Through home visiting, you can receive information on child development, health, and well being. You can also learn about available services such as developmental screenings, mental-health supports, and early intervention services. To find home visiting programs near you, select your state or territory and review the "Home Visiting" drop-down menu under the "Health and Social Services" tab: https://childcare.gov/state-resources-home.

EARLY INTERVENTION PROGRAMS

All states offer early intervention (EI) programs to help babies and toddlers who have developmental delays or disabilities. EI focuses on helping eligible babies and toddlers learn the skills that typically

What Is IDEA?

The Individuals with Disabilities Education Act (IDEA) is a federal law that guides programs for children with disabilities or suspected delays who may need supports and services. For children ages birth through five, the law identifies services for eligible infants, toddlers, and their families as early intervention (EI) (often referred to as "Part C" of the law) and services for eligible children ages three through five as early childhood special education (ECSE) (often referred to as "Part B, Section 619" of the law).

Early intervention programs help babies and toddlers with developmental delays or disabilities. The services are detailed in a plan called the Individualized Family Service Plan (IFSP).

Early childhood special education services help preschool children (ages three through five) with developmental delays or disabilities to support education needs. The services are outlined in each child's Individualized Education Program (IEP).

develop during the first three years of life, such as crawling, walking, eating, talking, and learning. To find EI services near you, select your state or territory, and review the "Early Intervention for Children with Special Needs" drop-down menu under the "Health and Social Services" tab: https://childcare.gov/state-resources-home.

We'll explore EI in more detail later in this chapter and in chapter 3.

EARLY CHILDHOOD SPECIAL EDUCATION SERVICES

States are required to provide early childhood special education (ECSE) services that help preschool children (ages three through five) with developmental delays or disabilities to support their education needs. The services typically are provided by the local public school where the child will attend kindergarten and elementary school. To find ECSE services near you, select your state or territory and review the "Education Supports for Children with Disabilities" drop-down menu under the "Health and Social Services" tab: https://childcare.gov/state-resources-home. We'll explore ECSE in more detail in this chapter and in chapter 4.

WHEN YOU SUSPECT THAT YOUR CHILD MAY NEED SERVICES AND SUPPORTS

If you're concerned about your child's development, you should ask for support and get help right away. Research has shown that acting early can make a huge difference in your child's lifelong health (Campbell et al., 2014; Barth et al., 2007; National Scientific Council on the Developing Child, 2020). Believe it or not, developmental delays are common. The Centers for Disease Control and Prevention (CDC) estimates that about one in six children has a developmental disability that could affect their health, learning, and overall success in life (Zablotsky et al., 2019; Boyle et al., 2011). Children whose developmental delays are identified as infants or toddlers can really benefit from early intervention services. Speech therapy, physical therapy, and other services are available in every state at little or no cost to parents. Sadly, more than half of the children with delays aren't identified until they start kindergarten (Glascoe, 2000). This doesn't have to be the case for your child! Let's start with the "big picture" steps to take, and then we'll explore some of these concepts in more detail. Here are the first steps to take when you have a concern about your child's development:

- **Use a checklist to better understand the typical things children do at your child's age.** The CDC website (https://www.cdc.gov/ncbddd/actearly/milestones/index.html) is a great place to go for information about developmental milestones in children ages birth through five. The website has a lot of helpful information about child development and the typical milestones that children reach during the early years and beyond. You can use the resources to track your child's development. When it's time to talk with your doctor or other health professional, write down questions you have and show the doctor the milestone checklist with information about the milestones your child has reached and the ones that concern you.
- **Talk with your child's doctor or go to a public health clinic to speak with a medical or other health professional.** You know your child best. If you review the milestone checklist and find that your child is not meeting the milestones for their age, talk with your pediatrician or other health professional. Don't wait! If your child's teacher, a family member, or close friend is concerned about how your child plays, speaks, acts or moves, speak with your child's doctor or other health professional right away.
- **Ask your doctor or other health professional about developmental screening.** *Developmental screening* is the term used for when you and your doctor fill out a formal checklist or questionnaire about how your child speaks, moves, acts, plays, and learns. Developmental screening is recommended for all children throughout the early years. These supports may also be available at your child's child-care program or Early Head Start or Head Start program. Screening gives the doctor more information about your child so that together you can figure out the best next steps to take. A next step might be a referral to a specialist who can take a closer look at your child's development in the area of your concern. If you do decide to ask for a referral to a specialist, make sure to reach out and make an appointment right away. It may be that the next available appointment is many weeks away, which can be really frustrating. Remember that you can call back every week to see if an earlier appointment has opened up. You can also let your child's doctor know that you're having trouble making an appointment, and they may be able to help. Getting your child the help they need as quickly as possible is important, so you'll have to be persistent.

What if your doctor tells you to wait and see? Children develop in lots of different ways, and many factors can influence the rate of development. Even different child-rearing practices or cultural expectations can influence how and when a child reaches a given milestone. For example, in some cultures, it is not acceptable for children to make frequent eye contact with others, so that milestone

RESOURCE SPOTLIGHT

The CDC has a set of resources for tracking developmental milestones, including checklists and a milestone tracker app for your smartphone (www.cdc.gov/Milestones). If you are wondering what a certain milestone looks like in the real world, the CDC also has a section on its website called "Milestones in Action," where you'll find a free online library of photos and videos of developmental milestones.

may emerge later. For this reason, some doctors or other health professionals are hesitant to make a referral to a specialist. However, if your child's doctor has told you to wait and see, and you feel unsure about that advice, reach out to another doctor for a second opinion. Trust your instincts!

REFERRALS AND EVALUATION FOR EARLY INTERVENTION AND EARLY CHILDHOOD SPECIAL EDUCATION

At any point in the process, you can also reach out for early intervention (EI) or early childhood special education services (ECSE) in your state. You do not need a doctor's referral to have your child evaluated for services. Family members, medical professionals, and teachers—including those from child-care, Head Start, or pre-K programs—can call the local EI program or local public school to ask about the evaluation process and make a referral for your child. Children can be evaluated only after the parent or guardian provides written permission. When you agree to an evaluation for your child, it does not mean that you are agreeing to receive services. It is just an agreement to find out more about your child's development and whether or not services might help.

> I had taken him to the pediatrician because he wasn't walking. My only point of reference was my oldest son, who started walking at twelve months. Phillip was a year and a half and still wasn't walking. The day that he took his first steps was so memorable. After he took them, I ran to him. I hugged him so tight, and I was just crying. As parents, if we could do it for them, we would. But there are things we just can't do.
>
> **—LATISHA R. STUCKEY, PARENT**

Whom do you call to receive a screening, evaluation, or special services? Each state has a Parent Training and Information (PTI) center or Community Parent Resource Center (CPRC) to answer questions and provide support for parents, family members, teachers, and other professionals. These centers are especially helpful, because most of the staff are parents of children with disabilities themselves. The parent centers can provide details about the referral and evaluation process in your area and will provide the name and phone number for the person to contact if you have a concern. To find the parent center in your area, go to https://www.parentcenterhub.org/find-your-center/.

In addition, the Center for Appropriate Dispute Resolution in Special Education (CADRE) maintains a map of the United States with links to the EI and ECSE contacts for each state and US territory (www.cadreworks.org/find-state-agency-parent-center-information).

We'll get into the details about EI in chapter 3 and ECSE in chapter 4, but all the services available start with a *referral* and then an *evaluation*:

- **Referral:** A parent, family member, teacher, or other professional may ask that a child be evaluated to see if the child is eligible for early intervention or early childhood special education services. This request may be verbal, but it's best to put it in writing.
- **Evaluation:** Parents and professionals then seek to learn whether the child has a disability or developmental delay. For infants and toddlers, evaluations help to answer questions about whether or not the child would benefit from services to help with growth and development. For preschoolers, the focus is primarily on the child's educational needs.

If the child is eligible for services, the professionals will organize a meeting of the team that will discuss the services available for the child. Parents and family are important members of this team. Together, the team will make decisions about the services and will develop a written plan.

Now that you have the big picture about what to do when you have a concern, let's back up and take a deeper dive into what we mean by developmental milestones, developmental screening, evaluation, and assessment.

> Her development is not gonna go in a straight line. That was a huge boon for us to learn that development was gonna go with ups and downs, spurts, and lags.
>
> **—PATRICIA REEDY, PARENT**

WHAT ARE DEVELOPMENTAL MILESTONES?

To understand how to identify a possible developmental delay, we must first understand typical child development. Every child grows and develops differently, at their own pace. Some children develop quickly in some areas and a little more slowly in others. Skills such as taking a first step, smiling for the first time, and waving bye-bye are called *developmental milestones*. The CDC website (www.cdc.gov/Milestones) is a great place to go for information about developmental milestones in children ages birth through five. They even offer a free developmental milestone tracker that you can use to track your child's development.

You'll find checklists organized in four key developmental domains:

- Social-emotional
- Language and communication
- Cognitive
- Movement and physical

Each domain is important, and each supports, and is supported by, the others. Here is a brief explanation of each domain and some of the related milestones. You can find a more expansive compilation of typical milestones in child development at CDC's Developmental Milestones website.

SOCIAL-EMOTIONAL

This domain is about how children interact with others and show emotion. Examples of milestones include:

- Smiling spontaneously, especially at people
- Cooperating with other children
- Showing affection for friends without prompting

LANGUAGE AND COMMUNICATION

This domain is about how children express their needs and share what they are thinking, as well as understand what is said to them. Examples of milestones include:

- Cooing and babbling
- Pointing to show others what they want
- Singing a song from memory, such as "Itsy Bitsy Spider"

COGNITIVE

The cognitive domain—learning, thinking, and problem solving—is about how children learn new things and solve problems. It includes how children explore their environment to figure things out, whether by looking at the world around them, putting objects in their mouths, or dropping something to watch it fall. This domain also includes "academic" skills such as counting and learning letters and numbers. Examples of milestones include:

- Reaching for a toy with one hand
- Exploring things in different ways, such as by shaking, banging, and throwing
- Building towers of at least four blocks

MOVEMENT AND PHYSICAL

This domain is about how children use their bodies. It includes many milestones that parents excitedly wait for, such as:

- Crawling
- Catching a bounced ball most of the time
- Eating with a spoon

Some developmental milestones fit more than one domain. For example, playing make-believe can be a social-emotional milestone as well as a cognitive milestone. Following instructions can be a language and communication milestone as well as a cognitive milestone. Playing peekaboo can be a cognitive as well as a social-emotional milestone (CDC, n.d.).

> A moment that I think about a lot is the first time June held her own bottle. She was considerably older than what the developmental progression said she should be. But it was really this first moment of, "Oh, wow! She's really gonna do this when she's ready." Every little bit that they are able to become more independent is almost like a little sigh of relief.
>
> **—JACKIE JOSEPH, PARENT**

Children reach milestones in predictable ways. There are typical stages when children learn how to speak, act, move, play, and learn, but every child is different, and there are variations based on the child's culture and experiences as well as individual differences. How children develop is based on a combination of factors, such as the characteristics they are born with, the culture they live in, and their experiences within their family and in other settings. Each of these factors is important in a child's growth

and development, so these are important considerations as you think about supporting your child's development and learning.

I love this anonymous quote, "Every child is a different kind of flower, and all together make this world a beautiful garden." This quote reminds me that I have many flowers in my garden, and they don't all bloom at the same time. I don't expect my tulips to flower in December, because I know it is not their nature to do so. Children are the same way. Some children may take their first steps when they are one year old, and others may take them later. Child development also occurs in "spurts and lags" or "waves and cycles" (NAEYC, 2022). These metaphors are used because development is not as straightforward a process as we once believed. Child development happens in an overlapping fashion, and it is difficult to assess skills and behaviors within the rigid boundaries of developmental domains. Children develop in different ways and the progressions are often hard to explain. This is why some doctors will default to the wait-and-see approach. For example, my own son would achieve several developmental milestones all at once, and then it seemed as if he suddenly put the brakes on. Sometimes it seemed like a "two steps forward, one step back" type of pattern.

Keeping all those considerations in mind, you can still use the developmental milestone tools as a way to keep track of development and learn about when your child may be experiencing a developmental delay.

WHAT IS DEVELOPMENTAL SCREENING?

Screening (or developmental screening) is a brief assessment that can be completed by a parent, educator, or trained professional to determine whether or not concerns support a referral to early intervention or special education systems. **Screening does not identify or diagnose a developmental delay.** It only provides a snapshot of how your child is functioning in a particular area at a point in time. Remember those vision and hearing tests that you had at the beginning of elementary school? Those were screenings.

You might have also heard the term *developmental monitoring.* This is different from developmental screening because it is done by parents and educators on an ongoing basis. The American Academy of Pediatrics (AAP) recommends that children receive ongoing developmental monitoring as well as a developmental screening with a medical professional when the child is nine, eighteen, and thirty months of age (Committee on Practice and Ambulatory Medicine et al., 2019; Lipkin et al., 2020). The AAP also recommends that screenings be conducted with a validated screening tool by medical professionals or other staff who have special training. Both developmental monitoring and developmental screening look for developmental milestones and are important for tracking signs of development and identifying concerns.

Disparities in Access to Screening

Children who receive early and regular developmental screenings and access to high-quality early care and education demonstrate lasting improvements in social competence, emotional regulation, and cognition and often achieve long-term health and educational benefits (Cole, Trexberg, and Schaffner, 2023). For children at significant risk, early intervention (EI) can serve as a protective buffer against influences that may slow optimal development (Campbell et al., 2014). Developmental screening leads to early identification of concerns so that they can be addressed as soon as possible. Unfortunately, access to developmental screening is not the same for all children. The Zero to Three *State of Babies Yearbook* (Cole, Trexberg, and Schaffner, 2023) states, "parents reported low rates of basic developmental screening for infants and toddlers (34.2% overall), with particularly low rates for those with low income (29.5% compared with 37.3% for babies in families above low income)." Racial and cultural disparities exist as well. *Our Youngest Learners: Increasing Equity in Early Intervention* (2021), a report by The Education Trust, the National Center for Learning Disabilities, and Zero to Three, found that Black and Latino/a children with developmental delays are 78 percent less likely than white children to be identified as such and receive early intervention services. The report also says children of color often have less access than white children to programs such as high-quality health care and early childhood education in which specialists are trained to use screening tools. This results in fewer screening opportunities for children of color. Families can reach out to professionals such as an early childhood teacher, or medical provider, to ask about screening services available in their community.

Usually, the screening process involves assessing your child by using a small number of items and, depending on the tool, a screening can be completed by you, your child's teacher, a home visitor, or other trained professional. Most developmental screening tools provide a quick look at major developmental milestones to show whether or not your child is on track developmentally and if a closer look by a specialist is needed. Most children who have the recommended well-child visits with a pediatrician or primary health-care provider will also have a series of developmental screenings.

> I remember when we were looking for the right diagnosis. We were kind of in a race to help him. We were thinking, "Okay, so we have time, but we don't have that much time because he's growing up." So I was pushing a lot with the doctors. They had to be saying, "Here she comes again." Now I realize that I was running the sprint, but I needed to be running a marathon.
>
> **—ANDIE AMOSSON, PARENT**

WHAT IS EVALUATION?

Evaluation is how we determine eligibility for services. Evaluations must be:

- conducted with parent consent.
- timely, comprehensive, and multidisciplinary.

- conducted by qualified personnel.
- not culturally or racially discriminatory.
- in the native language of the child.
- conducted so that no single source is used to determine eligibility.

This last point is really important. When professionals are determining whether or not your child is eligible for services, they must gather information from multiple sources, using multiple methods, across multiple domains of development. For example, a local school-system evaluation team might observe your child, interview you or other family members, review your child's records, and reference questionnaires completed by you or your child's teacher. Evaluation is most effective when you are a partner with the evaluator. You have important information to share because you know your child best. To make informed decisions, evaluators need the information you have about your child's strengths and needs.

Early childhood special education laws require that your child be evaluated in "all areas related to the suspected disability, including, if appropriate, health, vision, hearing, social and emotional status, general intelligence, academic performance, communicative status, and motor abilities" (20 USC 1400, 2004). This is important because the evaluation must be comprehensive enough to identify all of your child's special-education needs, even if they don't seem to be related to the disability category that led to the initial referral. All areas of suspected disability must be examined, so other professionals are often involved in the evaluation. For example, your child may be evaluated by speech and language therapists, occupational therapists, physical therapists, and others. While the laws do not list specific tests that should be administered, they do set forth very clearly what *kinds* of tests should be used, how they should be given, and by whom. Tests should be given for the purposes for which they are designed and in accordance with the instructions provided by the publishers of the test. You should also expect that tests are administered by trained and knowledgeable evaluation staff.

In addition, the tools used in evaluations to determine eligibility for your child should be administered in your child's home language and should take into consideration your family's culture. Tests should not discriminate on a racial or cultural basis. Early childhood professional organizations have developed specific recommendations and guidance for the evaluation of children who are learning English and any other language that is spoken at home. One key point is that evaluators should avoid making assumptions. "Many factors—anxiety, hunger, inability to understand the language of the instructions, culturally learned hesitation in initiating conversation with adults, and so on—may influence a child's performance, creating a gap between that performance and the child's actual ability, and causing staff to draw inaccurate conclusions" (NAEYC, 2003). This careful process can take time. If the evaluation process is expected to be lengthy, you can request services to start while the evaluation and planning processes are carried out. For more information on disability laws, see appendix B.

WHAT IS ASSESSMENT?

Once the evaluation is complete and a plan for services is in place, teachers and other professionals will still need to assess your child's growth and development over time. *Assessment* happens through careful observation and gives teachers and other professionals information about your child's strengths and needs so they can provide ongoing support. This information is then used to plan an individualized approach for your child. Teachers and other professionals may observe your child to gather information that will guide planning, individualizing the curriculum, and modifying teaching practices or the learning environment. For example, if information gathered through assessment shows slow or no progress toward a goal in the classroom, teachers then can decide how to change lesson plans and activities to support the child's development. Early intervention and early childhood special-education staff are key partners in this process. Specialists can provide valuable support when a child with a disability needs specialized teaching techniques.

Where Do Services Take Place?

One of the key concepts in the IDEA legislation is that, in most cases, services should be provided in the place where the child would be if they did not have a disability. For many children, this is a child-care, prekindergarten, or Head Start program. The language used to describe this concept is different for each program:

- Early intervention services for eligible children birth through age two are to be provided in the child's "natural environment," which means the environment where the child spends the majority of their time, such as the child's home, child-care program, Early Head Start program, or grandparent's house.
- Early childhood special education services for eligible children ages three through five are to be provided, to the maximum extent appropriate, in the "least restrictive environment" (LRE) based on the child's unique strengths and needs. For preschoolers, this would likely be in a child-care program, Head Start or public prekindergarten program, or other regular early childhood education setting.

GETTING SUPPORT FROM TEACHERS AND OTHER PROFESSIONALS

Maintaining strong connections with professionals is important for many reasons, but these relationships are especially helpful when you have a concern about your child's development. If you have concerns that your child is not growing and developing in the same way as other children you know, the support from teachers and other professionals will be helpful to you and your child to access needed services.

CADRE, the national Center on Dispute Resolution in Special Education (www.cadreworks.org), helps state and local agencies and parent centers in preventing and helping resolve disputes. CADRE has information about disability laws and how to get the services you are legally entitled to receive in plain, "non-lawyer" language.

When thinking about how to approach these discussions, preparation is key. Before the conversation, you will want to collect information, organize your thoughts, and build your knowledge about the referral process and available resources. I also recommend that you practice the conversation with a friend or family member before you reach out to your child's teacher. Another strategy is to practice the conversation by yourself just looking in a mirror. It sounds strange, but it really will help you to feel more confident and comfortable when the time comes. Your confidence will project strength, which can help the professionals to trust your judgement and take action on your child's behalf.

Request a time to talk with the teacher outside of the busy program day, so that everyone can focus on the discussion and you won't feel rushed. This is not a conversation to have at drop-off or pickup time. Find a time that works for everyone and a place that is comfortable, quiet, and private. Ask at the start of the meeting that the discussion will remain confidential. Be ready with information about what you are noticing at home with your child and a list of questions that you have collected. If you come to the meeting with a clear description of your concerns, it will be easier for the teacher or other professional to identify the best next steps.

> In the beginning, my fears and worries were really about me and not about June. I worried a lot about what our life was going to be like. Another mom said to me, "Everything you worry about? Once you're there, it is not as hard as what you worried about." It's much more normal than I thought it would be. I love June exactly how she is. I don't want her to change. I don't want our life to change. I want the world around her to change.
>
> **—JACKIE JOSEPH, PARENT**

One of the best ways to prepare for these conversations and for future discussions about supports for your child is to become familiar with the laws and regulations pertaining to young children with disabilities. Knowledge is power! I know that it may seem intimidating to try to understand laws and the often-complicated language around anything related to the legal system. I have included information about the most relevant laws in appendix B.

PROCESSING YOUR FEELINGS

The feeling of responsibility that all parents have for their children is multiplied for parents whose children are struggling with medical or developmental concerns. We need to explore those feelings and be gentle with ourselves and with each other. The time of learning that your child may have a disability or delay, the time of searching for a diagnosis, and even the times of finding answers can be filled with intense, sometimes scary, feelings of fear, worry, and maybe even guilt. You may feel hopeful on some days, worried on others, then optimistic, then grief ridden. It's just a mixed bag. The parents I interviewed for this book shared some common themes:

Like my son, I also feel intensely about specific things and certain people. When you get rejected and you feel really strongly about people, it sucks. For me, that led to significant depression. I know that Jude also feels things really intensely. I'm just really worried about him going through what I went through.

—BEN RIEPE

There are the memories that have been really positive. There are fewer big moments of aha! or devastation, and more quiet moments of positivity and hope and then moments of real despair. That chronic kind of crashing feeling where you think, "This is really bad." It's just like an everyday kind of extra level of difficulty and worry.

—LEAH MULLEN

I'm very embarrassed to say, but the day my son was born was probably when I felt the most grief. We were unprepared for him. Looking back on it, unfortunately, I had never really been exposed to people with disabilities. They were hidden from me in school, and I think I was just completely unprepared for Emilio, and I realized that was a huge gap in my understanding of the world. Since then, I feel like I've come around, and I'm learning every day. But that was the hardest moment for me. That first day.

—OLIVIER BERNIER

This chapter started with the story of Ricky's preschool teacher sharing a concern and how helpful it was for me to hear that perspective. That is true, but I have to admit that I didn't feel so appreciative of that information at first. My child was remarkable! Think about how much he overcame. While he was in the orphanage, Ricky wasn't held as often as he should have been. He didn't get the loving words that he needed to hear. He didn't have that regular, dependable person who was consistently in his life. He was alone in every sense of the word. I could only marvel at how remarkable it was that he grew to trust me by the end of that very first day.

> You may worry. You may have fears and or concerns. You may experience grief or sadness. These things are a part of the parenting journey, whether your child has a diagnosis or not.
>
> **—LATISHA R. STUCKEY, PARENT**

On the plane ride from Simferopol to Kiev, Ricky sat on my lap, and we looked at each other and smiled and giggled the whole way. I was completely enchanted by him. I made raspberries with my lips and pretended to nibble on his hands to make him laugh. He laughed so hard that at one point, no sound came out. That moment was sheer bliss for me and is imprinted in my mind. I can *feel* that moment as clearly as if it were yesterday. How could it be that this little sweet person could accept *this* little person as his mother so instantly? so soon? so completely? He was my son from the moment I saw him. I recognized him as my son that I was looking for. Here he is! We finally found each other! And everything he did was magical to me. Most of all, the way he approached life, with zest, pure and simple zest, was magical to me. To be able to brush off that feeling of being completely alone and approach life with zest? Incredible.

With all of that in mind, I felt some strong feelings about Miss Amy sharing with me that she had concerns about Ricky. Concerns? Do you have any idea how amazing my kid is? How smart? How funny? How capable? How resilient? As parents, we want to protect our child from anything that feels like criticism. Even our own concerns can sometimes feel like betrayal.

For your sake and for your child's sake, please be gentle with yourself. Take time to reflect, not just about the concerns you have or the results of a screening or evaluation but also about the feelings you're having. You are not alone. Reach out for help if you need it. Find your local parent center (www.parentcenterhub.org) so you can connect with other families who are going through similar experiences. We can connect virtually through technology now, so it's easier than ever to reach out.

*****

On the next page, you'll have the opportunity to reflect on your own child's development. This is the first activity in the book, and I'm hoping these pages will help to make this information real for your own family situation. Take a moment to learn about developmental milestones and where your child fits within the continuum. Remember that these are just averages, and that development isn't always as predictable as these screening tools make it seem. They do offer a great place to start though. You're on your way!

ACTIVITY: REFLECTING ON MY CHILD'S DEVELOPMENT

DIRECTIONS

Focus on your child's development and take a moment to reflect. You now have information about screening, evaluation, and assessment, so let's put that information into practice.

First, gather some data by using one or more of these free resources:

- CDC Milestone Tracker App (www.cdc.gov/MilestoneTracker) or the printable CDC Milestone Checklist (www.cdc.gov/Milestones) for your child's age group

  Note: If your child was born prematurely, adjust by calculating your child's developmental age using your child's *estimated* due date in place of the date they were actually born preterm. During the first two years, using your baby's corrected age will give you a better idea of when they should reach common developmental goals.

- Ages and Stages Questionnaires, Third Edition (ASQ-3) (https://www.easterseals.com/mtffc/asq/) Provided by Easterseals, ASQ-3 is one of many general developmental screening tools that are widely used in early intervention programs and Head Start.
- Survey of Well-Being of Young Children (SWYC) The SWYC is a free comprehensive screening instrument for children younger than five years of age. The SWYC was written to be simple to answer, short, and easy to read. The entire instrument requires 15 minutes or less to complete and is straightforward to score and interpret. Find the form that applies to your child's current age at this website: https://pediatrics.tuftsmedicalcenter.org/The-Survey-of-Wellbeing-of-Young-Children/Age-Specific-Forms

Be sure to share the completed questionnaire(s) and results with your child's doctor.

Next, once you have completed the milestone activity, record your thoughts to the following prompts:

I noticed the milestones my child has already achieved are: ______________________________

____

I noticed the milestones my child is still working on are: ______________________________

____

Completing the milestone tracker or checklist made me feel: ______________________________

____

I would like to talk with my doctor or health-care provider about: ______________________________

____

Some ideas I have for supporting my child are: ______________________________

____

CHAPTER 2

Advocate—Your Most Important Role

I consider myself a parent advocate. As a parent of a child with a disability, you have to become a parent advocate, to step outside of your comfort zone. Children can feel voiceless and choiceless. They have to do what the adults in their lives say they have to do. I try to let them know that their voice matters and that they should speak up and speak out and speak their truth.

—LATISHA R. STUCKEY, PARENT

Being a parent is hard work! I remember the concepts I had about motherhood before I became a mother and how much they changed when motherhood became my reality. I had a master's degree in child development. I had worked as a nanny and as a preschool teacher. I would be the "Mary Poppins of Motherhood," right? Wrong. I made many mistakes. I placed many tearful calls to my own mother asking for advice and endured many moments of sitting on the front steps with a pounding headache and desire to just curl up into a ball. Why was this so hard?

When Ricky was little, I read a book by Susan Maushart called *The Mask of Motherhood: How Becoming a Mother Changes Our Lives and Why We Never Talk about It.* The premise of it is that motherhood is hard, and often it is difficult for women to be honest about the challenges they face in this new life stage. People don't want to hear about how stressed out you are or about how the lack of sleep is making you crazy or about how you struggle to keep your worst impulses at bay. Typically, people want to hear, "He is the light of my life," or "I can't imagine what life would be like without her," or "She makes my world complete." They want to hear that it's all flowers, rainbows, hearts, and little imprints of baby feet and hands, which at times were my experiences. But not always.

> I had a moment where I realized that she was going to be different, that things were going to have to be different. We were invited to a birthday party for a friend whose youngest child was the same age as Mazie. I was thinking: there will be kids, she'll love it and she'll have fun. But there were so many people in the house, she could not handle it. She kept getting overstimulated, and we ended up having to leave. I realized how much more careful I had to be with the situations that I put her in. I'm going to have to be a different mom than I planned to be.
>
> **—AMANDA LOVETTE, PARENT**

In addition to ADHD, Ricky struggled with what the experts call *sensory processing disorder* or *sensory integration disorder.* Certain features of everyday life that relate to how we experience the world through our senses were challenging for him. He tended to overreact to sensory information related to sight, sound, and touch. For example, loud noises could turn even the most fun experience into a stressful event. Bright, overhead fluorescent lights seemed to affect his behavior and create anxiety. A scratchy tag on his shirt collar felt unbearable to him. A fun trip to Disney World? We're going to see Winnie the Pooh! Yay! Um, not so much. In addition, Ricky was extremely impulsive and would dart into the street as soon as I opened the car door. His nonstop energy left me exhausted and filled with constant worry. My carefree days before motherhood were gone in an instant, and I mourned the loss of my former self. When I did confide to my closest friend about these feelings, she responded with, "But this is what you wanted! You went across the world to find him! And he is just so adorable." All true. And good grief, I didn't want to send him back! He was *exactly* what I wanted, and motherhood was exactly what I

wanted too. I just didn't expect to feel this incompetent. I didn't expect that parenting would be so difficult.

I could really relate to Maushart's book. I thought that being the mother of a child with a disability wasn't just a mask of motherhood but a hazmat suit! I struggled with many things that seemed above and beyond the typical motherhood experience. In addition, it just isn't human nature to admit to the things that make you feel inadequate. Why would a parent want to be honest about the things that aren't going well?

In this chapter we'll take a look at how to become an advocate for your child, which includes:

- Finding resources
- Talking with your family about your child's disability
- Understanding Part C and Part B, Section 619 of IDEA
- Creating a vision for your child
- Building on your child's strengths
- Affirming your child's accomplishments and self-esteem
- Counteracting external and internal ableism

> It was difficult for our families. It was just too much for them. They would think he's spoiled or he needed to learn to control himself. They thought he wouldn't do these things if he was in control of himself. My thinking was that if he were developing typically he wouldn't be doing it.
>
> **—ANDIE AMOSSON, PARENT**

FINDING RESOURCES

Before Ricky was diagnosed, we were trying to understand whether the impulsive behaviors were typical or were a product of our parenting skills. Does he have a real condition that could be due to the way his brain is developing? Do we need to improve our parenting practices in some way? I may understand child development, but I absolutely did not feel like a parenting expert. I didn't want to admit these struggles to most of my family, neighbors, and friends. In some ways, the worries I had were too frightening for me to admit even to myself. I felt alone.

I later learned that I was not the only one who feels this way. The research backs me up on this point. For example, Whittingham (2014) found that parents of children with disabilities often face unique challenges, such as an increased burden of care and greater parental stress. Whittingham also found these parents are more likely to experience anxious and depressive symptoms. In our society, we often blame the parents—the mother in particular—for the child's behavior (Peer and Hillman, 2014).

That fact was why it was difficult for me to be honest about my challenges as the mother of a child with ADHD.

It doesn't have to be this way for parents and families. Resources are available to help! Linking with other families through a parent center or other community resource, or even reaching out to your child's teacher can help as you learn to navigate the early intervention and special-education systems. Sometimes, we really just need a listening ear and friendship. Reaching out to form these kinds of relationships is especially important if you are part of a family that lives in a rural area, tribal community, or even an urban area with limited resources. In some areas of our country, community resources are almost nonexistent. In these cases in particular, parent groups and the support from teachers and other professionals can be critical to our own well-being and to the well-being of the important child in our lives.

> We just want Kelsey to be happy and live a meaningful and fulfilling life. I think most parents have some kind of dream of what could be for their child. You know, when you are pregnant and before you even meet the child, the sky is the limit and they have all the potential in the world. A diagnosis of a developmental and or intellectual disability changes the potential, and it takes a little while to see that it's just a change and not the end of all possibilities. Finding a support organization helped me get to know other families like mine. It was especially the families with older children who were being successful that were inspirational to me. Kelsey also led the way once she found something she liked and decided that's what she wanted to do. So, we found ways to incorporate cooking and baking into her life.
>
> **—TERRI LEYTON, PARENT**

Regardless of where you are in the process, navigating the early intervention (EI) and early childhood special education (ECSE) systems can be stressful. Knowing that this is true, the Office of Special Education Programs (OSEP), which is under the U. S. Department of Education, provides funding to support a network of parent centers across the country, so that families can access support regardless of where they are in the process. There are nearly one hundred Parent Training and Information (PTI) centers and Community Parent Resource Centers (CPRC) in the United States and its territories. The hub for these is the Center for Parent Information and Resources (www.parentcenterhub.org), which is staffed by people who are not just advocates by profession but also have a personal stake in the work as parents, siblings, spouses, and so on. You can find lots of information on the hub to better understand your rights as active participants in your child's education.

TALKING WITH YOUR FAMILY ABOUT YOUR CHILD'S DISABILITY

Sometimes, the most difficult conversations happen within our own families. Your child may have a sibling who will need to know about the differences in their brother's or sister's development.

In addition, you may have extended family members who do not understand the concerns you have about your child's development. They may not understand how these concerns affect your life and day-to-day responsibilities, but you can teach them. When family members know about your child's strengths, therapies, preferences, fears, and interests, they are better able to support you. These conversations open the door so family members can ask questions and you can provide concrete examples of how they might support your family. Your family members may also have information to share or connections to make. For example, a family member might know an early intervention specialist or have experience with a supportive child-care teacher who might be willing to help or answer questions. Only you can determine if, when, and how to share information about your child with family members, but it can be helpful to share to some degree so they can understand your perspective and provide support. Parent Andie Amosson told me how she first became an advocate for her child, starting with her family:

> *When Iggy was younger, the family did not respect our boundaries. So, I wrote a long email. I said, "We are working really hard. We really need you to please read these rules." And I sent them a bunch of rules. Like, nobody could just touch him without telling him, because he had all these triggers.*

RESOURCE SPOTLIGHT

The Sibling Support Project (https://siblingsupport.org/) offers lots of resources for talking with siblings as well as ideas for ongoing support, such as online support groups and "Sibshops." These are events for siblings of individuals with disabilities and offer opportunities for siblings to meet other siblings who may have shared experiences.

The Sibling Support Project offers these suggestions for conversations with siblings:

- Talk with the sibling(s) in their language, using words and phrases they will understand.
- Emphasize their brother's or sister's strengths and what they like to do and enjoy. You can also brainstorm simple ways to include their brother or sister in everyday life, routines, and activities.
- Share books with the sibling(s) about their brother's or sister's disability.
- A list of related articles, books, videos, podcasts, and other resources can be found on the Sibling Support Project website.

> *He had to have a very specific schedule, like when he was going to bed or when he was eating. All of that had to be respected very clearly. But family members would just walk into the each other houses, and I knew we couldn't do that. I got some not-so-fun reactions from them at first. But we knew some of his triggers. We really had to control his environment. I had to tell them that this was important. This is how I can keep my son safe. And it worked. They didn't like it, but they said they would respect the rules. I spoke up for myself. To be a mom of a child with disability, sometimes you need to find your voice.*

As a family member or parent, you are an enduring presence in the life of your child. You serve as the most important partner for early childhood educators, early intervention specialists, early childhood special educators, and other professionals. Given this important role, you should know what your rights are and how you can contribute to the decision-making process as your child's advocate. This role is one that you will take on when you first suspect that your child may benefit from services or supports.

KNOWING ABOUT PART C AND PART B, SECTION 619 OF IDEA

The Individuals with Disabilities Education Act (IDEA) is an important federal law that governs how states and U. S. territories, jurisdictions, and public provide services for infants, toddlers, preschoolers, and school-aged children with disabilities. IDEA supports providing early intervention services to eligible infants, toddlers, and their families and providing a free appropriate public education (FAPE) through special-education services to eligible children ages three through twenty-one. Part C is the portion of the law that pertains to services for infants and toddlers; Part B, Section 619, is the portion of the law that pertains to services for children ages three through five. Both Part C and Part B, Section 619 require multidisciplinary teams to evaluate and develop service plans for eligible children. However, many differences exist. For example, eligibility criteria, timelines, and types and locations of services available to children and families differ. The basic differences between Part B and Part C come from different underlying goals:

- Goal of Part C: to support families in supporting their children; services are detailed in the Individualized Family Service Plan (IFSP)
- Goal of Part B, Section 619: to support a child's access to the general curriculum; services are detailed in the Individualized Education Program (IEP)

We'll explore both of these areas of service in chapters 3 and 4, and you can read more about the details of important disability-related legislation in appendix B. For now, this high-level description is a frame for you to understand your role as an advocate for your child. As shared in chapter 1, the services and supports available vary depending on where you live. Unfortunately, these are also dependent to some degree on the parent's ability to advocate for their child. What does your child need to be successful? What services and supports are available for your child and your family? Where should services be provided? Will your child have the opportunity to learn alongside their peers, or will the service agency suggest a separate or segregated setting? All of these questions are unknown at the beginning of the process. However, the IDEA is clear that parents are a key part of the ultimate decision-making team. As a parent, you have an important voice at the table. This is true during IFSP and IEP meetings, doctor appointments, home visits, parent-teacher conferences, and in any other space where decisions about your child's health, development, and learning occur.

This can feel very daunting. It reminds me of the time we chose to make a decision about ADHD medication for Ricky when he was in kindergarten. Before Ricky started taking medication, my husband was really hesitant about the whole thing. I said, "I think we need to try it. I think it could really help him." Then, the very first time Ricky took the medication he held my hand while we walked across the street, instead of trying to dart in front of the traffic. It was like a miracle. I felt such relief that this could help him focus and even keep him safe. My husband had been saying, "Jani, there's no magic pill!" Then after that he said, "I guess there is a magic pill!" We both had to laugh because it was like magic, and it continues to help him in ways that he needs desperately.

I share this story knowing that not all children respond well to medication and, for some families, medication might not be the best option. This decision was the right one for our family, and it wasn't made easily. From my perspective, we have been able to make good decisions as a family because we knew deep down that Ricky was smart, capable, and willing to try hard things. We always had a vision of success for Ricky, and he has always held himself to high standards as well.

What is the vision you have for your own child? To ensure your child has the services and supports they need, provided in an environment that is as inclusive as possible, start by imagining a vision for your child and their life ahead.

CREATING A VISION FOR YOUR CHILD

Before we delve into how you might imagine a vision for your child, let's explore one family's journey to creating a vision for their child. Olivier and Hilda Bernier brought their experiences navigating the EI and ECSE systems to life in their award-winning documentary *Forget Me Not: Inclusion in the Classroom* (Bernier, 2022). As loving parents to their son, Emilio, they present a true picture of what many parents experience when their child has a disability. Emilio has Down syndrome, and the film shows how Olivier and Hilda first learned about his condition in the hospital delivery room right after giving birth. The rollercoaster of emotions is clear throughout the film and is especially apparent when they search for an inclusive early childhood program for Emilio.

Even though Hilda worked as a special education teacher herself, she soon learned that Emilio would be most successful in an inclusive setting. Sara Jo Soldovieri is advocate who advised the Berniers during this process. During an interview with Sara Jo captured in the film, she says, "Inclusion early on almost guarantees inclusion later on. But segregation early on almost guarantees segregation in the rest of life" (Bernier, 2022). Segregation was not the vision that Hilda and Olivier had for their child.

During the film, Hilda shares the vision that she and Olivier wrote for Emilio during these difficult experiences of finding a program where he could learn alongside his peers in an inclusive classroom. The vision statement is told from Emilio's perspective.

My name is Emilio Andres Bernier. I want to be someone that grows up with the same opportunities as everyone else. I want to be surrounded by people that love me for who I am and all my strengths. I want to be as independent as possible, so I can explore all the beauty and diversity of this world. Most importantly, I have so much to offer, and can't wait to show everyone what I am capable of.

When I interviewed families for this book, I made a point to ask this question: "What are your hopes and dreams for your child? Did you have a vision for them early on? How did that develop?" Time and again, I heard from families that they just wanted their child to have the same opportunities as everyone else, to give love and be loved, and to find ways to share their gifts with the world. Here are some examples of vision statements from the interviews:

I want Wren to be happy and feel fulfilled. I would love for her to go to college in whatever type of program that matches what she wants. I just

want her to find what she feels good and confident at, and I want her to find a community, whether she lives independently or not. Maybe she lives independently near a sibling who can check in on her, but I want her to have her own life that she loves, if that includes work or volunteering. I just want her to love her life, and feel successful.

—KRISTIN JONES

My vision for Yaretzy is that she will be accepted and that her condition won't impact her life. I want her to be part of society and included in our community. She belongs in that community. She belongs in that.

—PAULINA VARGAS

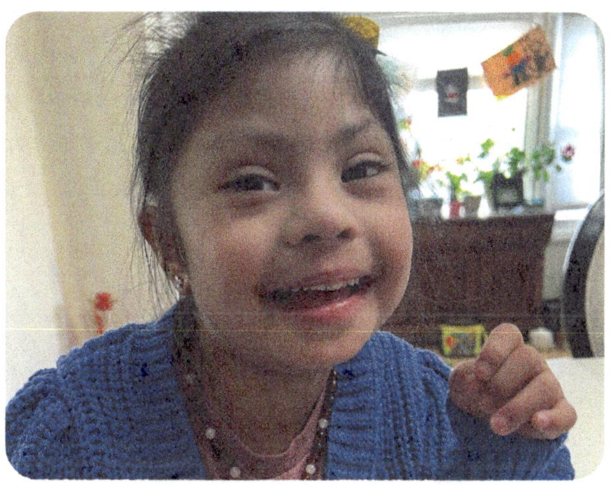

I want Phillip to experience love on a level that I can't provide. I desire for him to be married and have a family. I desire for him to have a job. He will be good at manufacturing. He loves loud noises, and he likes technology. I think the fact that he's affectionate and protective and loving will make him a good father and husband.

—LATISHA R. STUCKEY

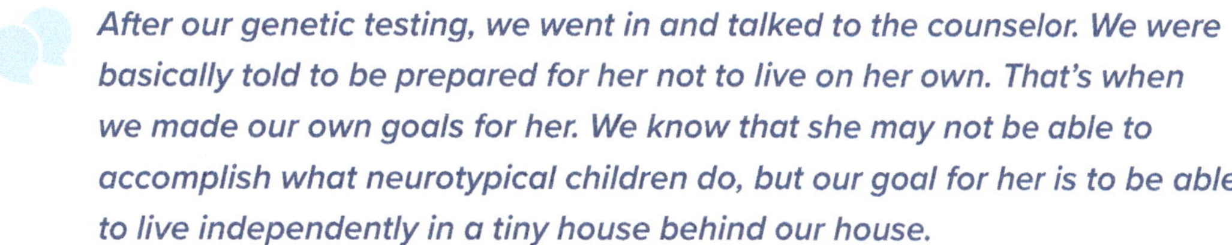

After our genetic testing, we went in and talked to the counselor. We were basically told to be prepared for her not to live on her own. That's when we made our own goals for her. We know that she may not be able to accomplish what neurotypical children do, but our goal for her is to be able to live independently in a tiny house behind our house.

—AMANDA LOVETTE

BUILDING ON YOUR CHILD'S STRENGTHS

We all have strengths and weaknesses. The frustrating thing for many families is that their child's weaknesses sometimes become the focal point in an IFSP or IEP meeting. It makes sense, because the purpose of the meeting is to identify supports needed, and a good description of the problems to address is the first step in identifying those supports. But these meetings are also a time to discuss a child's strengths. Their strengths are so important because these are the qualities and skills that the child will need to rely on as they make their way in the world.

During my interviews with families, I also asked the questions, "What are your child's greatest strengths? How do they use those strengths to help them reach their goals?" One theme that emerged from the family interviews was the strength of persistence and determination:

Jude is intense, three times cubed. He can be intensely sweet. And intensely upset about things. He can be intensely interested in different things and again it's laser focus, when he like zooms in on something, he's locked in on it.

—BEN RIEPE

Dancing is her thing. She's been doing a rock and roll dance this time, and her granddad built her a five-foot-tall jukebox. It plays old time rock and roll. She also loves her ballet class. She has a wonderful teacher who believes that she can do things to the best of her ability, and yet she

pushes her. She has high expectations. She pushes them as she works on their technique and their skills. She dances a lot. We're at the studio quite a bit. It makes her happy.

—PATRICIA REEDY

All the traumas he's been through and all the losses he suffered—I think it's amazing that he is who he is and he's as strong and as resilient as he is.

—JUDY DAVID

If we consider that the families who have been through "the thick of it" and have identified those strengths as highly important, then how might you nurture those qualities in your own child? Is it by stepping in and doing the hard stuff for your child? Of course not. Children build those skills when they have opportunities to be persistent and determined. Challenging situations or tasks are necessary for all children to develop those strengths that they will draw upon again and again throughout life.

AFFIRMING YOUR CHILD'S STRENGTHS, ACCOMPLISHMENTS, AND SELF-ESTEEM

When children are very young, they do not realize that they were born with strengths and abilities. This is true for all children, and so they form the concept of who they are and what they are capable of doing by taking in information from the adults in their lives. Self-reflection is just not available to a two-year-old. When children receive care, encouragement, affirmations, and affection from the important adults in their lives, they form a healthy self-image and learn how to love others. The research has found that maternal love is particularly vital (Feldman and Eidelman, 2009; Kingston, Tough, and Whitfield, 2012). Unfortunately, the opposite can occur as well. When adults are emotionally unavailable or dismissive of their child's needs, the child may interpret that information to mean that they are unlovable or unworthy (Barreto et al., 2017; Hauser Cram, Warfield, Shonkoff, and Krauss, 2001). Although we know that many factors can result in an emotionally unavailable parent, children are unable to see that whole picture. Children lack the emotional maturity to understand that these kinds of situations are not their fault. The only thing they think is that their parents don't love them and they are not good enough.

When we are emotionally open with our children, giving praise and encouragement, they develop self-assurance. Given that this is true for all children, it is especially important for children with disabilities (Hauser-Cram, Warfield, Shonkoff, and Krauss, 2001; Spiker, Boyce, and Boyce, 2002). As

Meg Zucker writes in her 2023 book, *Born Extraordinary: Empowering Children with Difference and Disabilities,* "[W]hen the world takes one glance at you and reminds you of everything you aren't, you need to rely on constant reinforcement at home to remind you of everything you are." Zucker was born with a physical disability that affects her arms, hands, and feet, and she is no stranger to the stares that I also encounter when I'm out in public. Zucker writes about her path to building her own sense of self-love, including a chance encounter with Golda Meir, the former prime minister of Israel, when Meg was young. Meir approached Meg and whispered in her ear, "You are enough," a bold action that startled Meg, mostly because she had previously only faced fear or pity from strangers. It was a defining moment for Zucker and is a good reminder of how influential our words are for young children. The families I interviewed shared similar sentiments related to how they work to affirm their children:

Theodore is resilience. He tries really hard, and he keeps coming back at things. His sense of humor and his memory are fantastic. He's also good with math. He's good at reading, and he remembers stories.

—LEAH MULLEN

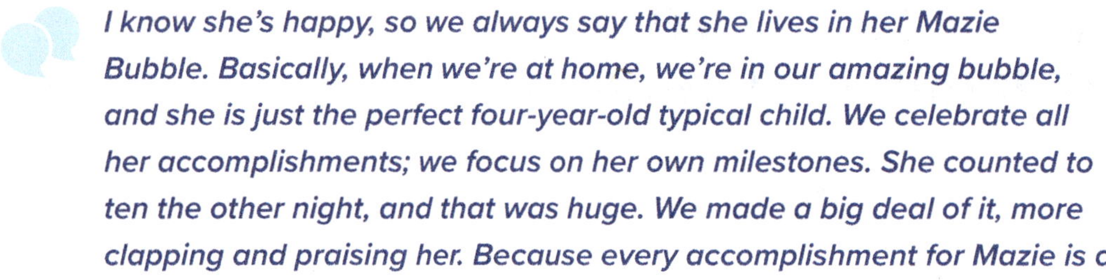

I know she's happy, so we always say that she lives in her Mazie Bubble. Basically, when we're at home, we're in our amazing bubble, and she is just the perfect four-year-old typical child. We celebrate all her accomplishments; we focus on her own milestones. She counted to ten the other night, and that was huge. We made a big deal of it, more clapping and praising her. Because every accomplishment for Mazie is a big accomplishment.

—AMANDA LOVETTE

Iggy's just a good kid, you know. Good heart.

—ANDIE AMOSSON

Kelsey trained very hard for her Special Olympics USA Games success last year. She went outside in all kinds of weather and either walked or ran and practiced her throws. Her hard work paid off!

—TERRI LEYTON

Yaretzy is strong and has the power to know exactly what she wants. And that has helped her to learn to do things on her own. And perseverance—if she really wants something, she will try and try and try until she achieves that.

—PAULINA VARGAS

COUNTERACTING EXTERNAL AND INTERNAL ABLEISM

Ableism is the intentional or unintentional discrimination against those with a disability. It can be defined as discrimination or social prejudice against people with disabilities based on the belief that typical abilities are superior. Ableism can manifest as an attitude, stereotype, or an outright offensive comment or behavior. When it comes to language, ableism often shows up in conversation as metaphors, jokes, and euphemisms: "My boyfriend is emotionally crippled," "That comedian was hysterical*!" "He is 'differently abled.'" Ableism is a difficult concept to consider as a parent of a little one that you love so much. But it does exist, so it's important to acknowledge this and do our best to parent in a way that counteracts that societal tendency. *Internalized ableism* is when a person with a disability holds negative feelings about themselves, and we want to keep our child from that kind of pain. How can we do that?

- Presume competence.
- Speak to your child directly.
- Respect your child's autonomy.
- Avoid making assumptions.
- Remain open about feelings.
- Give yourself grace.

Approach new situations with the mindset that your child is capable, and even though they may not be able to master a new skill right away, they should at least be given the chance to try. When you expect that your child is capable of just about everything, they may surprise you! It also means that you won't jump in to help as readily, because you'll expect they can do it for themselves.

Presuming competence has made all the difference for June, and we've always advocated for people to be around her who are going to hold high expectations and believe in her.

—JACKIE JOSEPH

*Hysteria is a type of neurosis "marked by emotional excitability" (Merriam-Webster.com, 2023).

We came up with a philosophy that if they ask me what Katherine can do, I say, "I don't know. Let's try it." And then we'll let her try. We tell her, "Katherine, you can do anything. It might take you longer, and it might look different. But you can do it." She doesn't realize she can't do things because she's been raised to say, "Try!"

—PATRICIA REEDY

Try to use language and tone of voice that you would use for any child their age. Avoid talking *about* your child when they are in the same room.

We've never limited our language with our daughter. June loves to know the rationale behind things, even if it's not what she wants to hear. She still has a lot of support needs related to feeding, and we say things like, "Okay, June, we can step back as long as you're safe. If you're not eating safe, then we're gonna have to come back in and help you, because you sometimes forget to chew. And if you forget to chew, you can choke." She's always just really appreciated an honest explanation.

—JACKIE JOSEPH

Your child's body is *their* body, so try to be sensitive about the physical contact you make and the way you treat their body, as well as their equipment and possessions.

Adults do not always know better, and your child may have skills and capacities that haven't surfaced for you yet. Here are some things the parents I interviewed shared about their children's skills and capacities:

We were at church, and we had a meet-and-greet time. It is a small ministry and everyone knows us. One day, a visitor who wasn't familiar with us or our story came up to us and greeted us. He saw Philip and said, "Hey, what's your name?" and Philip said "Pippa." That's how he says his name. He didn't even hesitate! I was just amazed. Wow, yeah, I was proud.

—LATISHA R. STUCKEY

We had a really cute moment when Theodore was little. He must have been two or three. He wasn't in a crib anymore; he was in a child's bed. It was low enough that we weren't concerned if he rolled out. The night that

we put him in there, we heard this clanging noise. Theodore had crawled out of bed and had gotten over to his garbage can and he was clanging the lid up and down. He was just playing around with it, and it was just such a funny experience for us, and it was really lovely to see him doing stuff for himself. It was the first time we'd ever seen him get out of a place by himself and do something that that maybe he wasn't supposed to do.

—LEAH MULLEN

When your child is able to communicate with you, verbally or nonverbally, make every attempt to ask before you help. Provide opportunities for your child to share feelings about their disability when they're ready, and find ways to manage your own feelings without putting it on your child.

When my daughter had her first surgery at age two, I had a spica cast made for her favorite doll so she could really understand what was going to happen. It helped her to be able to talk about it too.

—EILEEN SPAHL

If you make a mistake, just say you're sorry and move on. Every parent in the world makes many mistakes, and that's okay!

Continue to advocate for your child. You may not see their progress now, but it will happen later if you stick with the plan. My grandmother used to say, "Oh, it will come! Oh, it will come!"

—JACQUECE MOORE-LAW

KEEPING IT ALL IN PERSPECTIVE

This chapter began with the statement, "Being a parent is hard work," and I'm sure that rings true for you now as you learn about your role as an advocate for your child. In the times when it all feels like a heavy load, the best advice is just to keep the big picture in mind. This is just one point in your family's journey, which will surely have high points and low points along the way.

I kept a journal of funny things that Ricky said and did in the early years of his life. It is one of my cherished possessions. Lord knows that I never would have remembered all of those things if I hadn't written them down at the time. However, I remember thinking that I wasn't capturing the complete picture of my parenting experience, because I recorded only the positive memories. I had been worried that Ricky would come across that book as an adult and get the impression that parenting him was super challenging for me, so I recorded only the happy times. I took lots of photos and wrote down all of the cute, funny, and happy stories.

I kept this journal of happy stories and tried to erase the tough memories. The funny thing is that now I find those tough memories to be most informative. Those are memories that I look back on with pride because of how far Ricky has come. He has overcome adversity in his life and thrived and shined in spite of it all. I've come a long way, too, as a mother. With the benefit of years, I'm able to see that Ricky would have read stories of my parenting challenges with understanding and care. He remembers the hard times for me as a parent because they were hard times for him as well. Ultimately, I learned that parenting is about opening ourselves to all that our children are and about embracing the fact that we have both everything and nothing to do with who they are. Friends and family often say to me that Ricky has turned out really well. But children don't exactly "turn out" as if they were a pumpkin pie that you just took out of the oven. We all evolve, grow, and change through our entire lives. This is much easier to understand in hindsight.

In my current role providing technical assistance to state Part C and Part B, Section 619 coordinators, I often get emails from concerned parents who find my contact information online. They are looking for help for their child, and the desperation they feel comes through loud and clear even in an email. These parents remind me of the urgency I felt in those early years of trying to access services for Ricky. As parents, we all react in many different ways when we first become aware of a suspected delay or concern about our child. You may experience this awareness as a form of grief or loss. You may struggle to process information about it or may become angry or upset or receive information about it with indignation. The beautiful poem "Welcome to Holland" by Emily Perl Kingsley is a lovely tribute to those feelings that many parents experience. You can read it online. (See appendix C for a list of resources for this chapter.) Olivier Bernier, the father of Emilio, who is the subject of the movie *Forget Me Not: Inclusion in the Classroom*, has this to say about perspective. When the doctor told Olivier and Hilda that Emilio has Down syndrome, he also said something very powerful. Olivier shared it with me this way:

> ***The doctor said, "My parents didn't know if I would become a doctor, or if I would become a heroin addict. There's no way to know the outcome of your child. Don't try to predict the outcome of your child, just do the best you can do as a parent." That changed my whole perspective. From then on it was we are just Emilio's parents. Let's treat him like any other child. Let's try to be the best parents we can be.***

Regardless of how you feel when you start on this journey, you can be sure that you are not alone in feeling this way. You are not the only parent who is embarrassed by your child's behavior and lack of self-control. You are not the only family member who has internalized a sense of blame related to your child's disability. You are not the only parent who is worried that your child's actions are viewed by others as a sign that you have poor parenting skills. I was that parent. (Yes, even a child-development expert can be embarrassed by her parenting skills.) You are now part of a mighty fleet of parents, educators, service providers, and advocates who work to support young children with and without disabilities. When you talk with others and share your stories, you are creating a ripple in the water that will become a wave. Find others who share your values and passion. Lean on each other and build each other up. You will need those members of your fleet. Together we are strong. We have resilience, energy, and grit that are matched only by those qualities in the children we love.

> Every child should be their best self-advocate. That's my job—I want every kid in our school to have that when they leave, including Wren. I very much have taught her that.
>
> **—KRISTIN JONES, PARENT**

From my perspective, the fact that you are reading this book shows that you have already succeeded as a parent. It is a success to notice a potential concern for your child and to have the strength and bravery to take action. You are already well on your way toward becoming your child's best advocate.

ACTIVITY: WHAT IS YOUR VISION FOR YOUR CHILD?

DIRECTIONS

Take a moment to reflect on your child, their life now, and their life in the years to come. What is your vision for your child? Think about your child with a long view, beyond your concerns of today. Just as Hilda Bernier did for her son Emilio, think about the vision statement from your child's point of view and write it as though your child is telling it in their own voice. Use the prompts below to craft a vision that your child could share with the world.

My name is ______________________________ and I love to ______________________________.

I'm really good at ____________________________ and ______________________________.

My favorite things are _________________________ and ______________________________.

It used to be hard for me to ____, but now I can do it!

My family loves it when I _______________________ and when I ____________________________.

When I grow up, my life is going to be filled with ____.

Later in life, I'm excited that I will _________________________ and ___________________________

and ____.

Most of all, I want people to know that ____

____.

CHAPTER 3

Understanding Early Intervention: Services for Infants and Toddlers

It's your choice as a parent. Early intervention will come and work in a natural environment. They're gonna help you with things at home. They're gonna help you get a routine. They're gonna help you learn some of the behavior tricks that you're going to need to survive.

—PATRICIA REEDY, PARENT

As I shared earlier, given that I inherited my disability through genes passed down to me by my father, I was concerned about passing those genes to my own child. My husband, Rick, and I went through genetic counseling and learned that a biological child of ours would have a fifty/fifty chance of inheriting my disability. Even though in some ways it would have been amazing to have a child with some of our physical features, I remembered how guilty my father had felt about passing along the condition. Would I choose to give birth to a child knowing that he or she may well need multiple surgeries? Nope, not for me. Rick agreed, and we made the decision to adopt—the best decision of my life! By May 2000, I was the mother of Ricky Vadim Kozlowski. Life is full of irony, however.

Even though we were able to raise a child without an orthopedic impairment like the one I would have passed along, we did not have a path free from obstacles. (Is any parenting path free from obstacles?) But we were still lucky, right from the beginning and still to this day.

Ricky was seventeen months old when we adopted him from an orphanage in Simferopol, Ukraine. Simferopol is in the Crimean Peninsula. It is a beautiful place, right by the Black Sea and full of history, castles, and unfortunately, a great deal of alcoholism and poverty. We don't know much about Ricky's history before he joined our family, including his medical history. We just had to be open to the wonder and adventure that this little toddler brought to our lives.

What a wild adventure it was! While still in Simferopol, Ricky took his first wobbly steps from my husband's arms to mine. He was tentative and shy with us in the beginning. It seemed that most of the children in the orphanage spent a lot of time in their cribs, but it was hard to know for sure what his life was really like because we were just popping in and out for visits while we completed the necessary paperwork. On one visit, however, we came in to see one of the caregivers feeding Ricky through the bars of his crib. Did anyone ever hold him or comfort him when he was sad? I worried about this early deprivation. I remember being worried that he was only learning to walk at seventeen months, when most children take their first steps at around their first birthday. But his shyness did not last long. By the time we were back at the hotel in Kiev, he was running down the hallways, squealing with delight. Back home in the United States, Ricky continued to grow and develop at a surprising pace. He learned words quickly and was, as people say about most toddlers, *into everything.* His curiosity was unrivaled! He frantically grabbed any item within his reach and turned it over and over in his hands, smelled it, tasted it, eager to understand all these new discoveries in a suddenly wide-open world.

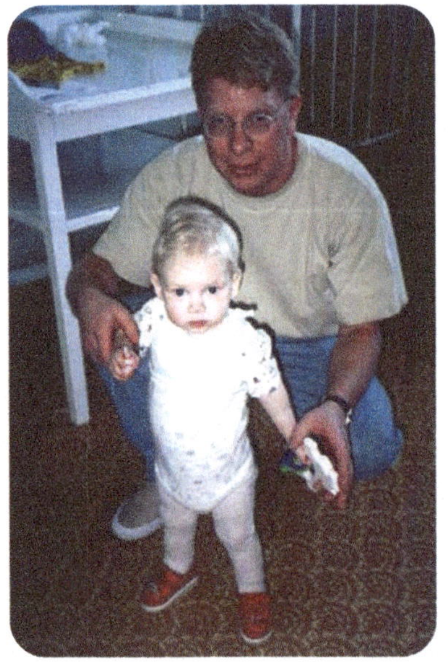

This curiosity was nonstop, and it was almost as though he couldn't stay in one place for long because there was too much to explore somewhere else. Ricky was in constant motion, running from toy to toy. He wanted to figure out how everything worked and loved to take things apart. I couldn't engage him in pretend play activities or, really, anything that didn't involve lots of movement. He didn't want to be held for long and would squirm away from us so that he could get down and explore. Mealtimes were over in an instant because sitting in his high chair during a calm activity like eating dinner was too much for him to bear. When we went out to eat, we immediately had to clear away the salt and pepper shakers and other condiments on the table, because Ricky would grab them and put them in his mouth.

I knew toddlers were curious, but this seemed excessive. It also verged on dangerous. He seemed to have very little fear and gravitated toward things that might hurt him. Fortunately, many of my friends are early childhood educators themselves, and they were happy to serve as sounding boards for me. They suggested that I reach out to the early intervention program and set up an evaluation. This led to an Individualized Family Service Plan (IFSP) and home visits that felt like a lifeline. What a relief to have someone validate my concerns and offer suggestions. It's worth mentioning that, despite my education and relative confidence as a parent, I still needed help. Reaching out in this way can be intimidating to families and educators alike. For our family, participation in early intervention set us up for success. We began a long road through systems of early intervention and early childhood special education that ultimately led to a successful high school graduation. We were fortunate to be able to access services for Ricky at the earliest age, when they could be the most effective. It all started with a referral—not from a doctor or a professional but a phone call from a mother who reached out for help. That was my first step.

In the following pages we'll explore the key features of early interventions and the steps in the process of obtaining services.

PART C—EARLY INTERVENTION SERVICES FOR INFANTS AND TODDLERS

Research has shown the most rapid period of brain development happens from birth to three years of age, and intervening early makes a significant impact on children's outcomes (Prenatal-to-3 Policy Impact Center, 2020). There are programs out there to help. The Program for Infants and Toddlers with Disabilities is also known as Part C of the Individuals with Disabilities Education Act, or simply Part C of IDEA (20 USC 1400, 2004). It is a federal grant program that helps states operate early intervention (EI) services for children from birth to age three and their families. Funding for Part C, however, is dependent on state funds to supplement federal funds. As a result, some states charge families a fee to access early intervention services. This varies greatly from state to state. Each state and territory has its own system for providing services under Part C, including an agency that oversees the EI system for children from birth to three years. The system includes such steps as evaluation and assessment, eligibility for Part C services, and the development of IFSPs. (These will be discussed later in this chapter.)

Where Do I Find Out about Part C Eligibility Guidelines in My State?

The Part C eligibility criteria for each state are listed on the ECTA Center's Part C eligibility page (https://ectacenter.org/topics/earlyid/state-info.asp). You can also find out about resources in your

Inequities in Access to Early Intervention Services

The Children's Equity Project and the Bipartisan Policy Center released a report titled *Start with Equity: From the Early Years to the Early Grades* (Meek et al., 2020). The report includes a collection of data related to the inequities in our early intervention and early childhood special education systems. For example, racial disparities exist in access to early intervention services. Children of color who are eligible for services are less likely to receive them and more likely to face challenges while receiving them. This is due to a variety of factors, including insufficient outreach and a lack of culturally competent services. According to Feinberg, Silverstein, Donahue, and Bliss (2011), Black children are five times less likely to receive early intervention services than white children. Early childhood leaders are working to address these disparities by collecting information from families to better understand the issues, raising awareness about the availability of early intervention services, sharing information with the public through social media stories and videos on YouTube, and supporting families if challenges arise.

state through your state Parent Training and Information (PTI) center. You can find your parent center online at www.parentcenterhub.org.

The law expects the services to be provided in a coordinated way across each state and outlines specific requirements that states must meet in order to receive funding (OSEP, n.d.a.). Let's take a look at these requirements.

RIGOROUS DEFINITION OF *DEVELOPMENTAL DELAY*

Young children and their families are eligible for Part C services if the child is under the age of three and experiences developmental delays in one or more areas of development or has a diagnosed physical or mental condition with a high probability of resulting in developmental delay. For Part C, each state must establish the criteria for eligibility. Thus, the law requires states to define what is meant by the term *developmental delay.* States also have the option of serving infants and toddlers who are *at risk* of developmental delay. The important point to remember here is that once states determine the definitions of *developmental delay* and *at risk,* they may serve only children who meet those definitions. The at-risk category includes children with a diagnosed condition that has a high probability of leading to developmental delay, as well as children who are deemed at risk because of other factors such as low birth weight, child abuse or neglect, nutritional deficiencies, or prenatal drug exposure (20 USC 1400, 2004). The definitions used in your state are important, because states are obligated to serve children who meet those definitions as long as the family consents to receive the services.

State governments make the policy decisions related to eligibility determination for Part C services. For example, states determine the criteria within Part C EI programs about whether or not to consider infants or toddlers who are at risk for a delay or disability as being eligible for services. As of 2023, only eight states actually support children who are at risk for a delay or disability, meaning that many children who would likely benefit from services are not eligible for them and are missing out on important interventions that would strengthen their development (U. S. Government Accountability Office, 2023). Including at-risk children in Part C eligibility and investing early in their growth would improve their developmental outcomes and prevent future learning and behavioral challenges. More federal funding for IDEA would likely increase the number of states that would include at-risk children in Part C eligibility.

The OSEP-funded Center for Parent Information and Resources ("Parent Center Hub") has a set of online modules called "Building the Legacy for Our Youngest Children with Disabilities" for parents and educators to help with understanding Part C. You can access the modules online at www.parentcenterhub.org/legacy-partc/. (See appendix C for a list of resources for this chapter.)

EVALUATION AND ASSESSMENT

States are also required to provide timely, comprehensive evaluations that show a child's current developmental level of functioning. In addition, Part C programs may also conduct a voluntary family assessment to determine the resources, priorities, and concerns for the family as a whole.

INDIVIDUALIZED FAMILY SERVICE PLANS

Early intervention (EI) providers in every state are required to develop an Individualized Family Service Plan (IFSP) with families to guide the delivery of services to eligible children. IFSPs are based on an in-depth assessment of the child's needs and the needs and concerns of the family. The IFSP itself is the written agreement with the family and all providers that details all the services and supports that will be provided. Developing an IFSP uses an interagency approach by involving representatives of several agencies and other resources that can help the child and family. Usually, a professional called the *service coordinator* is assigned to assist the child's family through the IFSP process. The IFSP clarifies the frequency of services, where the services will be provided, and who will be responsible for assisting the child and family. The IFSP includes child and family goals and outcomes

> It's scary right in the beginning; I didn't know what I was getting myself into. It took Yaretzy a while to walk, and she practiced, practiced, practiced—lots of therapies to help her, but no giving up. After walking, running, and now she's even jumping!
>
> **—PAULINA VARGAS, PARENT**

and must be reviewed and revised every six months, or more frequently if conditions warrant or the family requests a review.

RESEARCH-BASED EARLY INTERVENTION SERVICES

States must have a policy that ensures that services are research based and available to all infants and toddlers with disabilities and their families, including those who may live on an American Indian reservation or those who may be experiencing homelessness. These EI services include physical therapy, occupational therapy, speech therapy, audiology or hearing services, assistive technology, family counseling, medical services, nursing services, nutrition counseling, and service coordination.

SERVICES IN NATURAL ENVIRONMENTS

A key principle of EI is that infants and toddlers learn best through everyday experiences and interactions with familiar people in familiar contexts. This principle is supported through the IDEA requirement that services be provided in the *natural environment*. For infants and toddlers, a natural environment is any place the child and family live, learn, and play, such as the home, community, child-care center, or Early Head Start center. This works best for young children because they are more likely to learn, grow, and try new things in an environment that is familiar to them. Across the country, children are served through EI in natural environments in most cases, and other settings are used only when services cannot be achieved satisfactorily in a natural environment.

PART C OVERSIGHT

States must maintain oversight over their Part C programs in a number of ways, including having a system for identifying eligible children (also known as "Child Find"), staff professional development, safeguards for families, collecting data, supervision and monitoring, complaint procedures, and a state Interagency Coordinating Council (ICC). Here are some of the specifics about those requirements:

- **Child Find System:** The law requires states to maintain a central directory with access to information about services, resources, and experts, and to engage in public-awareness efforts so that other organizations know how to identify and refer children to the EI program. Part C emphasizes finding and serving children at the earliest possible age.
- **Professional development:** States must have a comprehensive system of professional development to make sure that staff who provide early intervention services are qualified and appropriately trained to understand a child's unique needs and are capable of supporting the family.

- **Procedural safeguards:** States must ensure that families are afforded certain legal rights related to confidentiality, prior notice and consent, due process, and access to services. All agencies that provide EI services must adhere to these legal safeguards that protect the rights of children and families, and they must ensure that families know their rights.
- **Supervision and monitoring:** State agencies must monitor programs to enforce the Part C obligations and report the results to the public. If there are issues, states must correct the issues.
- **State complaint procedures:** States must have written procedures to resolve complaints and establish solutions if a family is inappropriately denied services.
- **Interagency Coordinating Council (ICC):** Each state must have a state ICC that provides guidance to the program and includes representatives from early childhood programs at the state and local levels, as well as families who receive EI services.
- **Data collection:** Each state must collect information about its program and must report the data to the secretary of education within OSEP each year.

When Wren was a few months old, I got to meet a lot of other families with kids about her age with Down syndrome—the early intervention hosted an event for us. We made our own playgroup, and we all have kept it up. The group has gotten way bigger. There was a mom there who recommended the book *Kids Beyond Limits*. It totally shifted my thinking. It recommends taking a step back, meeting the child where they are in the moment. Instead of coming home, thinking I had to be her therapist, I was meeting her where she was, which made me enjoy who she was instead of who we needed her to be. It changed my life.

—KRISTIN JONES, PARENT

EARLY INTERVENTION STEP BY STEP

Now that you know some of the basics behind the legislation, let's look at it step by step and how the process might work for your child.

STEP 1. THE REFERRAL

Children are referred to EI in one of two ways: through the Child Find system or by referral of a parent or teacher, doctor, or other professional. Each state is required by IDEA to identify, locate,

What Is Child Find?

Child Find refers to the policies and procedures in each state that ensure that all children with disabilities, from birth through age twenty-one, who live in the state and need EI or ECSE are identified, located, and evaluated. Child Find procedures may include:

- Public announcements through newspaper, television, radio, and social media
- Meetings with private and homeschool representatives/ organizations
- Use of websites
- Community service fairs
- Parent mentors and collaboration with other public agencies

and evaluate all children who may benefit from EI services. When a child is identified as possibly having a disability and as needing special education, parents may be asked for permission to evaluate their child. Parents can also call the Child Find office and ask that their child be evaluated.

STEP 2. EVALUATION

Evaluation is the step in the process when parents and EI staff seek to learn whether the child has a disability that requires the provision of services. For EI, the question is whether or not your child would benefit from services to help with growth and development. Parental consent is needed before your child may be evaluated. Under the federal IDEA regulations, the evaluation must be completed within a specified time frame after the parent gives consent: forty-five days for EI (Part C). However, if a state's IDEA regulations give a different timeline for completion of the evaluation, the state's timeline is applied. The evaluation must assess the child in all areas related to the child's suspected disability or delay, and the results are used to determine whether or not the child is eligible to receive services.

STEP 3. ELIGIBILITY DETERMINATION

A group of qualified professionals and the parents look at the child's evaluation results. Together, they decide if the child has a developmental delay or disability as defined by federal and state laws and regulations, **and** they determine the supports necessary to meet the needs of the child. Keep in mind that, while IDEA does provide some guidance around eligibility determination, there are many areas where individual state governments make those decisions. It's important to know the guidelines in your own state. If you do not agree with the eligibility decision, as your child's legal guardian, you have the right to challenge it.

For Part C, children are deemed eligible based strictly on whether they have a developmental delay or a diagnosed physical or mental condition with a high probability of its resulting in developmental delay.

STEP 4. IFSP MEETING

Once your child is found eligible, the EI staff set up a meeting to determine the services that your child and family will receive. You are notified of the meeting, making sure that it is scheduled at a time and place that is convenient for you and your family. During the meeting, the team will identify annual IFSP goals and consider the services needed to support those goals. The team will also discuss where the services will be provided. If you consent to the services as described in the IFSP, your child can begin to receive services as soon as possible. If you do not agree with decisions outlined in the IFSP, you can ask for mediation or even file a complaint and request a hearing. (This process is described in more detail in chapter 5.)

STEP 5. PROVIDING SERVICES

Following the IFSP meeting, services can be provided as long as you give consent and the plan is carried out as written. You and your child's teacher should receive a copy of the IFSP. All members of the IFSP team should have access to the IFSP and know their responsibilities for carrying out the plan. The plan includes the accommodations, modifications, and supports that must be provided for your child and family. Remember that IFSP is a *family* service plan, so there may be services included that are intended to support you as your child's parent. (This is a key distinction from Part B, which focuses solely on the child and their educational needs.)

States are also required to provide services in a timely manner. How soon is *timely?* This is determined by the state, and clarification is provided on the state's early intervention website and in parent information materials.

STEP 6. PROGRESS MONITORING

The way the team will measure your child's progress toward the annual goals is also stated in the IFSP. You should be regularly informed of your child's progress and whether that progress is enough for your child to achieve the goals outlined by the end of the year. These progress reports must be given to parents at various points throughout the year.

STEP 7. IFSP REVIEW

The IFSP must be reviewed by the team at least annually, with a six-month periodic review to ensure that your child is making progress toward goals. If necessary, the IFSP is revised, and you would be invited to participate in these meetings as well. As your child's parent, you can make suggestions for changes, and you can agree or disagree with the services outlined in IFSP and where those services will be provided.

If you do not agree with anything in the IFSP, you may discuss these concerns with other members of the team and try to work out an agreement. Several options are available, including additional testing, an independent evaluation, asking for mediation, or a due-process hearing. You may also file a complaint with the state early intervention agency.

> My wife and I are working to do a better job at coming to consensus. Now we seem to come to consensus after we argue, and that's after [the children have] gone to bed. I wish we could do a better job of sitting down as a family and figuring the thing out together.
>
> **—BEN RIEPE, PARENT**

STEP 8. TRANSITION FROM EI TO ECSE

In almost every state, children with IFSPs must be determined eligible for continuing special education and related services. If eligible, before the child's third birthday an IEP must be developed in place of the IFSP for services to continue. In the next part of this chapter, we'll explore that transition a bit further.

TRANSITIONING FROM EARLY INTERVENTION TO EARLY CHILDHOOD SPECIAL EDUCATION

Transition is a natural part of all of our lives. In this context, transition is the process of a child moving from one location, program, or environment to another. Children experience multiple transitions in the early years. It may be the transition from playing in the home setting to playing in a center-based child-care setting. It may be from group to group within a setting, such as moving from playing in the infant room to playing in the toddler room. Or it may be the transition from a preschool program to a kindergarten program. Most of these transitions are expected or are due to a decision that the family makes; however, the transition from EI to ECSE at age three is due to changes in the systems that serve your family.

The transition between systems can be disruptive because it is dictated by the law rather than by the family's needs. Therefore, IDEA includes provisions intended to support families during the transitions from early intervention to early childhood special education and then to kindergarten.

Many families assume that their child will automatically receive ECSE services if they are already eligible for and receiving EI services. Unfortunately, this is not the case. In almost every state, children with IFSPs must be determined as eligible for continuing special education and related services at age three. If the child has been evaluated and is determined to be eligible for early childhood special education, an IEP must be developed in place of the IFSP before the child's third birthday so that services can continue. You can participate in the evaluation process and, if the team determines that your child does not qualify for special education services, you can learn about other community agencies that might be able to help.

The ECTA Center (https://ectacenter.org/) offers a series of practice guides and checklists related to transitions from hospital to EI (Part C) programs, from EI to ECSE (Part B, Section 619), and from preschool special education to kindergarten. These materials are available in English and Spanish. (See appendix C for a list of resources for this chapter.)

The EI-to-ECSE transition process typically happens at least six months prior to the child's third birthday. This can be anxiety producing, because just the thought of your toddler entering preschool for the first time is such a big deal. This transition also means that the focus on the whole family in early intervention will shift to the early childhood special education focus on the *child as an individual*. EI programs will work to support your preparation, participation, and decision-making obligations in the process, so you can learn about the different systems of support. These conversations give you a chance to share your thoughts, questions, feelings, hopes, and concerns. If you or a member of your family speaks a language other than English, programs will determine how to translate materials and set up interpreter services to foster effective communication as needed.

TRANSITION CONFERENCE AND PLAN

The first step is typically done through a transition conference with your EI service coordinator. This conference is set up to develop a transition plan with details about the steps in the process and information about early learning programs you may want to visit before making decisions about where ECSE services will be provided. ECSE services can be provided in a variety of locations, including a separate class at the public school, a public pre-K program, a Head Start classroom, a child-care classroom, and so forth. Your EI program staff can ask for information from the school district for you to review so you can take some time to consider the options and be prepared. You may want to find out information about services available, where services can be provided, the evaluation process, parent rights, and how the IEP is structured. Another option is to ask your EI service coordinator to invite a representative from the public school to join the transition conference so you can hear the information directly and ask questions.

RE-EVALUATION AND IEP MEETING

Following the transition conference, your child will be re-evaluated to determine eligibility, and if your child qualifies, an IEP meeting will be arranged by ECSE staff. Remember that you can invite others to join you for the IEP meeting. With parental consent, the EI program can transfer information about your child so ECSE staff will have access to the IFSP, recent assessments, and any other relevant information.

After the IEP is developed by the IEP team (details to come in chapter 4), you may want to visit the new program and meet the ECSE staff. Your child would benefit from these visits and may have questions of their own. You can support your child by giving plenty of opportunities to talk about the change, offering a visit to the new program, and reading books together about going to preschool. There may even be a way for you to set up playdates with other children who go to the new program. Explore all of these options with your EI service coordinator so the transition goes as smoothly as possible.

> When Jasmine was born, her legs were turned in and very weak and she was very fragile. She had PT and OT and saw many specialists. She didn't walk until age two; she kept falling. Finally, with the family around, she walked. I'm getting chills thinking about it!
>
> **—JACQUECE MOORE-LAW, PARENT**

Now that you have learned about early intervention, take a moment to look up the information about services in your state. To find EI services near you, select your state or territory and review the "Early Intervention for Children with Special Needs" drop-down menu under the "Health and Social Services" tab here: https://childcare.gov/state-resources-home. You'll use this information for our chapter 3 activity on the next page.

ACTIVITY: ALL ABOUT MY CHILD—INFANT/TODDLER

DIRECTIONS

Using the information about early intervention (EI) services you looked up (https://childcare.gov/state-resources-home), write all that you found out below.

Early Intervention Program: ____

Contact person: ____

Phone/Email:____

Early Education Program Contact (child care or Early Head Start) (optional):

____

Then, do some reflecting about what the EI professionals (service coordinator, therapists, teachers, and so on) would want to know about your child. Fill in the prompts below and share the information with members of your team when the time is right.

All About ______________________ (child's name)

The most important information that you should know about me is: ______________________

____

My greatest strengths are: ____

The things that are difficult for me right now are: ______________________________

I communicate with others by: ____

The language my family speaks at home is: ______________________________

I live with (people/pets): ____

The other children in my home or neighborhood are (names/ages/relationship to your child): ______

____

My favorite foods are:____

Foods to avoid giving me are:____

My favorite thing to play with is: ____

____

A thing that brings me comfort is: ______________________________

____

My favorite thing to do at home is: ______________________________

____

An important part of my daily routine is: ______________________________

____

Something to know about my eating routine is: ______________________________

____

Something to know about how I am around other children is: ______________________________

____

Something to know about how I am around other adults is: ______________________________

____

I am happy when: ______________________________

____

I am motivated to learn or try new things when: ______________________________

____

I get angry or upset when: ______________________________

____

I will let you know that I need something by: ______________________________

____

Other things to know about me are: ______________________________

____

CHAPTER 4

Understanding Early Childhood Special Education: Services for Preschoolers

When a family has a child with disabilities or a loved one is suddenly disabled . . . their only option is to include them. During meals, daily routines, visits with relatives, vacations, doctor's appointments, and the like. Each family decides how best to support that person . . . in whatever context should arise. Shouldn't this be the same with our schools?

—TIM VILLEGAS, DIRECTOR OF COMMUNICATIONS, MARYLAND COALITION FOR INCLUSIVE EDUCATION

Our son Ricky was diagnosed with ADHD early on. I have been to more IEP meetings than I can count. The ADHD affected his learning in many ways, but that really didn't show up until preschool. As I shared earlier, Ricky was always super-inquisitive, his curiosity on overdrive right from the start. At home, I kept him close by me to make sure he didn't get into danger, and he always wanted to help me with daily chores. I tried to put him to work in every way that I could think of.

At first, I really didn't think that the ADHD would be that much of a problem. We had lots of fun together as a family, and Ricky was a good-natured, sweet child. He had lots of energy, but how would that affect his learning? It was hard for me to understand, and I really bristled at the suggestion that he would need early childhood special education. Early intervention was one thing, but *special education?* Really? For my little boy? His preschool teacher insisted that it really could help him. But how? Why? His teacher told me that people would walk by her room and peek in with troubled faces. They told her that he really needed some help. I thought, "What? Who are these people? What was he doing that was so wrong?" She told me that when someone walked into her classroom at circle time, all of the children were sitting on their mats, crisscross applesauce, except for Ricky. Ricky could usually be found underneath the teacher's desk examining the hardware. That image painted a pretty clear picture for me.

We agreed to start the process and have an evaluation for special education. This was a whole new system to learn. We shifted from IDEA Part C services to Part B. It's a big shift.

PART B, SECTION 619—EARLY CHILDHOOD SPECIAL EDUCATION SERVICES FOR CHILDREN AGES THREE THROUGH FIVE

Now that you understand the services and supports offered through early intervention (Part C), let's explore the services available for children when they reach their third birthday and become eligible for early childhood special education (ECSE). As discussed earlier, IDEA's Part B, Section 619 provides information about how states deliver special education and related services for children ages three through five if they have a disability and need these services to be successful in school. In the 2022 annual report to Congress, OSEP reported that nearly 7 percent of preschool-age children received early childhood special education (U. S. Department of Education, 2022). In the following sections, we'll explore the key components of Part B, Section 619. We will also look at your rights as parents under IDEA and what you can do if you don't agree with the services and/or placement your child receives.

FREE AND APPROPRIATE PUBLIC EDUCATION

One of the ways that ECSE differs from EI is that states are required to offer ECSE services for free. ECSE services are provided as part of the state's education system, and IDEA states that every eligible child has the right to receive a *free and appropriate public education* (FAPE). Therefore, children with disabilities who have unique educational needs receive services at no cost to the family, if the child's IEP team determines that the services are necessary for the child to participate in the state education system.

IDENTIFICATION AND EVALUATION

As is true for EI, states are also required to have Child Find in place for ECSE. This requirement refers to the policies and procedures that ensure all children with disabilities who need special education and related services are located, identified, and evaluated. States offer support for families to help with the referral process and advocacy skills.

Qualified staff must administer the evaluations for ECSE, and the results are used along with other required information to determine eligibility. Note that it is *evaluations*—plural. No single measure or assessment can serve as the sole criterion for determining eligibility.

RESOURCE  **SPOTLIGHT**

The OSEP-funded Center for Parent Information and Resources ("Parent Center Hub") offers a set of online modules for Part B, Section 619 called "Building the Legacy." The modules are for parents and educators to help them understanding Part B, Section 619 of IDEA. You can access the modules online at www.parentcenterhub.org/partb/. (See appendix C for a list of resources for this chapter.)

INDIVIDUALIZED EDUCATION PROGRAM

I'm at this stage in my life where I finally have come to acceptance of what is to come: Ayden's going to grow up one day. So I just try to do my best to help him be able to navigate life, and I don't let anybody discourage me in my parenting.

—ARIELLE BRANCH, PARENT

The individualized education program (IEP) is a written document that outlines the educational needs and services to support the individual child. A team including the child's parents or guardian, regular and special-education teachers, a school-district representative, and others meets to review the assessment information available about the child and design a program to address the child's educational needs that result from their disability. You are a key partner in this process. In fact, states must meet regulations designed to ensure that parents are active participants in the process of developing their child's IEP and are involved in their child's education in an ongoing way.

IEPs must be reviewed at least annually. An IEP for a preschool-aged child includes information about the child's needs, annual goals, how progress will be measured, special education and any

A Note on IEP Terminology

What's the difference between *related services* and *supplementary aids and services? Related services* include speech, physical, and/or occupational therapy; interpreting services; counseling; mobility services; social-work services; and other similar services. *Supplementary aids and services* refer to the supports, such as accommodations, modifications, assistive technology, and so on, which help your child access and participate in learning activities in a regular early childhood program.

related services, supplementary aids and services, and necessary training for school staff. Supplementary aids and services include materials your child might need to be successful, support strategies, or modifications to the classroom environment or curriculum. Here are some examples of each:

- **Materials:** Large-print materials, graphic organizers, use of computers, use of computer-assisted devices, communication devices, book stands, highlighter tapes, fidget toys
- **Support strategies:** Preferential seating, peer tutors, recorded teaching demonstrations, reduced seat time, a notetaker, preteaching, use of a schedule or agenda, written directions. Support strategies can also include training for the general education teacher, special education teacher, and/or paraprofessional.
- **Modifications:** Visual supports, word banks, reduced number of items, hands-on models, pictures. Modifications can also include the assistance of a teacher or other professional with inclusive education training.

WHAT IF MY CHILD DOESN'T QUALIFY FOR IDEA SERVICES?

If your child received early intervention under Part C, they still must be evaluated to determine whether or not they qualify for early childhood special education under Part B, Section 619. Sometimes, children are eligible for EI but then are *ineligible* for ECSE. What are your options at that point? One strategy is to find out about available services through your family's health-insurance program.

Another strategy is to ask about services and supports available under Section 504 of the Rehabilitation Act. You may be able to access services if your child satisfies the definition of *disability* given in the Rehabilitation Act. Often called "Section 504" for short, this is a civil rights law intended to protect against discrimination based on disability. Your child may qualify for supports under Section 504 if they have a physical or mental impairment that substantially limits them in one or more major life activities. The law applies to students ages three through twenty-one and requires public schools and other federal programs to provide children with disabilities equal access to the program, with reasonable accommodations and modifications. If you learn that your child does not qualify for ECSE services, ask about services under a Section 504 plan. A 504 plan is used like an IEP to describe and document the accommodations and modifications your child receives. Although these accommodations are not considered "special education," they may be helpful to your child and their ability to succeed in the preschool setting. Look for more information about Section 504 and other disability laws in appendix B.

> I learned that it's okay to have tools to help Katherine do things, like turning on the lamp. Why does she have to work hard to twist a tiny little knob if she can just touch the bottom of the lamp? It was huge that we were learning that we could find those tools and those things did exist. If you need the plate that has the high rim on it, then it's okay to use that.
>
> **—PATRICIA REEDY, PARENT**

LEAST RESTRICTIVE ENVIRONMENT

During the IEP meeting, the team determines the services a child needs and where those services will be provided. IDEA emphasizes educating children with disabilities in inclusive settings alongside children without disabilities, with any needed supports to ensure that the child is successful in that setting. As discussed earlier, think about special education as a *service,* not a *place.* Therefore, to the greatest extent possible, special education services should be provided in the setting or environment in which your child would be educated if they did not have a disability. Sounds like inclusion, right? In the law, this is referred to as the *least restrictive environment* (LRE).

> I learned if I heard the word *no,* I think, okay, what's next? What other program? Just because somebody said no, then just go to the next person and get the help that your child needs. That's where I have come from.
>
> **—JACQUECE MOORE-LAW, PARENT**

For preschool-aged children, special education services can be provided in regular early childhood settings such as a public or private preschool program, Head Start, child care, Title I program, state pre-K, or other early care and education program. To determine the LRE, the team must first consider the supplementary aids and services the child would need in a setting to be successful alongside children without disabilities. Only when the team determines that the education of a particular child with a disability cannot be achieved satisfactorily in a regular early childhood educational environment, even with the provision of supplementary aids and services, can the team consider placement in a more restrictive environment. Placement decisions should be made based on the child's individual needs, the LRE, and consideration of family preferences.

PART B, SECTION 619 OVERSIGHT

Just as in Part C, the Part B of the law also specifies state obligations related to oversight. As stated in chapter 3, Part C refers to the portion of the IDEA pertaining to children ages birth to three years old. Part B refers to the services for ages three through twenty-one, and Part B, Section 619 refers specifically to the three-to-five age range of children. As a result of this nuance, each state has a leader known as the Section 619 coordinator or just 619 coordinator. The 619 coordinator is typically involved with state-level oversight around expectations related to data collection, supervision and monitoring, professional development for staff, and other activities. States must develop procedural safeguards that will protect the rights of children and families, such as the ability for parents to participate in meetings about their child, to request an evaluation, and to receive prior written notice if changes are to occur. Parents must provide *written* consent before their child is evaluated or receives services. The children's and families' rights are also protected if there is a disagreement between the family and the school system (OSEP, n.d.b.). These procedural safeguards are explained in further detail later in this chapter.

EARLY CHILDHOOD SPECIAL EDUCATION STEP BY STEP

Early childhood special education (ECSE) steps are quite similar to EI in the steps from a referral to the development of the IEP. Let's start with an overview of the steps and then dig in deeper to the specifics of ECSE.

STEP 1. THE REFERRAL

Children are referred to ECSE in one of two ways: through Child Find or by referral of a parent or teacher, doctor, or other professional. Each state is required by IDEA to identify, locate, and evaluate all children who may benefit from EI or ECSE services. When a child is identified as possibly having a disability and as needing special education, parents may be asked for permission to evaluate their child. Parents can also contact the Child Find office and ask that their child be evaluated.

STEP 2. EVALUATION

Evaluation is the step in the process when parents and ECSE staff seek to learn whether the child has a disability that requires the provision of services. For ECSE, the focus is primarily about the child's educational needs. Parental consent is needed before a child may be evaluated. Under the federal IDEA regulations, the evaluation must be completed within a specified time frame after the parent gives consent: sixty days for ECSE. However, if a state's IDEA regulations give a different timeline for completion of the evaluation, the state's timeline is applied. The evaluation must assess the child in all areas related to the child's suspected disability or delay, and the results are used to determine whether or not the child is eligible to receive services.

STEP 3. ELIGIBILITY DETERMINATION

A group of qualified professionals and the parents look at the child's evaluation results. Together, they decide if the child has a developmental delay or disability as defined by federal and state laws and regulations, **and** they determine the supports necessary to meet the needs of your child. Keep in mind that while IDEA does provide some guidance around eligibility determination, there are many areas where individual state governments make those decisions, so it's important to know the guidelines in your own state. If you do not agree with the eligibility decision, you or another member of the evaluation team may challenge it.

For ECSE, children are deemed eligible within a certain disability category, and then the IEP team must also determine whether the child needs special education. This is an important part of the team's decision because, for example, a child might meet the criteria by having a visual impairment but with corrective lenses does not require special education.

Disability Categories under IDEA, Part B, Section 619

IDEA lists thirteen disability categories under which individuals may be eligible for ECSE services:

- Autism
- Deaf-blindness
- Deafness
- Emotional disturbance
- Hearing impairment
- Intellectual disability
- Multiple disabilities
- Orthopedic impairment
- Other health impairment
- Specific learning disability
- Speech or language impairment
- Traumatic brain injury
- Visual impairment

Note: Developmental delay is also a category of disability in some states. Children who have a certain diagnosis, such as autism or a visual impairment, may also be placed into several different categories, depending on other factors.

Special Education Is a Service, Not a Place

What is the significance of this statement? This statement is at the heart of inclusion because, unfortunately, the special education system often places children with disabilities in a special school or classroom without first considering an inclusive service location option. The IDEA is clear that IEP teams must provide services in the least restrictive environment. Under section 612(a)(5) of the IDEA, IEP teams are directed to consider where services are delivered in this way: "To the maximum extent appropriate, children with disabilities . . . are educated with children who are nondisabled; and . . . special classes, separate schooling or other removal of children with disabilities from the regular educational environment occurs only if the nature or severity of the disability is such that education in regular classes with the use of supplementary aids and services cannot be achieved satisfactorily (§300.114(a)(2)(i))."

Therefore, if your child is currently attending a child-care, Head Start, or pre-K program, the IEP team must first consider that program as the place where ECSE services are delivered. You and your child should not have to choose between your current program and special education services. The IDEA is clear that your child and family can benefit from both services at the same time.

STEP 4. IEP MEETING

Once the child is found eligible, the ECSE staff set up a meeting to determine the services that the child will receive and where those services will be delivered. IEP meetings are usually arranged by professionals at the local education agency (LEA), which is usually the local elementary school. Parents are notified of the meeting, and it is scheduled at a time and place that is convenient for all participants. During the meeting, the team will identify annual IEP goals and consider the services needed to support those goals. (Chapter 5 offers a more detailed discussion about what happens during an IEP meeting.) If the parents consent to the services as described in the IEP, the services can begin as soon as possible. If they do not agree with decisions outlined in the IEP, they can ask for mediation or file a complaint and request a hearing. (This process is described later in this chapter.)

STEP 5. PROVIDING SERVICES

Following the IEP meeting, your child can receive services as long as you give consent and the plan is carried out as written. You and your child's teacher should receive a copy of the IEP.

The plan includes the accommodations, modifications, and supports that must be provided. For ECSE, local education agencies have up to ten school days to begin service delivery once the IEP is developed and signed.

STEP 6. PROGRESS MONITORING

Your child's progress toward the annual goals is measured as stated in the IEP. You should be regularly informed of your child's progress and whether that progress is enough for your child to achieve the goals outlined by the end of the year. These progress reports must be given to you at various points throughout the year.

STEP 7. IEP REVIEW

The IEP is reviewed by the IEP team at least once a year, or more often if you or the school staff ask for a review. If necessary, the IEP is revised. As members of the IEP team, parents must be invited to participate in these meetings. You can make suggestions for changes and agree or disagree with IEP services and/or where your child receives the services. If you do not agree with the IEP services and/or placement, you may discuss these concerns with other members of the team and try to work out an agreement. Several options are available, including additional testing, an independent evaluation, asking for mediation, or a due-process hearing. You may also file a complaint with the state education agency.

> A zillion times over the course of living with Ivan, I have learned to trust his timing and his intuitions. It's not always easy, and sometimes his timeline is not my timeline.
>
> **—JUDY DAVID, PARENT**

STEP 8. CHILD REEVALUATION

At least every three years, your child must be reevaluated. The purpose of this evaluation is to find out if your child is still eligible for ECSE services and to learn about any changes to the service and/or educational needs. Keep in mind that your child could be reevaluated sooner than three years if you or the school staff ask for a new evaluation.

TRANSITIONING FROM EARLY CHILDHOOD SPECIAL EDUCATION TO KINDERGARTEN

The transition from preschool to kindergarten is an important time in any child's life and can be especially daunting for families who have a child with a disability. How will she do in elementary school? Is she ready? Will other children accept my child? Will she be able to be successful in an environment with increased expectations? These are often family concerns, but in reality, the school should be ready for the child rather than expecting the child to be ready for school.

Sometimes, this transition can be stressful because children respond to the shift in different ways. Some children may become withdrawn and shy, while others may exhibit behaviors that are challenging to adults. In addition to supports provided by the early childhood educators, community programs may be available to support children with mental-health needs related to transitions, learning how to manage change effectively, improving social skills, and strengthening peer relationships.

Just as in the transition from EI to ECSE, communication between programs is the key to success. If your child and family's first language is not English, the school must make plans to support communication by translating materials into your home language and providing interpreter services. The transition team should include preschool and kindergarten staff, school administrators, family members, and others who come together to coordinate transition activities before the kindergarten year begins. The transition plan should describe the steps in the process and the differences between the program where ECSE services are delivered and the kindergarten program. If you are willing to give permission, it can be helpful for preschool staff to share key records with kindergarten staff and work collaboratively to design services and supports for your child in the new setting. Once education staff assignments are made, it will be important for you and your child to meet with the kindergarten teacher to learn about the curriculum and daily routine. The school might provide opportunities for you to learn about kindergarten policies and visit the new classroom. Once the school year begins, you should be allowed to be as involved as possible in your child's kindergarten classroom, and staff should provide ongoing communication about how your child is adjusting to the new setting.

> I think that we always want June to become the best version of herself and to have every opportunity to belong in every space that she wants to belong in. As her family, it's our job just to give her whatever opportunities and supports that we can to help her get there. I've learned a lot as June's mom.
>
> **—JACKIE JOSEPH, PARENT**

PARENT RIGHTS UNDER IDEA

As you learn to be your child's best advocate, it's important to understand the rights that parents have under the law. The IDEA law is clear that parents are their child's first teachers and should be the ultimate decision-makers about services for their child. What are the key parent rights under IDEA? Parents have the right to the following:

- Confidentiality
- An explanation of procedural safeguards
- Use of parent's native language or preferred mode of communication
- Opportunity to review their child's records
- Participation in meetings

- An independent evaluation
- Prior written notice of meetings
- Giving or denial of consent to services
- Opportunity to disagree with decisions
- Mechanisms to resolve disputes (CPIR, 2017; ECTA, 2012)

To learn more about the differences between IDEA Part C and IDEA Part B, see this resource on the eligibility and services delivery policies: http://www.infanthearing.org/earlyintervention/docs/aspect-idea-part-c-and-idea-part-b.pdf

As a parent of a child with a disability who had an IFSP and later an IEP, I can attest that the process often felt quite daunting. I received so many parent-rights handbooks that I could have wallpapered my house with them by the time Ricky turned ten! We were fortunate to have many caring and encouraging educators and service providers along the way. They helped us understand our role in the process as well as our parental rights before the evaluation, during the IFSP/IEP meeting, and after the meeting when services and accommodations were provided. I give a ton of credit to the educators who supported us along the way, and ultimately led us to a successful high school graduation.

Let's look at parent rights before the evaluation, during the IEP meeting, and beyond.

BEFORE THE EVALUATION

Before any evaluation can be completed, the agency that does the evaluation must provide you with *prior written notice* and with a *procedural safeguards notice*. The procedural safeguards notice was shared with me through those parent-rights handbooks that I mentioned. In addition, the agency must obtain *parent consent*. What exactly does all of this mean?

The term *prior written notice* refers to the ECSE agency's obligation to notify you in a reasonable amount of time before your child is evaluated (Küpper and Rebhorn, 2007).

The *procedural safeguards notice* refers to the explanation about all of the IDEA protections or safeguards in place for families. Schools must share this with you in writing at multiple points during the process (Küpper and Rebhorn, 2007).

Consent within IDEA has a specific meaning and is part of the requirements related to prior written notice. The school not only must notify you about an initial evaluation, but there is also a requirement that you are made aware of your rights, and you agree *in writing* to the evaluation before it takes place (Küpper and Rebhorn, 2007).

Once you have given consent for an evaluation, you can begin to think about the types of questions the team will discuss when it meets. Conversations and decisions about the services themselves and the place where services will be delivered are part of this process, so there are several things you and your family will need to consider.

The ECTA Center offers a list of questions that you can use for personal reflection when considering where your child will receive services. "Team Decisions for Preschool Special Education Services: Guiding Questions" (n.d.) is available online. (See appendix C for a list of resources for this chapter.) This is a good document to help you understand what to expect during the IEP meeting. The document is divided into four categories: child considerations, family considerations, curricular considerations, and support considerations.

- For child considerations, you'll find questions on topics such as where your child is spending her time now, what abilities and strengths she has, and what challenges she has.
- In the family considerations section, the guiding questions include prompts about what you have observed and would like to see happen.
- Curricular considerations include questions asking about your child's ability to participate successfully and work toward IEP goals, with or without modifications.
- Support considerations are just that, thinking about what supports are needed so that your child can participate in an inclusive setting.

You can review the document and think about the questions you have for the team, or even use the sample questions to practice how you might respond during the IEP meeting. If there is a particular question or consideration that you want to make sure to address, you can role-play with a friend or family member to practice sharing your thoughts. You can write down a list of items that are important to you, your child, and the family as a whole. Then, think about why each item is important and what your child needs to be successful.

> This doesn't have to have us, we can have it. He can grow. He can develop at his own rate. It doesn't have to have us. We can have it.
>
> **—LATISHA R. STUCKEY, PARENT**

In preparation for setting goals for your child, think about this question: What are your dreams for your child? Even a goal related to fun family time can be worked into the IEP in some way. For example, you might want your child to go fishing with you one day. That can be a goal written in your child's IEP. The IEP should be meaningful and exciting for parents and family members, too.

DURING THE IEP MEETING

Following the evaluation, the team will gather to discuss the results and determine a plan. The IDEA law is clear about parent rights during the IEP meeting and about how to ensure parent participation. To make sure that every parent has the opportunity to participate in the meeting, each public agency must:

- notify parents early enough so that they have the opportunity to attend;
- schedule the meeting at a mutually agreed upon time and place; and
- inform parents about who will be in attendance during the meeting.

These are the required members of the team according to IDEA:

- **Parents:** Parents or guardians of the child with a disability are vital members of the team, with an expertise to contribute like no one else. The IDEA recognizes this fact! You should be actively involved in every decision that will affect your child and family.
- **Special educators:** Special educators, with their knowledge of how to educate children with disabilities, are obviously an important part of a child's IEP team.
- **Regular educators:** If a child is participating in the regular education environment (or is going to be participating), then IDEA requires that at least one regular educator of the child be included on the IEP team.
- **Representative of the school system:** The IEP team must also include a representative of the school system who has the authority to commit agency resources.
- **Someone to interpret evaluation results:** Someone on the team must be able to interpret the evaluation results and discuss what they mean in terms of instruction.
- **Others with knowledge or special expertise about the child:** This could be another family member, friend of the family, or even your child's child-care or Head Start teacher.
- **Child:** The child should also be included in the IFSP or IEP meeting (Rebhorn, n.d.).

The team will make key decisions on behalf of your child and family. During a typical IEP meeting, each team member will take a turn in the discussion.

DISPUTE RESOLUTION

Once the IEP is written, the hope is that service decisions will be mutually agreed upon by the whole team, including the parents. Unfortunately, this is not always the case, and the IDEA law is clear that parents should have a variety of options to consider when resolving disputes. Every state has its own process for dispute resolution, but there are some requirements that must be followed, depending on the option used. These options are either informal or formal in nature, and a dispute-resolution guide has been developed for both Part C and Part B. You can find the links to the dispute-resolution guides in appendix C.

INFORMAL APPROACHES TO DISPUTE RESOLUTION

In all cases where your family and the school disagree, it is important for both sides to first discuss their concerns and try to compromise. Using a relationship-based approach, you should first try the informal options before moving to the options that might feel confrontational to the agency. The first informal option is to review your child's IEP together with the IEP team. If this still results in a disagreement, you can ask for a facilitated IEP meeting. This strategy of holding a facilitated IEP meeting is not mentioned in the law, but it is widely used by teams because it can be helpful to have an outside member of the team facilitate the discussion. An impartial facilitator can keep the team on track and address conflicts as they arise. A good facilitator ensures that everyone participates, clarifies points of agreement or disagreement, and models effective communication. Some agencies offer this service to families and cover the cost of the facilitator, but that is not required under the law.

Under IDEA, the school system or other public agency determines how frequently the IEP should be reviewed. This review must happen at least once a year, but parents have the right to request an IEP meeting at any time. If you are concerned about the services your child is receiving or your child's placement or any other related concern, you can work to resolve it through another meeting. At the meeting, members of the team would discuss your concerns and, hopefully, come up with a solution.

This is a strategy that I used many times over the years with Ricky's IEP team. Especially when he went to elementary school, it was hard to know the best way to support him. We did a lot of trial and error. Usually, the school system was open to this strategy and agreed to meet with us more frequently. I learned through experience that respect and honesty were key to the success of the IEP team meetings.

FORMAL APPROACHES TO DISPUTE RESOLUTION

If you and the school still cannot reach an agreement, there are formal ways to resolve the conflict: mediation, filing a complaint, and due process.

Mediation

In mediation, parents and the IFSP or IEP team meet together along with an impartial mediator. The mediator is different from a facilitator because the mediator must be qualified and trained in effective mediation techniques. IDEA requires that agencies offer mediation, and there are specific conditions that must be followed. The process must be voluntary and can't be used to deny or delay your right to a due-process hearing. The mediation process is similar to a facilitated meeting in that the team is encouraged to talk openly about the areas where they disagree and to try to reach agreement. In mediation, the meeting participants make the decisions about any changes that will resolve the dispute.

Filing a Complaint

Given the fact that services are provided at the local level, the state education agency (SEA) will not know if there is a dispute unless the parents file a state complaint. In this case, you would write directly to the SEA and describe in a signed document how the local agency has violated the law under IDEA. Every state develops its own form that parents must use, so it will look different from state to state. In most cases, the SEA must resolve the complaint within sixty calendar days and must send out a document that includes the reasons for the final decision. This method is different from mediation. In mediation the team resolves the conflict; when parents file a state complaint, the SEA makes the decisions.

Additional Resources for Military Families

The IDEA governs how states and public agencies, including the Department of Defense, provide early intervention, special education, and related services to eligible children with disabilities from birth through age twenty-one. The Department of Defense has developed a program called the Exceptional Family Member Program, along with an implementation manual for military families titled *Provisions of Early Intervention and Special Education Services to Eligible DoD Dependents* for clarification. The manual and other resources for military families can be found here: https://www.militaryonesource.mil/special-needs/educational-needs/moving-with-an-individualized-education-program

Due Process

When due process is used as a way to resolve disputes, parents and the school present evidence before an impartial, qualified person called a *hearing officer.* The hearing officer then issues the decision following a due-process hearing. A due-process hearing occurs in a formal, legal setting where both parties present their perspective through witnesses, documents, and other evidence. The process begins with parents filing a confidential complaint, and IDEA has specific guidelines for what the complaint must include. You can also hire an attorney to help with filing the complaint and representing your family through the process. IDEA requires that parents and the local agency must first hold a meeting to try to resolve the situation without having to go to the due process hearing, but if a due-process hearing is held, the hearing officer will make the final decision, and the school must implement the decision as soon as possible (CPIR, 2019; CPIR, 2008). Due process is the final formal option for dispute resolution.

Now that you have learned about early childhood special education, take a moment to look up the information about services in your state. To find ECSE services near you, select your state or territory and review the “Education Supports for Children with Disabilities” drop-down menu under the “Health and Social Services” tab (https://childcare.gov/state-resources-home). You'll use this for our chapter 4 activity on the next page.

ACTIVITY: ALL ABOUT MY CHILD—PRESCHOOL

DIRECTIONS

Using the information about early childhood special education (ECSE) services you looked up using the link on the previous page, write the information you found below.

Early Childhood Special Education Program: ______________________

Contact person: ______________________

Phone/Email: ______________________

Early Education Program Contact (child care, Head Start, or state prekindergarten) (optional): ______

____

Then, do some reflecting about what the ECSE professionals (service coordinator, therapists, teachers, and so on) would want to know about your child. Fill in the prompts below and share the information with members of your team when the time is right.

All About Me

The most important information that you should know about me is: ______________________

My greatest strengths are: ______________________

The things that are difficult for me right now are: ______________________

I communicate with others by: ______________________

The language my family speaks at home is: ______________________

I live with (people/pets): ______________________

The other children in my home or neighborhood are (names/ages/relationship to your child):

____

My favorite foods are:______________________

Foods to avoid giving me are:______________________

My favorite thing to play with is: ______________________

A thing that brings me comfort is: ______________________

My favorite thing to do at home is: ______________________________

An important part of my daily routine is: ______________________________

Something to know about my eating routine is: ______________________________

Something to know about my sleeping routine is: ______________________________

Something to know about how I am around other children is: ______________________________

Something to know about how I am around other adults is: ______________________________

I am happy when: ______________________________

I am motivated to learn or try new things when: ______________________________

I get angry or upset when: ______________________________

I will let you know that I need something by: ______________________________

Other things to know about me are: ______________________________

CHAPTER 5

Working as a Team with Your Child's Teachers and Other Professionals

I've learned to really trust my gut. You can feel so far out in the wilderness sometimes. You're hearing different viewpoints and different advice. But at the end of the day, you know what's right for your child.

—OLIVIER BERNIER, PARENT

Early childhood educators can be valuable partners as you navigate through the uncertain waters. Every time Ricky started a new class, I tried as hard as possible to form a strong, positive relationship with his teacher. My strategy was simple: compliments, presents, and baked goods. Offering to volunteer as much as possible helped too. I once had the privilege of attending a keynote presentation by acclaimed researcher Walter Gilliam of the Yale Child Study Center. Dr. Gilliam is an expert in preschool suspensions and expulsions, and he said that he had never known a case where a child was expelled from school when the parent also had a good relationship with the teacher (Gilliam and Shahar, 2006; Gilliam et al., 2016). I took that lesson to heart and attempted to do all that I could to nurture relationships with Ricky's teachers. When he started kindergarten, he went off to school with first-day "please be good to my child" presents for the teachers.

> It just feels sometimes like teachers are doing things not to help your kid out but to put him in a box, so they can explain it away. All I want from you as a teacher is for you to connect with my kid.
>
> **—BEN RIEPE, PARENT**

Forming relationships with my son's teachers didn't always come easy. Researchers have found that teachers' beliefs are influenced by their own personal experiences and their opportunities to spend time with people with disabilities (Avramidis, Bayliss, and Burden, 2000; Avramidis and Norwich, 2002; Barton and Smith, 2015a). In fact, the attitudes and beliefs that teachers hold are considered the biggest barriers to inclusion for children with disabilities (Barton and Smith, 2014; 2015a; 2015b). These teacher perspectives are difficult to address, in part because, as this image shows, the knowledge and skills that teachers hold are measurable and can been "seen," like the part of the iceberg above the waterline. But attitudes and beliefs about inclusion for children with disabilities are the hidden part of the iceberg.

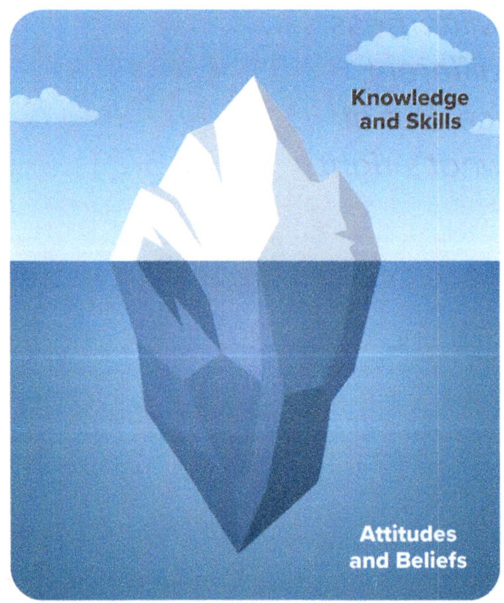

The negative feelings early childhood professionals may have about inclusion are not rational, but all the research and public policy in the world is unlikely to affect that perspective. I saw this firsthand when Ricky entered child care for the first time.

Before we were lucky enough to have Ricky in our lives, he spent much of his time during those early months confined to a crib. There was a lot of deprivation in my son's life. As discussed in chapter 1, the early years are extremely important. Human babies are born as a "work in progress," especially when it comes to brain development. They need varied experiences and opportunities to explore the world so that connections are made in their brains as they develop (Campbell, et al., 2014; Cole, Trexberg, and Schaffner, 2023). Now, it's also true that humans are extremely resilient, and Ricky is one of the most resilient humans I've ever known. But those early months of his life were challenging and difficult for him—and for us.

One of the important considerations for staff in the orphanage was the ability to maintain sanitary conditions. You might imagine that if one child became ill, the illness could easily spread to all the children in the orphanage. Therefore, caregivers were careful to keep children from sharing toys with one another, and we suspect that toys were withheld from the children to minimize the spread of germs. Infants and toddlers explore the world through their senses, and one way they do that is by putting toys in their mouths. Mouthing is a favorite way that babies use to learn about the object, which is a very germy situation to be sure!

Ricky could not explore his environment this way for the first seventeen months of his life, so when we adopted him and suddenly he was able to explore (clean) objects, he went to town! Books went into his mouth. The collar on his jacket went into his mouth. Toys went into his mouth. This was fine at home, but once he went to child care? Not so fine.

Just as in the Ukrainian orphanages, child-care centers in the United States also want to prevent the spread of illness. Educators spray down tables with bleach and water after meals or playtime. They clean toys if children put them in their mouths. This is completely understandable and a good health and safety practice.

But you might imagine what happened when Ricky started in child care. The toy mouthing was "over the top," according to Ricky's teacher. When I picked him up from school one day, she took me over to a sink filled with toys and soapy water and was exasperated to tell me, "These are the toys that Ricky has put in his mouth *just since noon.*" She was frustrated and I was mortified. "I promise that I'll have a talk with him," I said. He was a toddler at the time, but we would have a conversation about it. Right.

"It was so embarrassing," I sobbed to my friend who also happened to be an early childhood intervention specialist. She suggested, "Why don't you find something that he could have with him all the time to put in his mouth? Like a necklace he could wear made from those teething beads." We went shopping that night and bought some large, nontoxic, plastic beads and strung up a necklace.

"Now Ricky," I said, "whenever you want to put something in your mouth, just put this necklace in your mouth instead." He loved the necklace and, wearing it proudly, off to school he went. Yay for us—problem solved! When I picked him up from school that day, I was excited to hear how the necklace strategy had worked. But Ricky wasn't wearing the necklace. When I asked his teacher about it, she said, "Oh, that thing? It was nasty." She handed me a plastic bag with the necklace inside, and I wanted to crawl under her desk with shame.

Ricky's teacher was a pro. She taught me so much about Ricky and early childhood education in general. In our iceberg analogy, her knowledge and skills above water were on point, but her feelings deep down were that my son did not *belong* in her classroom. He didn't meet the expectations that she had in her mind for children his age, and these parts of the iceberg were a real barrier.

Ultimately, we figured out a solution by having Ricky wear a bandana around his neck. It was absorbent and so it worked better than the bead necklace. I have to say that getting to that place of compromise was heartbreaking for me as a parent. We had to fight for my son to be included. Inclusion is more than just having the ability to enter the building; it is also expressed by a sense of belonging.

I hope this chapter will give you some strategies so you can be better prepared for the inevitable challenges you will face as a family. You may even be able to avoid some of the challenges we faced. It is all about the relationships. For many families, these relationships begin during their first IFSP or IEP meeting. What exactly happens during an IFSP or IEP meeting? How should you prepare? Let's dive in!

ALL ABOUT THE MEETINGS

In this section, you'll learn about what happens during an IFSP or IEP meeting, how to prepare to participate in a team meeting, and what to do if you don't agree with some of your child's team members.

Each IFSP or IEP meeting will be unique and based on the strengths and needs of your child. However, early intervention (EI) and early childhood special education (ECSE) programs are required by law to cover certain topics during the meeting. Together, you and the rest of the team will make key decisions on behalf of your child and family. During a typical IFSP/IEP meeting, each team member will take a turn in the discussion. The discussion will include talking about your child's strengths; your concerns for enhancing your child's education; the results of the most recent evaluation of your child; and your child's academic, developmental, and functional needs (Rebhorn, n.d.).

What If I Do Not Want Services for My Child?

It is completely within your rights as the parent or guardian to choose to forgo resources and services for your child. Keep in mind that the IFSP and IEP meetings can be challenging for you and your family. It can feel like an emotional drain to process new information about your child, and that emotional reaction can sometimes affect the way you hear and understand the information. If it would be helpful, ask the team leader to repeat the information, answer questions, and share details about available resources. The IDEA law is clear that the family maintains the role of decision-maker. The team should respect that role. Over time, you may get additional perspective and process the information in such a way that changes your mind. It's okay to come back to the team for support, even if you deny services at first.

The team will also discuss whether your child would benefit from additional supports or services to be successful. The team might ask you questions like these:

- Does your child have communication needs?
- Does your child need assistive technology services and devices?
- Does your child's behavior interfere with their learning or the learning of others?
- Does your child have a visual impairment and need instruction in, or the use of, Braille?
- Is your child deaf or hard of hearing and have language and other communication needs?
- Does your child have language needs due to being a dual language learner? (Rebhorn, n.d.)

Depending on the answers to these questions, the IFSP/IEP team will discuss supplementary aids and services for your child, which can be accommodations and modifications to the Head Start, child-care, or pre-K curriculum, the way content is taught, or even how your child's progress will be measured. The services can also include support and training for staff who work with that child. The aids can include specialized equipment such as wheelchairs, computers, software, adaptive communication devices, special eating utensils, or even restroom equipment. Decisions about which supplementary aids and services would be useful are made on an individual basis, but the team may ask questions about the activities the child can participate in without

I learned that, in my area, you can have a life coach when you have an appointment. The coach comes and meets you when you go to your doctors' appointments and helps coach your child while you're checking in. They play with them and keep them busy. One day I had to have Ayden coached to get out of the car because he was unfamiliar with the place.

—ARIELLE BRANCH, PARENT

extra support, the activities that would require extra support, and the extra supports that would be needed as a way to make those decisions (ECTA Center, n.d.).

The relationships we build are very important. But you may be wondering about some of the details for these collaborative meetings. Whether it is a teacher-parent conference, a "getting to know you" gathering, an IFSP or IEP meeting, or some other gathering, the questions are often the same: What do I do to prepare? How can I stay on track and contribute? What should I do if we disagree about something? Let's consider all of those questions and how you might navigate the situation most effectively for your child and family.

HOW DO I PREPARE TO PARTICIPATE IN A TEAM MEETING?

The best way to prepare for a family-professional meeting is to think about the information you want to share about your child and the information you want to find out to help you to support your child. Let's start with what you want to share. What are some of the questions that you might expect a teacher or other professional to ask? What kinds of information might be helpful for you to share about your child? Start with the prompts from the All about Me pages in chapters 3 and 4. Then, add some additional questions that can help guide you personally. Your child's team might want to know the answers to these questions:

- What parts of your child's learning experience have been most challenging for you?
- What parts of your child's learning experience feel supportive and helpful?
- What services could be put into place that would support you in your parenting experience?
- What is your vision for your child? for employment? for family?
- What is your dream for your child?

In addition to thinking about the information you plan to share, you'll also want to reflect on the information you hope to gather during the meeting to best support your child. You might consider prompts like these:

- I need to know how to . . .
- I really could use some resources about . . .
- How have other families managed . . .
- How can I support my child to ____________________ over the next six months?
- How can I support my child to increase ____________________ over the next six months?
- How can I support my child to decrease ____________________ over the next six months?
- How can I support my child to make progress with ____________________ over the next year?
- How can I support my child to gain skills like ____________________ over the next year? over the next five years? over the next ten years?

Here are some other general suggestions for how you can prepare for meetings and make sure they are as successful as possible.

- **Try to attend all meetings.** By showing up, you not only are able to advocate for your child, you also will build relationships and common understanding with the team. If you are unable to attend, let the team leader know as soon as possible. If the meeting is an IFSP/IEP meeting, the team should schedule it during a time that is convenient for you and your family. Keep a calendar so you can have easy access to upcoming meeting dates and times.
- **Ask for the meeting agenda ahead of time so you can prepare.** If there isn't a formal written agenda, you can still ask the team leader to share key topics they plan to cover during the meeting.
- **Reach out to other parents. Ask** other families about strategies they use to prepare for meetings and where they find information on the topics and issues you care about.
- **Organize your thoughts.** Think about what you want to say and what you want to ask. Doing so will really help you to feel prepared.
- **Learn the lingo that the team may use during the meeting.** The glossary in appendix A is a good place to start. EI/ECSE systems are full of words and abbreviations that are not commonly known outside the early childhood field. By taking time to read through and study these words and abbreviations, you'll be able to understand the conversation better. Write up a cheat sheet that you can use during the meeting.
- **Take notes.** Write down in your own words what was discussed at the meeting. Keeping notes can help you remember important points. You might make a list of follow-up items and questions to ask. Then, before each meeting you can review your notes from the last time you met, or read through meeting minutes if they are available.

Remember that you are an equal member of the group, so it's important that you share your thoughts and ideas. When you do not understand what is being said, ask for the speaker to repeat the statement, or try to repeat what you heard and then ask, "Is that right?" This gives the speaker a chance to clarify or add more information if it is needed.

If you feel that bringing an advocate to help you with note taking and asking important questions, you can get some help from your local parent center. You can also be matched with another parent who can serve as a mentor while you become comfortable with the process.

Stay organized by choosing a way to keep track of all the information you will receive at each meeting. I used to keep a file folder for every school year, where I would keep a copy of Ricky's IEP or other important documents. Nowadays, you can use electronic folders to organize the information on your computer. Ask for help if you're not sure how to manage the files, or just use a file folder. Whatever works for you is what works.

WHAT IF WE DON'T AGREE?

While we all hope that team meetings will be collegial, friendly, and full of team spirit, that is not always the case. Conflict happens. It's actually likely to occur at some point, and that's okay. If you practice your skills at dealing with conflict by staying calm, listening, and trying your best to understand the other perspective, you will navigate your way through. Here are some tips to help work through challenging situations.

- **Do your best to keep an open mind.** Sometimes, conflict happens because we just do not understand the other person's perspective. If you stay open, you might learn a different way to handle the situation. Even if you still do not agree, if you know that you have listened with an open mind you'll be able to make decisions confidently.
- **Try not to take things personally.** Sometimes, decisions are made based on staffing, funding, legal requirements, or organizational policy. It's easy to jump to conclusions, but you'll learn more and make better decisions if you take it slow and ask questions to find out more. Find out information by asking lots of questions starting with *who, what, when*, and *why*.
- **Stay on topic.** Stay focused on the topic; refer to the agenda as a reminder if necessary. This will help you as well as the other members of the team. You may want to remind the team about the purpose of the group during stressful times. Ultimately, you are on the same team and all want the best for your child. Keep your child and their health, well-being, and learning at the center of the conversation. This will lead to one thing you can all agree upon, and finding one area of agreement usually leads to another and then another.
- **Take a break.** If things start to feel uncomfortable, take a break. It's okay excuse yourself for five minutes to collect your thoughts. Find a quiet place, take some deep breaths, and regain composure. I would sometimes pull out a photo of my son during those times because seeing his sweet face reminded me of the greater purpose of the meeting.
- **Bring an advocate.** Sometimes, families report that the meeting feels as if it is "us against them." If you feel that way, it might be best to reach out for an advocate to join you in the future. Your local parent center (www.parentcenterhub.org) can give you resources for this.

> If I could do something over, I would not request a certain teacher for Kelsey in one of the school years. By doing so, we unknowingly put her into a team of teachers who were not ready (and maybe not willing) to have a student with more significant needs in their classroom. The teacher we requested was great, but there was another teacher in that team who was not a good fit for Kelsey. It ended up being a very difficult school year.
>
> **—TERRI LEYTON, PARENT**

BUILDING RELATIONSHIPS WITH YOUR CHILD'S TEAM

Now that you have an understanding of what to expect in IFSP/IEP meetings, let's shift to the important work of building relationships with your child's team. In the following pages, we'll explore the relationship-based strategies you can use as you navigate these important relationships with EI/ECSE specialists, therapists, early childhood educators, and other professionals. You may be paired with a teacher or service provider who is from a culture or speaks a primary language that is different from your own. We'll discuss ways that you can engage with these professionals through difficult conversations and share information about your legal rights through the EI/ECSE process and even after the development of the IFSP or IEP. And if this happens through relationships, what can you do to build those strong, healthy, trusting, and open relationships?

FORMING CLOSE BONDS ON YOUR CHILD'S BEHALF

Forming a partnership with your child's teachers or other professionals is dependent on a strong relationship, but as parents, we are often particularly vulnerable during the early days of learning about our child's disability. I certainly was! This is normal and okay. In fact, our own vulnerability can be a strength if we learn ways to share it with members of your child's team.

In order to form open and close relationships with partners, we need to share and be vulnerable with each other. When you share information about yourself, your child, and your family, it will lead to greater understanding and empathy. Your child's service coordinator or teacher may not know how to ask you about these kinds of things that will build a close relationship. But you can open the door to share.

> You go out and become vulnerable: discussing your concerns, your traumas, your mishaps, the good and the bad. You come to acceptance and to be vulnerable with where you are in your lives.
>
> **—ARIELLE BRANCH, PARENT**

Here are some aspects of your family that you may want to share with a supportive member of your child's team when the time is right:

- **Preferences for feeling respected and valued:** How would you like to be involved in the services and supports your child receives? How often do you want updates about your child's progress? Would you prefer to communicate by phone, email, text, or another way?

- **Past experiences with service providers:** What are some of your past experiences with other providers either related to your child's disability or related to another social service or community resource. What worked well? What did not work well for your family?
- **Your hopes, expectations, and worries about the services:** What are your pet peeves when it comes to the way that other adults treat your child? For example, one family hated when their child got messy at school. They dressed their child in good school clothes, and the child came home covered with grass stains or paint. Consider asking the team to identify one person who will serve as your primary liaison to the team. Sometimes it's easier to connect deeply with just one person on the team, and you can reach out to the other members when you have questions related to their area of expertise.
- **Proven strategies:** What approaches work well for your child, and what do not work? For example, does your child need repetition, lots of opportunity to practice, or plenty of time outside to get their energy out?
- **Current life circumstances that may affect your child or family:** One thing we know for certain is that life comes with its own challenges, whether that be a divorce, death of a family member or pet, birth or adoption of a child, a new housing arrangement, or another source of family stress or joy. Those changes can affect everyone in a household.
- **Your culture:** What are your home language(s), family values and traditions, holidays and celebrations, and religious beliefs? Differences between home and school cultures can lead to misunderstandings. Our own willingness to address cultural misunderstandings is essential. A service provider, teacher, or therapist who may have different beliefs, attitudes, or behaviors than we do can often take us out of our cultural comfort zone. If you share information up front, you could open the door to having some helpful conversations and avoid misunderstandings.
- **Important friends and family members:** Include friends of the family who truly are just like family and important traditions such as family meals, reunions, and outings. What are some of the things that you love to do with family and friends, such as going to the beach or library, shopping, going on picnics, visiting museums, or taking walks in the neighborhood?
- **Important family stories or memories:** What are the memories or family stories that are most frequently shared during family gatherings?
- **Household chores:** How does your family negotiate and manage these tasks?
- **Favorite movies, TV shows, or music:** What do you like to watch and/or listen to? Be sure to include child and grown-up preferences.
- **Funds of knowledge:** What are your family occupations? What special skills do your family members have? We all have special skills and abilities, and your child's team might be able to connect with you to a greater degree when you share this information about yourself. Try

to open up about your special skills, such as singing, knitting, dancing, exercising, cooking, coaching sports, gardening, decorating cakes, bird watching, and so on.

INTERSECTIONALITY AND CONFRONTING BIAS

We all have multiple social and cultural identities. We view the world and interpret reality through that lens, and our perspective changes over time as we learn and grow. If your child and/or your family is also a member of a marginalized group, there will be stereotypes and bias beyond ableism. This is a concept called *intersectionality,* "the overlapping and interdependent systems of oppression across, for example, race, gender, ability, and social status" (NAEYC, 2019).

The unfortunate result is that you and/or your child may face bias from teachers and other professionals. Often, this bias is unconscious. Staats and colleagues (2015) use the term *implicit bias* as "the automatic and unconscious stereotypes that drive people to behave and make decisions in certain ways." Human beings use mental categories to sort the world as we try to make meaning out of all that we encounter. This tendency to sort people into categories in an unconscious way can bring along negative biases from our childhood into adulthood and can create a difficult situation for you to navigate. You depend on the teachers and professionals in your child's life. They all play a critical role in helping your child grow and develop with a positive sense of self, so it can be concerning to find that someone on your child's team views your child through a cultural lens that leads to biases, stereotypes, and misunderstandings.

What is the solution? It starts with our ability to recognize bias within ourselves and the members of the team and to reflect together about how our biases might influence the partnership. These conversations can be difficult, so reach out for support through your local parent center if you need help. You may find a parent who has had a similar experience and had learned lessons to share. Even though this is difficult, your child needs you to confront the issue and address it with the team, especially if it has caused, or could cause, pain for your child.

Once you begin to share and open up with each other, you become part of an even stronger team with your child's teachers, therapists, and other professionals. Effective teams have been studied for many years, and the research on EI/ECSE teams has lifted up some key characteristics that help us understand how successful teams function (Rausch, Bold, and Strain, 2021; Sheldon and Rush, 2013). Many of these characteristics are within our control. Think about what you can do as a member of the team to make sure these relationships are successful.

What Makes a Team Successful?

Family members are an integral part of the team. You should feel that you are an equal partner and serve as an active participant in setting goals and making decisions about your child's development, well-being, and learning. This is called *choice and voice.*

- The team includes individuals from multiple disciplines.
- Teams meet on a regular basis. Communication occurs frequently and is considered to be a two-way street.
- The team shares information in an easy-to-understand format.
- The team has a clear and common purpose.
- One team member serves as the lead for the family.
- The team works together by combining knowledge, skills, and resources.
- Services are individualized for families in a respectful and culturally sensitive way. You should experience responsive relationships, and your family story and the partnership you bring to the table should be valued.
- All members share responsibility for implementation of the IFSP or IEP.
- All members evaluate outcomes and make changes to the plan as necessary.

Remember: You are your child's first teacher. You know your child best. You are at the table to be a voice for your child. You are entitled to have an interpreter at the table if you need one.

You can suggest changes for improvement. The whole system works better when good ideas are shared. Sharing articles, websites, or films can help build the capacity of the team. What you encounter today will not always be your reality. Relationships can improve, and your child will also learn, grow, and change. You are working to create a bright future for your child; this is the most important work of all.

ENGAGING WITH TEACHERS AND OTHER PROFESSIONALS FROM A DISTANCE

The COVID-19 pandemic taught us a great deal about engaging with teachers and other professionals from a distance. We learned that doing so can be especially challenging, even under the best circumstances. However, there are certainly benefits as well. Children with some types of disabilities or children who are medically fragile may need remote educational services, regardless of whether in-person programming is available. This may also be true if your family lives in a rural location where it is difficult to join an IFSP/IEP meeting in person. For example, during the pandemic, EI providers tried new strategies to support families such as distance coaching, gathering, and reviewing videos taken of the child during daily routines, and sharing videos of effective strategies for families to watch during a convenient time for their family. We have all become better at communicating via email and text, and some families have become skilled with using collaborative virtual workspaces (Rao, 2021; Steed, Stein, and Charlifue-Smith, 2022). What are the considerations for connecting with professionals to receive support in a virtual world? Here are a few things to keep in mind:

> I'm very proud of my husband and me. We sought out help early, and we were open to what the doctors were saying, even if we didn't like it. Our pediatrician referred us to a neurologist . . . who put together an entire team for Mazie.
>
> **—AMANDA LOVETTE, PARENT**

- **Start by sharing your preferred method of communication.** Do you prefer email, phone calls, texts, or online video meetings? Let the professional know your preferences in the beginning of the relationship. Some of us do not have a stable internet connection, or we may have a limited data plan. Let the professional know about those issues so that they may keep cost considerations in mind. Programs may have funding to help with these costs. If you do not have access to a computer in your home, let the professional know that. It may be easier to connect with a phone call or text. In addition, educators or specialists can drop off lessons and materials for your child, with detailed instructions for parents and other family members. You can ask that they check back with you after a time to see how the lessons worked.
- **If you are able to connect with a video call, practice the technology ahead of time if possible.** Some educators share videos with families as preparation. For example, you might need support with entering the virtual meeting room or classroom, muting and unmuting the microphone, or changing the background of the screen. Ask for this kind of help if you need it. We all can benefit from a little technology support from time to time.
- **To the greatest degree possible, ask for information ahead of time.** Make sure to let your child's teacher or therapist know as soon as possible if there is a schedule change.

THE CIRCLE OF SUPPORT

Think about all the people in your life who are available to support you and your child. This includes the closest in your circle, such as family members and friends, as well as neighbors, teachers, and the EI/ECSE professionals. Some early intervention programs engage with families in the first few meetings by completing a diagram known as an *ecomap*. An ecomap is a concept that started with researcher Urie Bronfenbrenner. He studied the idea that that child development occurs within a complex system of relationships and human connections (Bronfenbrenner, 1986). In early intervention, ecomaps are often used to show how a family is connected with extended family members, friends, neighbors, as well as EI/ECSE professionals and other supports (McWilliam, 2010; Ray and Street, 2005). In the best case, your child will be surrounded by two rings of support: your close family and friends in the inner ring, and an outer ring of professionals, such as your child's service coordinator, teacher or caregiver, medical provider, therapists, and other forms of support. This circle of connectedness among the important people in your child's life can have a huge impact on the way your child grows and develops.

> We were living in another country where we didn't have family or friends around. So I would call my mom. At that time, she was still working as a nurse. She would give us help. I would say, "Mom, I have all these medicines, and I'm getting all lost," and she would say, "Okay, let's make a calendar." She helped me a lot from far away. Ultimately, for me it was all about finding my people. I didn't have my family around, so I made my village through the doctors, the psychologist, psychiatrist, occupational therapist, and physical therapist. It had to be like that because we were all alone."
>
> **—ANDIE AMOSSON, PARENT**

The circle of support is most effective when the important adults in your child's life have developed and nurtured their own relationships with each other, so that your child can be supported in all environments. This is a powerful strategy to leverage all of the relationships in your child's life. For example, you might tell your child's therapist that over the weekend you were thinking about the strategies they shared and how much they seem to be helping your child progress. We feel connected when we share those kinds of sentiments with each other. Take some time to reflect on your own circle of support with the activity on the next page.

ACTIVITY: CIRCLE OF SUPPORT

DIRECTIONS

Consider who makes up the circle of support for your family. Write their names into the diagram below. You don't need to have all circles filled in to create a circle of support, but seeing these names in this image will serve as a reminder that you are not in this alone. You have a team in your child's corner that is ready to help!

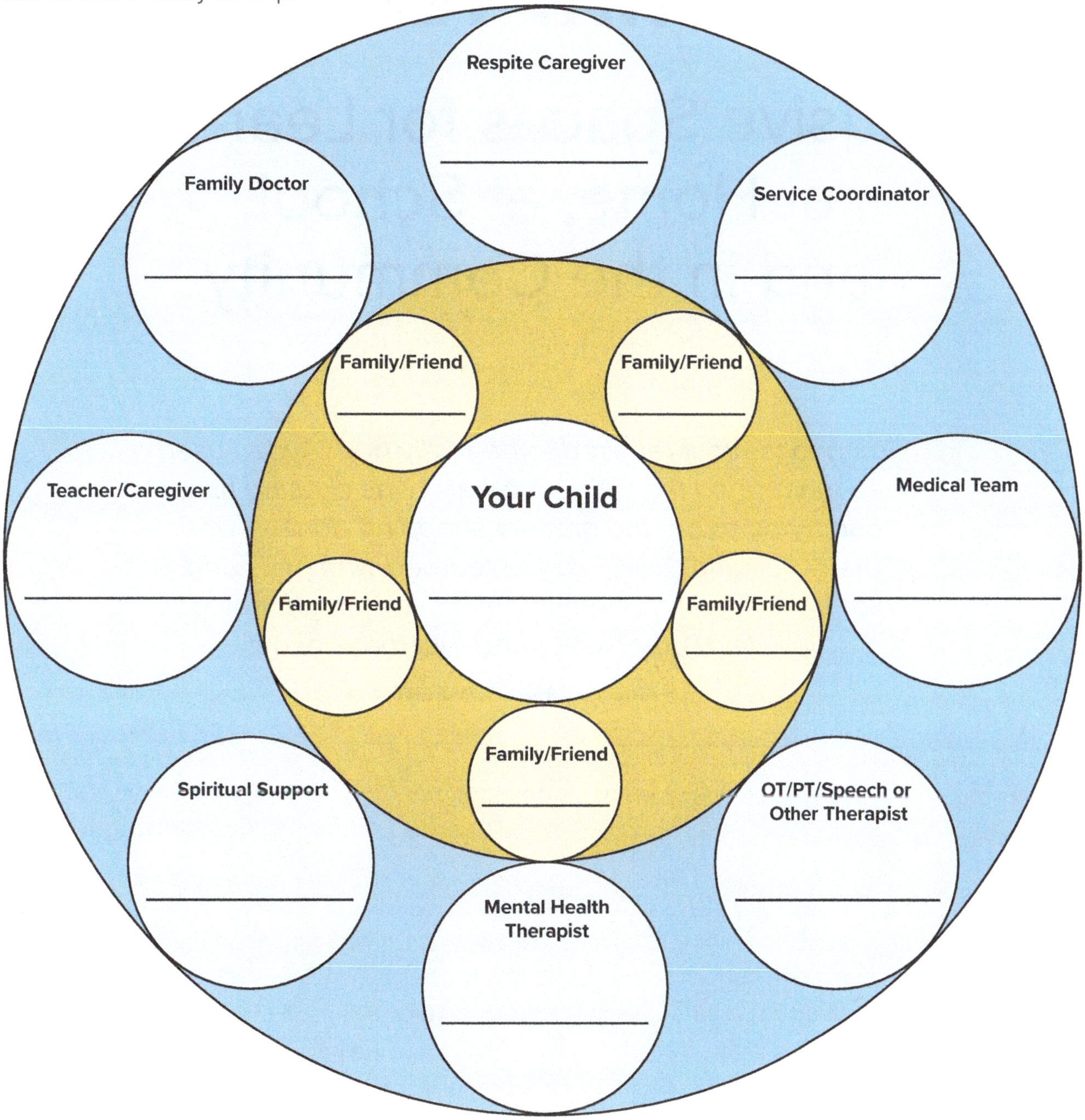

Respite Caregiver

Family Doctor

Service Coordinator

Family/Friend

Family/Friend

Teacher/Caregiver

Your Child

Medical Team

Family/Friend

Family/Friend

Family/Friend

Spiritual Support

OT/PT/Speech or Other Therapist

Mental Health Therapist

CHAPTER 6

Inclusive Spaces for Learning at Home, at School, and in the Community

Going to the market used to be really bad. Ayden used to run around the whole market. I was chasing him and trying to get the grocery shopping done. It was overwhelming. Now I've just learned who he is and what he needs in that environment. This might not look like what other kids need, but that's okay!

—ARIELLE BRANCH, PARENT

I'll never forget an image I once saw on the back of a magazine. It was a photo of a young boy running along the beach on a dark and stormy kind of day. The image was in black and white, and the storm clouds overhead made for a striking photograph. But the caption at the bottom of the photo is what really made an impression on me. It explained that the boy had always struggled in school and had difficulty sitting still in class. His parents found that when they took him to wild places in nature, he achieved a sense of calm and stillness. Then it said that the year was 1908, and the boy in the photo was Ansel Adams.

Ansel Adams was a famous photographer best known for beautiful nature scenes and landscapes. After seeing the image on the magazine cover and reading the caption, I looked him up and learned that, as a child, he had been described as hyperactive and socially awkward. He grew up in northern California and was always out in nature, collecting insects and exploring the bluffs near his home. How remarkable that by taking Adams to all of the wild places in nature, his family not only supported his needs to be active, but they also gave him early experiences that ultimately led to his career and success in life. Adams's parents gave their son the freedom to grow and become the best version of himself, as he wrote: "I am certain [my father] established the positive direction of my life that otherwise, given my native hyperactivity, could have been confused and catastrophic. I trace who I am and the direction of my development to those years of growing up in our house on the dune, propelled especially by an internal spark, tenderly kept alive and glowing, by my father" (Adams and Alinder, 1996).

> I want to keep fostering whatever Wren is interested in. She really likes to hunt mushrooms. She's probably the only five-year-old kid with Down syndrome out there who can identify mushrooms, spot them, and know which ones we pick and don't pick. (I still don't let her eat them.)
>
> **—KRISTIN JONES, PARENT**

This perspective is useful to consider when we think about learning spaces with appreciation for children's strengths and interests that will provide opportunities for growth and learning. It's an important consideration for all children, including children with disabilities, who will likely benefit from an individualized approach to the design of the learning environment. This was certainly the case for my own son, who approached learning differently from the other children in his class.

Right after we came home from Ukraine, my friends from work sent me a toy for Ricky. It was a plastic tower with a ball that you could drop into the top, and the ball would spin 'round and 'round until it got to the bottom. This seemed like the perfect toy for my little scientist! I put it together and showed Ricky how it worked. He dropped the ball in one time, watched it go around and around, and then took the whole thing apart. Why couldn't he just play with it the way that you were supposed to? The package on the front showed two children playing with the tower and delighting in the way that the ball rolled around and around to the bottom. Why was my child different? Why didn't he follow the rules? Looking back, the whole thing seems really silly, and the toy must have been boring to him. But at the time, I just wanted him to be okay. I worried that by not following the "rules" of the toy, it would lead to a lifetime of waving away the rules. My friends said, "Don't worry about it, Jani! Let him play with it however he wants to!" Sure, that would be okay at home, I thought, but what about at school? Would the preschool learning environment accommodate this lack of structure that he seemed to favor?

Preschool was a challenge in many ways. His teachers complained that he wandered off during group activities. He mostly played alone and didn't engage in pretend play. When the class activities became a bit rowdy, he became *too* rowdy. In kindergarten, the challenges were heightened because the expectations increased. When Ricky was engaged in active play at school, it was all good. But sitting at a desk all day? Not so much. He didn't see the point in doing something that wasn't interesting. Exploring critters in the dirt on the playground? Interesting. Sitting at a desk and coloring? Not interesting. To do well in school, concentration and focus are essential. For Ricky, the school environment was just not that interesting, and his ability to concentrate on the uninteresting stuff was pretty much nonexistent. Later, we learned that he had fine-motor delays that affected his ability to hold a pencil or a crayon. No wonder coloring wasn't very fun!

> Although we are our child's first teachers, we should aim to learn from them, so that we can better teach them.
>
> **—LATISHA R. STUCKEY, PARENT**

On one of his first days in kindergarten, I took him into class and was planning to volunteer for a while that day. The teacher showed me that she had put Ricky's desk far away from the other children because he was "distractible," and she felt that he distracted the others. There was my sweet child, off in the corner by himself. This is not inclusion, I thought. To make matters worse, the teacher had given the children a worksheet to do. Mind you, they couldn't read, and she didn't explain it, but there they were with worksheets and pencils. Ricky looked at the paper and looked at the pencil, wrote a few scribbles, and then looked up at me with the most worried face and asked, "Mommy, is this right?" It was awful. No child should experience that level of uncertainty about his own competence in kindergarten. I believe that those early years were the most challenging of all for Ricky. He decided early on that he didn't like school.

In later years, when I read over the stories in my journal and remembered the wise comments he made as a small boy or how keenly he noticed and responded to the world around him, I felt so sad. Before Ricky entered school, he was engaged with the world, learning, laughing, and growing. Then he went to school—and they took my smart, inquisitive child and made him sit in a chair for hours on end. Again and again and again, he was faced with all kinds of things that he couldn't do well. Fortunately, he is resilient and succeeded in spite of the challenges. We switched schools and connected with caring and knowledgeable educators, and the situation did improve. School was never easy for Ricky, but he worked hard and his persistence paid off. Once he graduated from high school, Ricky was able to concentrate on learning about the things that interest him. He still likes to take things apart, but now he gets paid to do it. Ricky graduated from a program at the community college where he learned how to fix giant diesel engines like the ones found in farm and construction equipment. He works as a mechanic, and he loves his job.

The stories from Ansel Adams and my own son's experience are evidence that children tend to thrive given access to a learning environment that will best meet their needs and build upon their strengths and preferences. In the following pages, we'll explore considerations for the learning environments your child will experience in the home, school, and community. We'll discuss concepts such as universal design and assistive technology, think about adaptations and accommodations, and explore strategies to support your child's curiosity and engagement.

Key Questions in Universal Design for Learning

- **Multiple means of engagement:** What options does your child have that encourage engagement and motivation to learn?
- **Multiple means of representation:** How is information provided to your child so they can perceive and understand it?
- **Multiple means of expression:** What opportunities does your child have to show what they have learned?

UNIVERSAL DESIGN FOR LEARNING

Developed by the Center for Applied Special Technology (CAST), Universal Design for Learning (UDL) is based on the understanding that children learn in different ways. Therefore, parents and teachers should use multiple methods for imparting information, multiple ways of asking children to share and demonstrate what they are learning, and multiple ways of engaging children. Children learn best when they have choices for activities so that learning is based on their interests. Rather than a single approach, UDL is all about providing multiple ways to learn so as to meet the needs of all learners. UDL is a framework that can help us think differently about expectations for how children learn, engage with the environment, and show competence. As you consider the spaces where your child is learning and growing, you can use the key UDL questions below to reflect on the play materials, the experiences, and opportunities for showing learning.

Think about your home as a learning environment. How have you set up the physical spaces in your home to maximize your child's learning potential? The following four strategies are ones that you can consider when you design spaces in your home using UDL principles to meet the needs of your child:

- Provide optimal positioning.
- Modify the response.
- Stabilize materials.
- Offer larger or brighter materials.

PROVIDE OPTIMAL POSITIONING

Think about the child who uses a walker to walk. Can she reach all the materials in her bedroom? Can she maneuver effectively between rooms in the home? Does she have options for how to engage with toys and other learning materials? We can think about the position of materials as a way to promote access and engagement. As you know, I am a very petite lady, so optimal positioning is an easy principle for me to understand. I have a step stool in pretty much every room of my house. Thinking about my own experience helped me to consider the environment from a child's perspective and support the need for independence. Consider how you place learning materials in your home so your child can access them without having to ask for help.

MODIFY THE RESPONSE

Is there only one right way to do things? Of course not! You can individualize the environment by being open to a variety of ways to do things and to use materials. For example, when tying shoes is too difficult, there's Velcro. If your child is nonverbal but can move her fingers, perhaps she could use a switch device to press a button to communicate with you. She might also benefit from using visuals such as a Picture Exchange Communication System (PECS), which is a strategy that is used widely in K–12 special education. PECS is a set of pictures that represent items or actions used frequently during the course of an everyday routine. A child can point to the pictures as a way of communicating with

peers or adults. The use of visuals is a great way to modify response.

We can individualize the environment by being open to the fact that there are a variety of ways to accomplish tasks and use materials. Some children with sensory issues might not like fingerpainting, for example. The feeling of the paint on their fingers is just too icky. In that case, painting with a cup, a dowel with a sponge attached, a small toy car, or a cotton ball might increase their comfort level. We can change our perspective and realize there are lots of ways to do something. In this photo, little Nora is painting with a green pepper.

There are also many ways to show knowledge, an idea that uses the UDL approach and the component of multiple means of expression. When we want our child to communicate something to us, we can be open to all types of communication: sign language, pictures, electronic communication devices, gesturing, nodding, and so on. All the forms of nonverbal communication are considered *augmentative and alternative communication* (AAC). AAC refers to all of the ways we can communicate without talking. Think about the ways your child can respond to you during story time. They may respond by using spoken words but may also be able to respond by pointing to pictures or simply by helping you to hold the book or turn the pages. Your child might benefit from the use of technology at story time. This way, they can help to turn the pages of a book by using the arrow keys on a computer or other electronic device. These bright round buttons can be programmed to make a particular sound that your child can use as a way to respond during play or mealtimes.

We can think about this strategy as not only modifying the response of your child but also as modifying our own response and expectations. For example, if your child becomes anxious when joining a large-group activity like story time at the library, you could find a quiet area near the activity to give your child time to observe and build familiarity until they become comfortable with the group.

STABILIZE MATERIALS

Some children with disabilities may not have good motor control, so making sure learning materials are stable can increase participation. How can you ensure that puzzle pieces are stable and don't move all around or fall off of the table as your child tries to put the puzzle together? You can use rubber padding under the pieces, or you can put the pieces on a tray. An art project can be clipped to a slant board for easier access on a tabletop. A book might be placed on a bookstand or a toy might be clamped down so that it doesn't move around too much. Toys can be adapted with hand splints or straps so that a child with limited mobility is able to grasp them. You might attach Velcro to the bottom of a bowl or plate so it can attach to the table at mealtime. This will allow your child to eat independently without the bowl sliding around.

OFFER LARGER OR BRIGHTER MATERIALS

Some children might benefit from using materials that are larger and easier to grasp. For example, chubby crayons are easier to use for children who do not yet have the fine-motor skills to use the small skinny crayons. My son had fine-motor delays, and we tried all sorts of pencils, pens, and crayons until we found the ones that worked for his specific needs. Children with visual impairments may benefit from using brighter colored materials. A zipper pull on your child's jacket could be altered so that it is larger and easier to grab. Spoons and forks could be modified with larger handles or made wider by taping foam padding around them, so that they are easier to grab and will allow your child to eat independently. Playing cards can be glued to pieces of foam or cardboard so that they are thicker and, therefore, easier to handle.

> My son Jude is on the [autism] spectrum. Whatever his interest is, he gets really excited about it. It's just an absolute blast, now that he's older, for him to share what he talks about or what he's interested in. Now, he likes fantasy stuff, and he's been really geeking out about it and that's been fun.
>
> **—BEN RIEPE, PARENT**

ASSISTIVE TECHNOLOGY

Another way of thinking about the supports you can provide your child is to consider assistive technology options. *Assistive technology* is defined as "any item, piece of equipment, or product system, whether acquired commercially off the shelf, modified, or customized, that is used to increase, maintain, or improve functional capabilities" (Sandall et al., 2005).

The use of assistive technology tools and other strategies can help children gain access to, and function more independently within, activities and routines. These tools can be as high tech as a voice output device for communication or as simple as Velcro to fasten sneakers. Assistive technology can be used for communication, play, art activities, mealtime—the possibilities are endless.

The PACER Simon Technology Center (www.pacer.org/stc) helps children and adults with a variety of disabilities to use assistive technology to enhance learning, work, and independence.

AbleNet (www.ablenetinc.com) provides assistive technology, curriculum, and services to help individuals who have disabilities lead productive and fulfilling lives. (See appendix C for a list of resources for this chapter.)

ADAPTATIONS AND ACCOMMODATIONS TO LEARNING SPACES

How can we make sure that the learning spaces in our home and community are accessible for our child? *Adaptations* and *accommodations* are types of support given to make the environment or an activity within the learning environment accessible for different learning needs. The terms are often used interchangeably, but there is a distinction between their meaning and use, especially for school-age children. For preschool children, the differences are more subtle because children under five are working on a wide variety of developmental skills in many areas.

A Note on Terminology

- **Adaptations:** An overall term for any assistance required by a child with a disability to be successful or to experience the same opportunities as typically developing peers
- **Accommodations:** Adaptations that help a child access or participate in the activity without changing the activity itself

Adapting the physical environment is kind of like being a detective, thinking about the world through your child's eyes and accommodating not only your child's needs but also their preferences, thoughts, and feelings. In making decisions, we sometimes forget that children have their own unique perspectives on the world too.

One strategy that can be helpful regardless of the activity is to give children choices. Having choices gives children a sense of control over their environment. As adults, we take it for granted that we have choices throughout the day, but children do not typically enjoy those same freedoms. You can put materials out that are within your child's reach so they can independently make their own decisions, or for activities that require your help, you can offer choices verbally and/or nonverbally. A father might ask, "Claudia, would you like to play with the musical instruments or the blocks this afternoon?" In another family, four-year old Mariano is not yet able to speak, so he uses picture cards and an electronic speaking device to communicate his choices.

ACCESSIBLE HOME AND COMMUNITY SPACES

What do we mean by the term *accessible*? The concept of access comes up frequently when I think about environments and activities that are fun and enriching for all children, with or without disabilities. The Merriam-Webster dictionary defines *accessible* as something that is "capable of being used or seen, capable of being reached, and capable of being understood" (Merriam-Webster, 2023). We might think about accessibility in the way that a building is wheelchair accessible, but the concept is much broader because our home and community spaces are about so much more than ramps and curb cuts. Think about the way you learn through reading. You are able to access information in this book by reading the words on the page, but you might also access the information by having someone read it to you or by listening to an audiobook. Children also access information in many different ways, and as your child's first teacher, you can help them through the supports you provide, the way you adapt toys or other materials, or even through the experiences you offer. For example, when my son was a toddler and we were living in Michigan, I wanted him to experience the fun of playing with snow. I scooped up some snow and brought it inside in a plastic bin. Ricky was able to play with the snow, feel the coldness, scoop it up with a spoon, and spread it out on the table, all within the warm coziness of our kitchen. That activity was a way that I made snow accessible. Children are always learning about the world around them, and sometimes it takes a bit of creativity to make all of the learning possibilities within their reach. Here are some examples of strategies you might try to make your home and community spaces more accessible and fun.

SAND, WATER, AND SENSORY PLAY

Young children learn about the world through their senses. They take in information through their eyes, ears, tongues, noses, and skin. Over time, their minds and senses help them to understand the world. The senses develop independently, and then around their first birthday, babies are able to process information from multiple senses together. This is called *sensory integration.* In early childhood, many connections are made between the mind and the senses. Therefore, it's important to offer lots of opportunities for your child to explore the world through different and surprising sensory experiences.

This is why many early childhood classrooms have a piece of equipment called a *sensory table.* This long plastic bin is set up at child height so they can stand and touch the different textures inside. The table height may be adjusted so a child sitting in a wheelchair can reach in to play as well. The sensory table can be filled with sand, water, or even shaving cream, and provides the experience of different textures, temperatures, and other sensations. You can adapt this practice for the home by offering your child experiences to play with sand, water, or other materials such as slippery beads in water or soapy bubbles. These activities can be made accessible and engaging when you offer a variety of cups and spoons of different sizes, materials that are bright in color, and materials that can be easily grasped. Your child can practice pouring with pitchers or can wring water from sponges and cloths.

The STEM Innovation for Inclusion in Early Education ("STEMIE") Center (https://stemie.fpg.unc.edu) is a great place to find resources about STEM (science, technology, engineering, and mathematics) learning opportunities for young children with disabilities. You'll find resource briefs with activity and materials adaptations, ideas, tips for using storybooks, and much more. (See appendix C for a list of resources for this chapter.)

Think about your child's interests and preferences when planning for sand, water, and other sensory play activities. I remember when I was teaching in the classroom and a little girl named Ginny joined my group. At first, she was hesitant to engage with her peers, but I learned from her father that Ginny was interested in dinosaurs, so we turned the sand table into an archeological dig site. We added small shovels, rakes, fine-mesh sifters, paintbrushes, and plastic dinosaurs and made sure that the young scientists also had access to clipboards and markers for recording field notes. Ginny wouldn't have been interested in the sand table at all, but when I added things that piqued her interest, the sensory experience became accessible to her.

If your child is squeamish about touching strange textures, put beads or uncooked rice in the bins. You can hide toys in the material for your child to find or place a variety of textures together. Fill bins with swatches of fabric, a variety of wooden beads, or puzzle pieces to touch, talk about different textures, or match by color, size, or texture.

ART AND CREATIVE EXPRESSION

Art projects give your child the opportunity to express themselves and can be set up to promote independence as well. Your child may want to paint at an easel if sitting still at a table feels too confining. Experiment with lots of different types of materials, from markers to crayons to pencils to chalk to watercolor paints. Adapt these materials to make them easier to grasp if necessary. Markers make thick lines and need less pressure than crayons. They may be a good adaptation for children who may not see thin crayon lines or who cannot press hard enough with crayons.

You can lengthen, shorten, or widen paintbrush handles, paint rollers, and so on with foam pieces. Attach a handle to your child's hand using a Velcro strap, or attach a handle to a glove with Velcro on the palm. Tape paper to the table if more stability is needed. On an easel, use tape, paper clips, or binder clips to hold the paper to the surface.

Painting offers lots of options and can be made accessible in many different ways. For example, children can paint with sponges that are easy for children with motor issues to grasp but are also usable for any child. If your child is squeamish about touching fingerpaint, you might let them paint using raw potatoes, small toy cars, squeeze bottles, or drinking straws. Another option is to put a small amount of paint into a plastic bag for your child to touch, hold, press, and squeeze. If messy and wet materials are stressful, start out by playing with dry textures—or use squeeze bottles filled with puffy paint or glue. Creativity galore!

> Jasmine is definitely "artsy." She loves music, art, and dance. She has a love of drawing. Her doctors told me that she could never hold a crayon or a pencil, but now she loves to draw a lot. It's not just a scribble-scrabble type of thing—it's great art!
>
> **—JACQUECE MOORE-LAW, PARENT**

PRETEND PLAY

Pretend play with dress-up and make-believe activities are great ways for your child to experiment and play. They can imagine themselves in the real world taking on specific roles and responsibilities, such as playing a clerk in a grocery store or a doctor in a hospital. Dress-up activities can also help with fine-motor skills if you have clothing available that uses a variety of fasteners, some easy, others more difficult. Include dolls with disabilities, dolls with different skin tones, and dolls that represent different cultures as part of the family of dolls available.

For my own son, pretend play did not come naturally. This was surprising to me, because I had fond memories of playing with Barbie dolls as a little girl. I remember making up elaborate stories and then building on those stories when friends came over. At first, Ricky behaved as though he didn't understand what the dolls or plastic play figures were meant to do. When I would act out scenes with the figures, he would look at me with a puzzled face. Over time, I would offer a figure to Ricky and ask questions such as, "What do you think the cow would say to the chicken? Should the animals go back into the barn and go night-night?" You get the idea. It feels kind of silly to play make believe at first, but this kind of modeling is important, especially for many children with disabilities. Through this adult support, your child will learn how to play with other children cooperatively, as well as on their own. This practice that your child has during playtime with you will be a benefit now and later when they are in school or when you are not there to play alongside them.

STORY TIME

Some of my fondest memories as a parent have been the times when Ricky and I snuggled up to read a book together. As a toddler he would say, "Again! Again!" at the end of a good story. When he grew older, I would choose books that would lead to a conversation. "Why do you think the mouse acted that way when he got a cookie?" or "What would you do if you went to the place where the wild things are?" The best books were the ones that led him to ask me questions. This was such great practice for learning how to be assertive in school when he might need extra help.

All that time we spent reading stories led to Ricky's ability to tell a story. The ability to tell a story and describe your thoughts and experiences is a powerful tool. My absolute favorite children's book author is Robert Munsch. We still quote lines from *Pigs, Mortimer, Thomas' Snowsuit,* and *The Paper Bag Princess* to this day. There are all kinds of benefits for children when you read together each day. Children learn the right way to hold a book, that letters are more than just scribbles on a page, and that language has rules. Letters have sounds associated with them, printed words have meaning, and (in English) we read sentences from top to bottom and left to right. Your child will learn from these experiences that you are someone who knows what the letters and words say, and their vocabulary will expand to boot.

If your child is nonverbal, story time is even more important. I hear from parents all the time that they know that their child can understand so much but just hasn't developed the skills to communicate verbally. If this is your child, first of all, you are not alone. Many children with disabilities struggle with communication skills, and there are lots of assistive technology tools out there that can help. One idea is to make audiobooks available so that your child can access stories independently and frequently. Not only is this a strategy for children with visual impairments, but it can also be useful for a child with autism or ADHD who might not have an interest in sitting still for long or who may be sensitive to too much human-to-human contact. You can try an audio player with large buttons or adapt one to turn on or off with a large switch. Some children might benefit from color-coded buttons or ones that use textures to identify "play" and "stop" buttons.

> Phillip picked up sign language at age two in preschool. His play therapist was signing to him, and she said that by the end of the thirty-minute session, he was signing to her to sing. He will try to say *apple*, and he will sign it and say it too. If you don't know the sign, then you can kind of make an approximation of what he's saying from the sign and by what he verbalizes. He does both of them. He picked it up so fast! It's his strength and a way to express himself.
>
> **—LATISHA R. STUCKEY, PARENT**

Make book pages easier to turn by modifying the pages with a paper clip for easy grasping. Or you can attach a small piece of foam to each page so there is more room to slip in a finger and turn pages. The EI and ECSE folks call these "page fluffers." Another strategy is to offer board books or books with squishy foam pages.

Homemade books can be a great way to add sensory materials to the story time experience, as well. Make a squishy book with scrapbook materials by filling plastic bags with hair gel and the "content" of your choice. You can include laminated photos, foam letters and numbers, small soft objects, pieces of fabric, and more. Make sure that each bag is sealed well, and then place it in a plastic protector sleeve before adding each page to a three-ring binder.

Homemade books can also be useful when you are working on a specific task or skill, and so the book can have a story related to your own family routine or a family activity. This is a type of book called a *social story*. Social stories (also called *scripted stories*) help children understand social interactions, situations, expectations, social cues, the script of unfamiliar activities, and/or social rules. They are brief descriptive stories that provide information regarding a social situation (Broek et al., 1994). You can use pictures, objects, or pieces of material that relate to your child's life. If your child is nonverbal or has a speech delay, they can share information about their interests or perspective about home life by pointing to the objects. Social stories can also help with reinforcing expectations you have and reminding your child about the rules around daily transitions, schedules, and routines. You can find sample social stories online that you can download and print. (See appendix C for a list of resources for this chapter.)

The key is to tap into your child's interests and preferences when selecting books. We tend to be interested in learning about the things that spark our own curiosity or about the things that are part of our own daily life. Therefore, you might want to focus on insect books if your child has suddenly become fascinated with ladybugs, but you also might include books about the challenges your child is facing. For example, you can add books to your story time about children with disabilities in general, or if you can find them, books that reflect your own child's lived experience. For example, you may want to include books that use sign language to tell the story if your child uses sign language to communicate. Check out appendix C for some book lists to explore.

It's helpful to try out books that might appeal to children at all levels along the developmental continuum. As I shared earlier, my son was always interested in construction and farm equipment. He had a book that was designed for very young children that was a collection of images of tractors and construction equipment with the name of the vehicle below the picture. That book was a favorite of his through elementary school. Don't worry so much about whether a book is developmentally appropriate. Early on, the main goal is to read, read, and read some more. In addition to early literacy skills, your child will develop a love of books and stories that can lead to an interest in communication in general.

BLOCKS AND SMALL TOYS

Blocks and other small toys are another home staple that can lead to learning for all children. When young children play with blocks, for example, they use their imagination to create things and problem-solving skills to figure out construction dilemmas. Mathematical concepts are explored involving comparison, estimation, balance, and so on. How can I make this tower higher without having it all fall down? Blocks and other building toys can offer a place for your child to express themselves creatively. This happens when children move blocks around or connect them together in a creative way, as well as when other play materials are added to the fun. What can I use to build a home for my plush toys?

> When Mazie wants to achieve something, she works very hard for it. One of the milestones that she reached recently was stacking blocks. She was concentrating really hard, even if it was just to stack two blocks. She would really focus on that until she got it.
>
> **—AMANDA LOVETTE, PARENT**

To avoid frustration, you can think creatively about this type of play depending on your child's specific needs. You might want to attach Velcro to blocks to help them stay together easily. Or find blocks that are easier to stack or easier to grab. Blocks and other building toys can be light, heavy, squishy, make noise, or fasten together using snaps or magnets. Experiment with a variety of blocks and building materials to match the developmental and physical needs of your child. You can even make your own blocks by wrapping shoeboxes with butcher paper and then decorating them with your child's help.

Mix in other toys to expand the play options. You might add a bin of play figures of people and animals near the blocks where your child plays, so they will be naturally inclined to build the settings for those play figures. If your child has difficulty holding small toys, help them to grasp the toys better by building up handles with sponge hair curlers or pieces of foam or by attaching the toy handle to your child's hand using a Velcro strap. Some puzzles already come with knobs or handles for infants and toddlers, but you can also adapt more advanced puzzles for older children by attaching inexpensive knobs from the hardware store. Most electric or battery-operated table toys can be modified to turn on or off using a switch. Partner with an occupational therapist to learn more about the options for your child.

Consider the way that real-life items are, in fact, puzzles to young children. As adults, we are experts at turning a doorknob, but your child is just learning these skills. How might you use these items for play and learning opportunities? The following photo shows a board that was created using lots of

> Ayden is highly intelligent in math, and he has this passion for building. He can take Legos and build them into anything with just memory and no directions. I took him to a Lego center, and they showed how to connect motors and lights and make things spin. He's been growing his passion from there. Now that he's mastering the Lego skills, he's been moving up to robotics.
>
> **—ARIELLE BRANCH, PARENT**

items with buttons to press, knobs and dials to turn, and latches to unlatch— all with everyday items! Activities that are relevant to your child's everyday life will be much more engaging and will serve a variety of purposes.

PLAYING OUTSIDE

In addition to the learning spaces in your home on the inside, it is just as important to consider accessibility and engagement in outdoor spaces in your community and your own backyard if you have one. Outdoor spaces promote physical activity and provide an ideal setting for all sorts of activities. I have found that just by going outside, children are more physically active and expend more energy. That is a huge stress reliever—for children and adults! And the options for outdoor play are endless. Your child can spend time gathering objects they find such as stones, leaves, and pine cones (you can help if your child has a visual impairment or limited mobility).

We are finding that more and more communities are creating inclusive outdoor playspaces. There is even a free app for your phone called Playground Buddy (https://www.playgroundbuddy.com) to help families find nearby playgrounds. If your child is able to use them, swings are an excellent outlet, especially for children with sensory concerns. Swinging provides a certain kind of feedback that is calming for some children. Children with sensory concerns also benefit from what specialists call *heavy work*. Heavy work routines are thought to provide a calming effect on the nervous system. The outdoor playspace is perfect for this type of stress relief. Heavy work includes any activity that uses the whole body and provides resistance, such as carrying heavy objects or large boxes, pushing a scooter or shopping cart around, or pulling a friend in a wagon.

The outdoors can be a place for all sorts of activities, not just those that encourage physical activities. Just bring a blanket and toys outside for a safe outdoor playspace. Bring a box of books outdoors. Paint or draw outside. The play figures that are usually indoors might have fun in the sandbox at the park, or in a sandbox created in a plastic bin. Outdoor spaces can truly be an extension of the learning environment for your child. This is true in all kinds of weather, just as long as the right clothing is available. On hot days, we loved to find a shady spot for a picnic and some story time.

The Early Childhood Technical Assistance (ECTA) has developed a collection of checklists for families that focus on adapting the environment for children with disabilities. The environmental adaptations checklist includes information about how to determine the type of environmental adaptation needed to promote participation in learning activities. You'll also find checklists related to child physical activity, natural environments, and environmental arrangements. The checklists and related practice guides are available in English and Spanish. (See appendix C for a list of resources for this chapter.)

Adaptations and accommodations are ultimately about being creative and responding to the needs of your child. Recognize that it may take a few attempts to find what works. When you find success with one adaptation in a particular setting, you might consider whether that same adaptation might work in a different setting. For example, if using the big spoon is working well at mealtime, then maybe a big crayon might work for coloring. Use your creativity to figure it out.

ACTIVITY: OPPORTUNITIES FOR PLAY AND LEARNING

DIRECTIONS

Think about all of the play materials your child has access to in your home and in the community. How might you acquire materials that you are missing?

Remember that your state may have equipment loan programs available for free. To find resources, select your state or territory and review the drop-down options under the "Child Development and Early Learning Resources" tab (https://childcare.gov/state-resources-home).

How might you adapt the materials you have to best meet your child's needs? Consider this question for the different types of play we explored in this chapter. Which accommodations might be helpful for your child? What do you need to do to make the play more accessible for your child? How might you promote engagement? Add to the list as other ideas come to mind and then reference it later when you have a rainy afternoon at home and need some creative suggestions. Make a list of ideas you would like to try under each category of play.

Sand, Water, and Sensory Play

1. ____

2. ____

3. ____

Art and Creative Expression

1. ____

2. ____

3. ____

Pretend Play

1. ____

2. ____

3. ____

Story Time

1. ______________________________

2. ______________________________

3. ______________________________

Blocks and Small Toys

1. ______________________________

2. ______________________________

3. ______________________________

Playing Outside

1. ______________________________

2. ______________________________

3. ______________________________

CHAPTER 7

Working on IFSP or IEP Goals at Home and in School

Ayden was nonverbal at the age of three. So watching him have a conversation with me is my happiest moment. I still smile to this day when I notice different words that he uses or different expressions he puts together.

—ARIELLE BRANCH, PARENT

Working together as a team with educators, service coordinators, and therapists is very important. Creating a supportive learning environment is also important, and putting all of that together can be the magic that leads to progress for your child. Children are eager to apply what they learn in one environment to all of the other parts of their life. For example, when we were working on self-care skills during his preschool years, my son was eager to do the "grown-up" tasks as well. For Christmas one year, we gave him a little push vacuum because he loved to see the results of his efforts sweeping up the floor. As I did housework, Ricky was always close by and ready to help. Moving clothes from the washer to the dryer was something he could do to help, and that led to Ricky doing his own laundry off and on throughout childhood.

We can move our children toward more independence and make learning goals fun by integrating the goals into the everyday routine. This is true for the routine in child care or preschool, but also for the routines we have in the home environment. In this chapter, we'll look at your daily routine at home and how you can help your child work on their Individualized Family Service Plan (IFSP) or Individualized Education Program (IEP) goals in your home environment. You'll learn what to teach and practice at home, when to teach and practice the goals listed in your child's IFSP/IEP, and how to practice them.

DAILY ROUTINES

How do routines make children feel? The answer is simple—they love routines! Young children thrive in an environment built around predictability and consistency. Adults are the same way, really. We generally like to know what is coming next in our daily lives. As adults, we maintain a certain sense of control over our schedules and routines because we keep calendars of our events, wear wristwatches, or check our temporal lives on our cellphones. Young children don't have the advantage of those tools, and as a result, the world can seem like an uncertain, scary place without predictable routines. Children thrive when the daily routine is clear, consistent, and predictable.

DAILY SCHEDULES

What are the main events of your family's daily schedule? Is it the same for every day of the week, or do you alternate between a weekday schedule and a weekend schedule? How does your schedule change throughout the year? Is your winter schedule the same as your summer schedule? This type of planning is typically guided by the needs of the adults in the household, and that's okay. However, when we consider how important routines are for young children, it makes sense to find ways to share information about the daily schedule so that your child can feel secure. When children are brought into the planning of daily schedules, it gives them a sense of trust and safety. Schedules help children feel a sense of control, and they lead to the development of independence when schedules are used to prepare for what's ahead. When children know what to expect of the day, it helps them transition from one activity to the next more easily. Schedules create a sense of safety and predictability.

You might use pictures to show your child the daily schedule, and help them understand what will happen throughout the day. Each event in the routine might have a set of pictures as well, to remind your child about expectations within that routine. Your child can look to the schedule on their own to find out what is coming up. The daily schedule should be visible throughout the day: include a photo

or graphic for each daily activity, posted at your child's eye level, and have some way to show the passage of time. For example, you and your child can put the daily routine on note cards and then remove or flip over the cards for events once they have occurred. The photo shows an example of a daily schedule that a preschool teacher created, so the children can manipulate the activities of the day and better understand which activities come first and which come later. The pointer graphic attaches with Velcro so it can be moved from activity to activity throughout the day.

Teaching your child about the daily routine also makes it easier to explain when something out of the ordinary is going to take place. For example, if you're planning a trip to Grandma's house over the weekend, you'll need to make sure to let your child know about this ahead of time. No surprises equals a predictable environment and a happy child.

ROUTINES WITHIN ROUTINES WITHIN ROUTINES (ROUTINES^3)

A daily schedule gives your child a sense of the main events of the day, but they often need more specifics. Your daily routine is made up of more than just wake up, get dressed, eat breakfast, play, eat lunch, play, eat dinner, bathe, read a story, and go to bed. There are routines within each part of your routine. For example, your child might have a getting-dressed routine with multiple steps. Your expectations might begin with your child getting out of bed, washing their face, brushing their teeth, combing their hair, picking out clothes, putting on each item of clothing . . . you get the idea.

> I've learned that Ivan is an astonishingly visual learner. I used to have a big whiteboard, and I would draw pictures using little stick figures: today is the day you have swimming lessons, or you're playing soccer, or you're going over to a friend's house.
>
> **—JUDY DAVID, PARENT**

In some homes, brushing teeth starts with taking out the toothpaste, putting it on the toothbrush, looking in the mirror, brushing for as long as it takes to sing the ABC song, rinsing out the toothpaste, and putting the items back in the drawer. This concept is known as Routines to the Third Power (Routines[3]) (Strain and Bovey, 2011). We have routines (events such as getting dressed) within routines (activities such as tooth brushing) within routines (steps within the tooth-brushing activity). Regardless of the details, the most important thing about the routine is that each activity happens in the same order every day. There is a rhythm and a pace to the events of the day that your child can expect. They know what is coming next and are more likely to be ready to engage with that activity as a result. And if you add some playful elements to the routine, you might even notice a reduction in challenging behaviors. In the tooth-brushing example, singing the ABC song in a silly way can help your child enjoy brushing their teeth because they want to hear the song. Think about the way you feel when listening to a favorite story that a family member has told a million times. You know what is coming next, and that is part of why you are on the edge of your seat. You think, "Oh, I love this part!" Children can feel the same way about an event within the daily routine and the routines within that event. If you add silly, fun, or playful elements, the routine can become something to look forward to. We know that the silly part of our routine is coming, so get ready to giggle together! This is critically important for young children and can be a helpful tool for children with attention needs as well. Routines help children answer these key questions:

- What am I doing now?
- How do I know I'm making progress?
- How do I know when I'm finished?
- What comes next?

Take a look at your daily schedule and the various routines nested inside. Where are the opportunities to embed learning opportunities into these planned, consistent, and predictable routines? Finding those opportunities for teaching and learning will offer your child some chances to practice the skills they are developing throughout the day.

There are lots of examples of visual supports on the Head Start Center for Inclusion website (https://headstartinclusion.org). You'll find examples of a picture schedule of a typical home routine as well as transitions that might benefit from a "first-then" schedule. For example: "First you will do your exercises for physical therapy, then you can play on the tablet." Or, "First get dressed, then we can have breakfast together."

Depending on their age and abilities, you can also try the strategy of teaching your child how to use a timer. This gives children a sense of control and predictability because the timer lets them know how much time is left in a visual way before an activity ends.

The other day I was at June's school at the end of the day, and I was helping her through the bathroom routine. Then, she stands up and pulls up her pants all on her own! At home, I would have pulled up her pants. I just didn't realize that she was going through those types of routines so independently.

—JACKIE JOSEPH, PARENT

LENGTH OF DAILY ACTIVITIES

Another aspect of the daily routine to consider is the length of time your child spends in a given activity. You may find that even after implementing predictable daily routines, your child is still wiggly during story time. Your expectations around how long your child can stay still and pay attention to a story may need to be reevaluated. That's okay. It's just a matter of recognizing this about your child and adapting to shorter books or books that are more likely to capture their interest. The trick is to find a recipe for each activity that works for your child. Make sure you persist in presenting a new activity again and again. Just because your child is not ready to attend to a full storybook today doesn't mean that they won't be ready next week. Assume competence and give your child many opportunities to try.

Here are some suggestions for supporting routines at home:

- **Start with simple routines of just three or four steps:** Think about the task as having a beginning, middle, and end. For example, a bathtime routine might include the steps of getting in the tub, washing your body, washing your hair, rinsing off, getting out of the tub, and drying off with a towel. You can take a photo of your child doing these steps and use the photos to make a poster that you can they tape to the bathroom wall. Morning and evening routines are highly effective for families to address, and following these routines with consistency can be a great starting point.
- **Think about how you might involve your child in planning the day:** If you are a parent who works from home, this can be a helpful strategy for the days when your child is home with you during a preschool holiday. "Do you want to play with blocks or watch a show while I work?" or

"Do you want to take a walk before or after my phone call?" Providing choices when possible gives children a sense of some control over their environment.

- **Engage siblings within routines:** Siblings can be effective teachers, especially when peers are not available.
- **Prepare for changes to routines:** Like many families, your family likely has changing work and life schedules that can make it difficult to implement a consistent routine. You can help your child adapt to those daily or weekly changes by creating visual cues for the schedule for that day or week.

TRANSITIONS DURING THE DAY

Often, the times of transition from one activity to the next can be the most difficult for young children. Think about it from their perspective: "I'm in the middle of pretending to be shopping in the grocery store with my friend Lois, and suddenly I'm told that I have to put away my apron and clean up. The nerve!" You can smooth transitions between activities by using some intentional practices.

One strategy is to develop transition routines. Transition routines can help children to prepare for the change by making it predictable, giving them advance notice, and in some cases, offering opportunities for making choices. First, you teach your child the routine and the expectations you have for the routine at a time when your child is calm and focused. Try teaching routines with puppets, role-play, or a story. Make it playful and fun! For example, let's say that you want to build in a weekly story hour at the library. However, past attempts at making the transition of getting out of the car and walking quietly to the story area have not worked well. Your child is loud. They fall to the ground and writhe around on the floor when you tell them to use a quiet voice in the library. We have all been there. Instead of assuming that your child knows the expectations, try taking time at bedtime when your child is calm to read a story about going to the library. Then, at breakfast the next day, act out a silly story about your child going to the library for story time—how they quietly get out of the car and then tiptoe and use a quiet voice going into the library. Pretend that you are the fork and your child is the spoon as you act out the breakfast "going to the library" play. Get creative over the next few days as you playfully prepare your child for the event. When time comes for the weekly story time, your child will know what to expect and will have had time to practice what it means to live up to your expectations.

Your child might benefit from a transition warning. For the library example, you can talk about the expectations on the drive over to the library, and let your child know how many minutes are left until you get there. This is where that timer comes in handy. You can use a simple timer or hourglass, so they have a visual for how much time is left before the transition happens.

The National Center for Pyramid Model Innovations (NCPMI) (https://challengingbehavior.org) has a huge library of visual supports, including transition cards to help children manage transitions appropriately. You can download the cards, print them, and laminate them to use in your home. It also has developed a resource that families can use to help children learn, practice, and integrate household expectations. You can access the materials and related visuals online. (See appendix C for a list of resources for this chapter.)

CLEAR EXPECTATIONS

When children enjoy the same advantage that adults have in knowing what is coming up through the course of the day, the results can be huge. When we couple that advantage with teaching children the expectations for each point in the daily routine, we really have the secret sauce! Children appreciate rules because they feel pride when they are able to meet the expectations that adults have set for them. For example, your child will likely feel proud when they come home at the end of the day and know where to hang up their jacket and put their backpack away.

When setting expectations for your child, it's wise to focus on what they can and should do rather than using words like *don't*. You might say, "Let's use gentle hands," instead of saying, "Don't hit." Keep expectations positive and brief. Figure out which three to five household rules would be important for your family. You can think of these as a "family motto," keeping in mind that you'll want to focus on rules that apply to situations where your child typically needs reminders. These choices should also be things that you can teach your child to do and that are appropriate for their age or stage of development. For example, your family might function based on three key expectations:

1. Use listening ears.
2. Use gentle hands and feet.
3. Clean up messes.

Whichever rules you decide on, make sure to put them into a chart and add a picture of your child as they are following the rule. Your child may want to help you make the chart or at least watch as you make it. To get started, you can find printable posters online with these rules along with the meaning behind the rules (See appendix C for a list of resources for this chapter.) For example, "Be respectful," means that we have gentle hands, take turns, and use quiet voices and listening ears. Your household expectations should be posted at your child's eye level, with visual representations for each rule.

Once you have made the chart together, find a time to teach your child the rules when they are not distracted. Talk about the rules together. Keep it relaxed and fun. This is not the time to scold your child or to talk about the times they did not meet expectations. This is the time to talk about what the expectations actually are. What does it look like to follow the rule? What are the smaller steps your child might need to take? Take turns with your child showing what it looks like when you DO follow the rule, and what it looks like when you DO NOT follow the rule. You can use puppets or stuffed animals, make up stories or songs about the rules, play a game to see if your child can remember the rule—the possibilities are endless! Focus on the teaching, and allow lots of time for your child to practice. You may want to think about possible scenarios from your family life and give your child a chance to problem solve how they would respond if they were following the rules.

NCPMI has developed a guide for families with strategies to manage tricky situations in the everyday routine at home. The guide includes prevention strategies and suggestions for how to teach new skills. You'll find strategies for the common routines and activities that occur during your family's week, such as getting dressed, going to a restaurant, cleaning up, and so on. It's called *Positive Solutions for Families: A Family Routine Guide* (https://challengingbehavior.org/docs/Positive-Solutions_Family-Routine_Guide.pdf)

Understanding consistent rules and expectations promotes independence and self-control in young children. When those rules are consistent over time, across settings, and between educator and family, children learn about boundaries and how to meet expectations. Then, celebrate success! When your child does meet expectations, make sure to provide frequent, positive descriptive feedback. Give your child lots of praise and encouragement when they have learned how to follow the rules. You know the saying, "Catch 'em being good!" When children get that feedback, it is reinforcement that will lead to meeting expectations in the future. The positive verbal feedback or praise can be paired with other kinds of feedback, such as a hug or high-five, for maximum impact. How much positive feedback is necessary to make a difference in this way? It really depends on your child and the relationship you have built together. I like to suggest a ratio of a minimum of five positive statements, such as telling children how awesome they are and catching children being good, to every one negative statement. Experiment with your own child; you might be surprised by how well some words of affirmation can work.

> June just has always had this social maturity. If somebody is not following the rules in the classroom, she'll look to an adult and just give a look, like "I know, what are you gonna do?"
>
> **—JACKIE JOSEPH, PARENT**

WHAT TO TEACH AND PRACTICE AT HOME

As we discussed in chapter 5, the goals in your child's IFSP or IEP will be individualized based on your child's strengths and the skills the team believes are within reach for your child. For older children, goals might have to do with academic achievement like improving their algebra test scores. Obviously, that is not the case for early childhood. What do IFSP/IEP goals look like in early childhood?

For preschool-aged children, IEP goals often focus on social skills and how your child is forming positive social relationships. They may also relate to how your child communicates, or skills related to language and early literacy. For example, if your child is nonverbal, the team may suggest that they learn some basic signs from sign language to communicate. In many cases, your child's goals will be related to what your child is working on in the context of everyday living. These are known as *functional outcomes*. Functional outcomes are intended to measure how your child is able to carry out the important activities in their daily routine. These might look like a collection of behaviors across many aspects of development that your child needs to know or do to be successful in everyday life. Want to learn more about functional child outcomes? The ECTA Center developed a helpful infographic; see appendix C for more information about this resource.

> Kelsey is somewhat competitive. That tends to make her work hard at whatever she wants to achieve. We just remind her of the goal that she wants to reach and point out how she can get there if she really wants it.
>
> **—TERRI LEYTON, PARENT**

WHEN TO TEACH AND PRACTICE: USING EMBEDDED LEARNING OPPORTUNITIES

Shared responsibility is important because when team members use this approach, it is possible for your child to make progress on IFSP or IEP goals throughout the day, every day, regardless of the setting. The child is at home? Work toward goals! The child is in the Head Start or preschool program? Work toward goals! The child is in speech therapy? Work toward goals! This approach changes the intensity of the intervention equation. And from the child's perspective, it is much less confusing because all the adults in their life are consistent in how they provide support. This also provides an opportunity for the child to rehearse the knowledge and skills they are working on during therapy or in school, using more authentic ways and in a different context.

> Families should set their priorities, and use those priorities for the child and the family as a guiding point for all the decisions that are coming with it. Once you know your priorities, it's not a straight path forward, but you can find different ways to achieve your goals as a family, and help your child get where he or she wants to be.
>
> **—HILDA BERNIER, PARENT**

Individualized goals can be practiced in the context of daily routines and activities. As we described in chapter 6, your child might practice skills during daily routines such as meal preparation, household chores, engaging in a phone conversation with a family member, or even while watching television. This strategy is called *embedded learning opportunities* because the skills to practice are embedded into natural settings like the home or community. This gives children authentic opportunities to work on their individualized goals. What do we mean by authentic? It means that the task is meaningful for the child or relevant to what is happening in their world.

In addition, using embedded learning opportunities allows more time for the child to apply knowledge and practice new skills. The following chart highlights how this strategy can result in much more time to practice for the child. It provides a breakdown of the amount of support two children receive over the course of a week, comparing pull-out therapy with support provided throughout the home and classroom routine. You can see that Michael receives one hour of pull-out speech and language therapy with a speech/language provider (SLP); Miguel receives three times that amount in his home and classroom settings, where his parents and teachers prompt him to use his receptive-language skills to communicate during mealtimes, routines, transitions, and learning experiences even though he is not yet verbal.

	MICHAEL		MIGUEL	
Day	**Activity**	**Minutes**	**Activity**	**Minutes**
Monday			• Points to his selection of breakfast items when asked, "Cereal or yogurt?" • Nods when his teacher ask if he is all done, wants more, of if he is enjoying his meal • Practices signing *more* when he wants more to eat at mealtimes • Makes finger and hand motions to fingerplays and songs at school	5 mins. 10 mins. 15 mins. 10 mins.
Tuesday	Points to picture cards and reads books with therapist	30 mins.	• Raises his arms when caregiver asks, "Can we change your diaper now?" • Brings his coat over when Mom says, "Let's go outside to check the mail." • Points to several animals when Dad makes their sounds during a bedtime story • Makes finger and hand motions to fingerplays and songs at school	5 mins. 5 mins. 15 mins. 10 mins.
Wednesday			• Makes finger and hand motions to fingerplays and songs at school • Points to his body parts when named during diaper change • Signs *more* during afternoon snack time • Raises his arms when caregiver asks, "Can we change your diaper now?"	10 mins. 10 mins. 5 mins. 5 mins.
Thursday	Points to picture cards and reads books with therapist	30 mins.	• Makes finger and hand motions to fingerplays and songs at school • Points to his choice when asked which T-shirt he prefers to wear: dinosaur or tractor • Points to the mouse on each page of *If You Give a Mouse a Cookie* during afternoon playtime with his teacher • Raises his arms when caregiver asks, "Can we change your diaper now?"	10 mins. 5 mins. 15 mins. 5 mins.
Friday			• Practices signing *more* when he wants more to eat at mealtimes • Walks to his cubby when it is time to collect his things and leave with Mom, selects his coat, and hands it to Mom • Raises his arms when caregiver asks, "Can we change your diaper now?" • Makes finger and hand motions to fingerplays and songs at school	15 mins. 5 mins. 10 mins. 10 mins.
Total time		**1 hr.**		**3 hrs.**

You've got to really balance what you want for your child with letting them be an actual kid. Your child isn't a project; your child is a person who is going to not want to do things and is going to be developing in ways that you wouldn't expect.

—LEAH MULLEN, PARENT

This strategy works for teaching social skills and expectations as well. Parents and teachers can use everyday routines to help children practice the skills they need to be able to communicate with others, manage their emotions, get along well with others, and engage in learning in ways that will lead to success.

As family members, we know how important it is to advocate on behalf of our child. This may lead us to think that we should try to advocate for an extra session of one-on-one specialized services for our child. This may very well be needed, but another option we might consider is that a specialist could work with us directly and/or with our child's classroom teacher to find ways to embed activities throughout the routine of the day. This doesn't mean every minute of the day, but you can see from Miguel's example that your child could potentially have many more opportunities to practice and master skills to reach milestones and desired outcomes with an embedded approach. An additional benefit is that your child may then more easily generalize the skills when they are learned and practiced during regular, everyday activities.

HOW EMBEDDED LEARNING HELPS CHILDREN

Let's explore this further. If we consider that an advantage of this approach is that your child is able to generalize skills from one setting to another, what might that look like in real life? Let's use the speech-therapy example. Sam is working on the use of rhyming words such as *hat* and *cat.* He would certainly practice that skill during speech therapy, but with an embedded learning approach, he is also practicing at home and in child care as well. Sam points to his furry friend and says, "Cat!" and his mother says, "Yes! Cat! What rhymes with *cat,* Sam?" The next day, Sam walks into his child-care classroom and his teacher is wearing a silly hat. Sam points and says, "Hat!" His teacher says, "Yes! Hat! What rhymes with *hat,* Sam?" Now, Sam is thinking about words that rhyme across all the settings and with all the people who are important in his life. He has lots of opportunities to practice new skills.

> Our educational goal right now is for her to continue to stay in an inclusive program to get the social aspect of everything, to gain skills, and then to live independently.
>
> **—AMANDA LOVETTE, PARENT**

This approach is also empowering for us as parents because family members are considered an essential part of the team. We have the most knowledge about our child, are the constant in our child's life, and we will be the decision-makers when choices about services are presented. The specialist can support us and our child's teachers by providing information about our child's condition and practical strategies to facilitate our child's development.

HOW EMBEDDED LEARNING HELPS SPECIALISTS

Early intervention (EI) and early childhood special education (ECSE) specialists benefit from this approach as well because they are able to serve in more of a consulting role to support and provide resources to families and teachers. EI and ECSE specialists can use their time to:

- provide services to a child within the program or classroom;
- share information about a particular disability with the family or early childhood educator;
- provide information about typical child development;
- give suggestions for activities to embed learning into the daily routine, activities, or transitions;
- demonstrate therapeutic techniques;
- observe children and provide feedback;
- suggest available resources or related services in the community; and
- answer questions and provide written information and resources.

Efforts to coordinate service delivery in this way will likely vary depending on the needs of your child and family, but this approach has shown that working together is better. Teams have found that, through this coordination, they have been able to discover new and better ways for meeting the needs of the child and family. Once roles are determined, it works best to put any specific agreements into writing, so that the specialist, family, and early education provider understand the expectations. The team may also decide to review agreements on a regular basis to make sure that all partners are on the same page. I can personally attest that a team approach really works. As a parent, it felt extremely supportive to have several people whom I could connect with if I had questions about my son's progress toward his IEP goals.

> We try to respect her timeline, her strengths and preferences and interests and loves. That means sometimes accessing every possible therapy support. However, just because we could do more doesn't mean we should do more. We have to let June guide that for us. She is secure in her timeline.
>
> **—JACKIE JOSEPH, PARENT**

To facilitate this collaboration, teachers, therapists, and parents can engage in honest communication about what is working and not working at school, in therapy, or at home.

- What does the child do? What does the child do independently? When does the child need adult assistance?
- What does the child seem to enjoy? (What makes the child smile, laugh, or get excited?)
- What is difficult for the child?
- When are there opportunities for the child to practice new skills during the everyday routine?

The answers to these questions will give you information about what to teach and practice and about when to teach and practice the skills.

HOW TO SUPPORT YOUR CHILD WITH EMBEDDED LEARNING OPPORTUNITIES AT HOME

So, if we have identified what to teach and practice, as well as when to teach and practice the skills, our next step is to think about the how of the process. Of course, how is individualized and will depend on many factors, such as your own family context, your child's specific needs, and your child's IFSP/IEP goals. However, there are some helpful strategies that you can try. In the early childhood learning environment, these are called *curriculum modifications,* but they are also just helpful ideas for supporting your child as they learn new skills. Five strategies that work especially well for parents and families to use at home are *scaffolding, activity simplification, response prompting, peer support,* and *child preferences.*

SCAFFOLDING

The term *scaffolding* is used to describe a method of helping children move to more independence as their skills develop. The concept comes from researcher and psychologist Lev Vygotsky's zone of proximal development, in which adults provide just the right amount of help so that the child can be successful, without taking over and doing the task for the child (Crain, 2010). Think about the scaffolding set up by builders during construction. The supports are there while all of the sawing and hammering happens, but once the building is in good shape, the scaffolding is removed. The building couldn't have been built with such strength or risen to such a height if the scaffolding had not been present during the building process.

The first step is to learn what your child is able to accomplish on their own, what they cannot accomplish on their own, and how they might be able to accomplish the new skill with some assistance. Scaffolding happens when we provide supports that can help the child follow instructions and learn. Some ways to scaffold learning include the following:

- **Communicating expectations in a way that your child can understand:** You can do this through simple language, role-playing, and use of supports or repetition to explain concepts, rules, or tasks.
- **Using a variety of pictures or visual supports geared to your child's different learning needs:** Photographs with captions, posters, calendars, and to-do lists are all ways that your child may be able to understand home expectations.
- **Using scripted stories or social stories:** You can write down a simple story that describes a situation that your child may encounter and the behaviors your child should use in that situation. Scripted stories can be illustrated with photographs of your child or with graphics found online. Broek et al. (1994) advise that we can use these simple stories as tools to prepare your child for a new situation, for addressing challenging behavior, or for teaching new skills.

(See appendix C for a list of resources for this chapter.) Scripted stories can be particularly useful when teaching social-emotional skills, which we discuss in more detail in chapter 8.

- **Using a variety of reinforcements, including signals, such as visual cues, songs, or other reinforcements:** How often you use them will vary depending on the needs of your child. Communicating with your child in ways that will expand their learning by commenting about things that interest them so they are more likely to respond to or repeat your comment, asking questions that require more than a yes-or-no answer, and expanding on something that your child says to build vocabulary. For example, your son says, "Truck," and you say, "Yes, you have a green dump truck."
- **Setting up situations to capture your child's attention and encourage conversation:** You can do something that is outside the typical routine, such as holding a book upside down to read to your child, so they will say, "No! This way!" and then they can show you how to read a book the right way. We all love to know the right way—and it's fun for your child to correct their parent. Another example is a strategy called "snack talks," which are visual supports intended to encourage conversations during mealtimes (Gauvreau, 2017). The idea is that you share a snack-talk topic with your family at the dinner table, and then you all use it as a topic of conversation. You might include topics such as favorite songs, toys, books, or food—whatever is of interest to your family. (See appendix C for a list of snack-talks tips.) When Ricky was younger, we used to have a dinnertime routine of sharing something great and something not so great. It was a way to learn about each other and get past the typical, "So, how was your day?" question that typically ends with an answer like, "Fine."
- **Providing opportunities for challenge:** This approach might involve placing a favorite toy in such a way that your child will need to work on a skill to obtain it. For example, if your child is working on fine-motor skills, you might put a favorite toy in a container that is tricky to open. Your child has the challenge of opening the container to get to the toy.
- **Creating opportunities for choice:** Your child will need to use their brain and their communication skills when they have to select from multiple options. For example, you might offer two different types of fruit during snack time so your child learns the words for the fruits and has the chance to use the new words when you ask them which one they want to eat. Providing choices is also a way to give your child a sense of control while still making progress toward a skill.
- **Modeling a task from beginning to end:** By hearing your explanation step by step, and by watching your actions, your child will learn to think through a task and to understand what needs to happen first, next, and so on. When it is your child's turn to try, you can coach them along the way to reinforce learning.
- **Allowing many opportunities for repetition and practice:** All children use repetition and practice to learn about the world, and your time and patience will allow this to happen so that your child can be successful.

ACTIVITY SIMPLIFICATION

A strategy that can be helpful for teaching many different types of new skills is known as *activity simplification*. This is the concept of breaking a complicated task into smaller parts or reducing the number of steps or parts. For example, Tracy turns away when a large number of puzzle pieces are put in front of her, but she stays engaged when the puzzle pieces are given to her one at a time. Another example is that Jake is learning the steps to wash his hands. He uses a process chart that breaks down the handwashing process into steps that he can follow.

I love using this strategy when engaging children in pretend play. As I shared earlier, pretend play doesn't come easily for all children. It may seem strange to teach your child to play, but you'll be surprised by how fun it is when you give it a try. For example, Marcy engaged with her daughter in a game of "doing the laundry." She created a visual of step-by-step directions for using a pretend washer to wash doll clothes. She included photos of her daughter telling the doll that it was time to wash clothes, removing the doll clothes from the doll, putting the clothes in a cardboard box decorated to look like a washing machine, shaking the washing machine to get the clothes all clean, and taking the clothes out and hanging them on a clothesline. This activity taught her daughter important pretend-play skills, as well as how to follow step-by-step instructions during a playful and nonthreatening time.

RESPONSE PROMPTING

In addition to scaffolding and modeling, prompts can be effective in early childhood, both in the classroom and as a strategy for use at home. The Barton Lab (n.d.) at Vanderbilt University defines *prompts* as "instructions, gestures, demonstrations, touches, or other things we can do to increase the likelihood that children will respond how we want them to. Prompting helps children complete tasks that might otherwise be too difficult or contain multiple or complex steps. Supporting children using prompts (and providing positive descriptive feedback) helps them learn to complete tasks independently."

You are most likely already doing this. For example, you might tap your child on the shoulder when they are deeply engaged in a puzzle to let her know it's time to clean up and have lunch; that is using a physical prompt. You might also say, "Angel, it's time for lunch!" which is a verbal prompt, and you might even point to your watch or the clock, which is a gestural prompt.

We Carry Kevan

Kevan Chandler is a charismatic, empathetic, smart, and funny young man who took a trip across Europe in 2016. This may not sound that amazing, but Kevan has a rare neuromuscular disease called spinal muscular atrophy, and he uses a wheelchair for mobility. Throughout the European trip, Kevan's friends carried him on their backs in a backpack that they designed especially for him. It's an incredible story, and Kevan continues to be an advocate for thinking about accessibility as a cooperative effort. (See appendix C for a list of resources for this chapter.)

Response prompting, made popular by Wolery, Ault, and Doyle (1992), is used to describe the process of using prompts to support learning in a specific way: ordered from most to least or least to most. A most-to-least strategy is used to support your child as they learn a complex task. You first provide a lot of help and then gradually reduce the support as the child learns the skill. Least-to-most prompting is used when a child already knows how to do something but must be supported to generalize the skill in new situations. For example, your child may be skilled at taking turns with an adult while playing peekaboo but is still learning how to take turns when rolling a ball back and forth with a friend. To use this technique, you start out by providing the least amount of help necessary for your child to successfully take turns but then add in additional support over time as needed for your child to be successful.

PEER SUPPORT

Does your child have a sibling? a neighborhood friend? a cousin or other family member close to your child's age? You might find that peer support can serve as a way to increase your child's engagement in a learning activity. Not only can peers provide support through praise and encouragement, but they can also model play strategies or demonstrate other activities that their friend is learning. This happens naturally in an inclusive early childhood program as peers watch each other throughout the day and as they do classroom chores, eat, play, and learn. Sometimes the child with a disability is being helped, and other times the child with a disability is the helper. This is a strategy that can work at home too. Here are two examples:

- Mary, LeeAnn, and Destiny work together on an art project. It starts when Mary makes a simple mark on the paper. LeeAnn adds to it by drawing a shape, and Destiny finishes the project by cutting a shape out from a page of construction paper and gluing it on the masterpiece.
- Judy is not eager to run through the sprinkler but is happy to do so when her brother Luke takes her hand and they run through together. When she makes it through, Judy is all smiles as Luke, Verla, and Aisha cheer her on.

CHILD PREFERENCES

Another effective way to support your child with learning new skills during everyday routines is by identifying and integrating your child's preferences into the task. You likely know what your child is interested in. These preferences give you clues for what will keep your child motivated to remain engaged in an activity. Consider the following examples of how to use child preferences as a way to motivate them:

- Sammy loves trains. At home, his parents have decorated his room with trains and even bought him a bedspread with trains on them because he loves them so much. Transitions are difficult for Sammy, but he was able to be successful when his father suggested that he chug like a choo-choo train when he puts his clothes on in the morning.
- Janice loves music. When she becomes bored with a puzzle activity, her mother sparks her interest in the activity by singing a song while they play together.
- Peter is anxious when going to new places or trying new things. His grandmother knows that Peter loves books and really loves it when she reads to him. Together they go to a new park and bring along a picnic blanket and Peter's favorite books to read.
- Josie is learning to identify and name common objects, but she doesn't seem very interested in most of the objects around the house. However, Josie is a natural "foodie," and she loves mealtime. Her parents use this preference by teaching Josie to name and identify fruits and vegetables.

> I can make myself so exhausted trying to push skills that matter to me. But that's not my job. I need to support June to be able to do what matters to her when she's ready to do it.
>
> **—JACKIE JOSEPH, PARENT**

Here are some questions to think about when considering your child's interests and preferences:

- What is a typical day like in your family?
- What does your child like to do in the morning? afternoon? evening?
- What is your child's favorite thing to do on the weekend?
- Which routines or activities does your child not like to do? What makes this routine or activity difficult or uncomfortable for your child?

> He tries his best and gives effort, his best effort when he's motivated. He is really good at sorting things. He'll scan the page to see which things go together. He does good with big puzzles. He has a very good memory.
>
> **—LATISHA R. STUCKEY, PARENT**

- If you could dream up a perfect family vacation, where would it be and what would you do?
- What is your child's favorite toy? Does your child have a particular attachment to an object at home?
- What is your child's favorite food? Are there certain foods you know to avoid?
- What holds your child's attention the most?
- What makes your child happy? When do you see your child smile or laugh?
- How does your child calm himself?

Use the answers to these questions to complete a planning matrix for your child (the activity for chapter 7). A planning matrix is a tool to use for organizing the ways that you can embed your child's IFSP/IEP goals into your everyday routine. The activity planning matrix can be a helpful way to organize embedded learning opportunities. (See appendix C for more resources on using a planning matrix.) You can use this tool as a visual reminder to take advantage of all the potential learning opportunities that occur each day in your everyday routine. Share it with your child's teacher, who may even want to create a similar matrix for use during your child's time in child care or preschool.

One special note to consider about all of this: even though it is encouraged and helpful for you to work on IFSP/IEP goals at home, you really need to give yourself grace in the process, as parent Hilda Bernier so wisely advises:

> ***I recommend that you just live a little. Don't believe that this [disability] is everything because your child is gonna get there at their own pace. Emilio started walking when he was just about two years old, and it took him a long time, but he got there. He asked me for his first cookie when he was past two. But he got there. Everything is going to happen when it has to happen, when the child is ready. And it happened with Emilio. If I would do it all over again. I would give myself and give Emilio some grace.***

You are, first and foremost, your child's parent or important and caring family member. Your number-one job is to keep your child safe and healthy and to promote happiness in every way possible. My friend Jackie Joseph said it best: "My job is not to be June's therapist. My job is to be June's mom." So true! You are not a therapist (unless you have been trained to be one). However, as a loving, kind, and caring influence in your child's life, you do have the ability to make a difference in their growth and development.

ACTIVITY: ACTIVITY PLANNING MATRIX

DIRECTIONS

Here's a sample planning matrix to try at home. The left column is where you will list the activities that make up your child's everyday routine—the when. The middle column lists the IFSP/IEP goal or outcome your child might work on during that time—the what. The column on the right indicates the specific adaptation or strategy to support your child—the how.

DAILY ROUTINES/ ACTIVITIES (getting dressed, mealtimes, playtimes, family outing, bedtime, bathtime, and so on)	IFSP/IEP GOAL (putting on shoes, using a cup, putting together puzzle pieces, listening to a story, cleaning up after playtime, and so on)	ADAPTATION OR STRATEGY (what we say or do, how many times we do it, use of visual supports, activity simplification plans, use of child preferences, modelling, prompting, adult support, and so on)

CHAPTER 8

Helping Your Child Make Friends, Deal with Big Emotions, and Get Along with Others

A lesson that I wasn't expecting is how much our boys learn from each other and value other people. I didn't expect that Jude, having gone through his own experiences and those of his little brother, would stand up for other kids like he does. I just couldn't be prouder of my kids.

—BEN RIEPE, PARENT

When I interviewed families for this book, a recurring theme that came up was the hope for their child to love and receive love in return. Ultimately, the ability to read, solve math problems, and perform independent self-help skills, as well as other important life lessons pale in comparison to our desires for our children to experience strong social relationships. This is often referred to in early childhood as healthy social and emotional development.

It's interesting to me that these areas of development are so closely tied together. Our ability to develop friendships and other relationships is dependent on our abilities to express and regulate our emotions effectively as well as to solve problems in a calm and relaxed way. Relationships are at the heart of what we teach our children simply by showing them how we relate to others and how we relate to our children as people. This is especially important if your child has a visible disability or behaves in a way that is different from other children. As a parent, you can play a huge role in helping your child to navigate through those feelings. It starts with understanding your child's behaviors and what they are actually communicating.

This chapter begins with a discussion about young children's behaviors as a way of communication and the importance of understanding the communication behind the behaviors. We then delve into teaching children social-emotional skills and explore ways that you can help your child understand and regulate their emotions, make friends, and solve problems. The chapter concludes with a section on managing those behaviors that challenge us.

Katherine knows she has cerebral palsy. She'll say, "That's why it's harder for me to write, and I can't run well." And she knows that she has Turner syndrome, and she'll say, "That's why I'm so short, and I have to take shots." We have learned that it's best to be matter of fact about it and to not be afraid to share.

—PATRICIA REEDY, PARENT

For a long time, of course, we knew his speech has been delayed, or that he has low verbal skills. But he's always talking and trying to converse. I always thought it was gibberish, like just a very little bit I could understand. And then he kept saying this one sound over and over, and I'm like, "What is it?" He was asking for something very adamantly. This is going on for weeks, maybe a month. Then, finally, I realized he was asking to listen to Bob Dylan! So cool! It made me realize that he's saying so many things. It's just that I'm not understanding what he's saying. This is my first time as a parent, and I realized that he is communicating. It's me that's not understanding him. It kind of changed my perspective.

—OLIVIER BERNIER, PARENT

BEHAVIORS HAVE MEANING

Thinking back to how we felt as a child can be challenging for us as adults. We have a lifetime of understanding what it is like to live in the world and manage the emotions that come up for us in our day-to-day lives. Children do not have the benefit of those years of experience and can easily become overwhelmed by the feelings that take over their bodies. Try to think about feelings from the child's perspective. A child who is lying down in the middle of the grocery store with tears and cries is a child who is having challenging feelings and thoughts. This is a child who is frustrated or stressed or angry or scared. She feels out of control inside her own body, and the behavior she uses to express that out-of-control feeling is really a cry for help. I always say that the more extreme the behavior, the more desperate the cry for help. Your child is not *giving* you a hard time, she is *having* a hard time. Young children do not yet have the ability to express themselves verbally, so often the communication happens through their behaviors. If we approach children's behaviors with curiosity and try to understand the "why" behind the behavior, we can respond in a more empathetic way and take advantage of a teachable moment.

As adults, we have learned over time to use words to communicate with others. Children let us know their wants and needs through their behavior long before they have words to express their feelings. They give us cues to help us understand what they want us to know. Infants might smile, cry, turn away, or arch their backs. Toddlers are beginning to communicate with words, but they also use facial expressions, crying, squeals, giggles, or running away. Preschoolers say words and sentences but also smile, scream, cry, kick, hit, laugh—and the list goes on.

Children will use certain behaviors until they learn new ways to communicate what they want and need. The behaviors they use depends on lots of things: their developmental stage, relationships with others, culture, and individual differences, including temperament and health issues. All behaviors have meaning, and for children with disabilities who may have special communication needs, it's important that we work to figure out what the behaviors are intended to communicate.

Each behavior has a form and a function. The *form* is the actual behavior that the child uses to communicate; the *function* is the reason or purpose the child is using that behavior. For example, an infant will cry (a form of behavior) when they are trying to communicate, "I'm hungry!" (the function of the behavior). A toddler will bite her friend (form) when they are trying to communicate, "I want the toy you have" (function). A preschooler will hit a friend (form) when they are trying to communicate, "I don't want to stop playing and clean up" (function).

Sometimes, we can figure out what the function of the behavior is, but other times it can be trickier. Typically, the function of every behavior is to help the child obtain something, such as a toy, attention, sensory need, or to get away from something, such as doing a task, unwanted attention, or sensory input. If we can remember that every behavior has both a form and a function, and when we can understand the function, we can start to address it and give the child more appropriate replacement options for the form of the behavior.

The function of the behavior determines how it should be addressed. That is, that we often need to look past the behavior itself to understand the motivation behind the behavior. For example, two children are making lots of noise during story time at the library. Angela may be motivated by a desire to escape, while Deshawn is motivated by a need for attention. The way that their parents successfully respond in each case is different. For Deshawn, his parent might try the "catch 'em being good" approach from chapter 6. But Angela may not respond to that; she might need a five-minute break from the story time instead. Gaining a better understanding of what the behavior *means* for the child can help us develop effective strategies that meet our child's needs.

What Do We Mean by Healthy Social-Emotional Development?

According to Zeanah and colleagues (2005), healthy social-emotional development, also described as infant and early childhood mental health, refers to the developing capacity of children ages birth through five years of age to:

- form close and secure adult and peer relationships;
- experience, regulate, and express emotions in socially and culturally appropriate ways;
- explore the environment; and
- learn all in the context of family, community, and culture.

When adults respond to children in a warm and supportive manner, children learn to understand, express, and regulate their emotions and behaviors. For example, Karlie tends to blurt out remarks while her mother is on the phone. Instead of saying, "That's rude!" her mother could say, "Karlie, I know why you are interrupting me. You have this awesome brain that's always filled with ideas, and you are excited to share them, so you want to say them right away before you forget. But you also

> I feel like I had to go through everything, all of my experiences, so that I can better help other people and my son. Even the sadness and grappling with the grief. Going through those phases, the fluctuating—that's a part of the process.
>
> **—LATISHA R. STUCKEY, PARENT**

know that we have a rule that you don't interrupt me when I'm on the phone unless it's an emergency. What can we do about that?"

Successful parents and family members approach challenging behaviors with curiosity, almost in the same way that detectives go about their work. Children don't come to us with tidy labels and operating instructions. By approaching your child with compassionate curiosity when they are experiencing stress, you can build trust and connection. Your child will know that their feelings matter to you. Together, you can build understanding of their feelings and find effective ways to manage them.

TEACHING SOCIAL-EMOTIONAL SKILLS

There is no sweeter child than my son, Ricky. I know that many parents out there would disagree and would insist, "No, *my* child is the sweetest child!" But let me just make my case with two examples. When Ricky was three years old, I was angry with him—I can't remember what I was angry about, but I was really, really angry with him. I sat him down with me on the couch and said, "Ricky, I'm really angry with you." He stroked my cheek and said, "Gentle, gentle." It really made me laugh because this was a strategy that I used when teaching him how to be gentle with our pet cat.

When he was in kindergarten, the school play had just finished. All the children came out to take a final bow. Then, as they all ran off the stage, one little girl tripped and fell down. The crowd gasped, and before any adult could react to help her, my son ran back on stage and helped her up and they both ran off, hand in hand. It was the perfect intersection between impulsivity and kindness.

Both of these instances are examples of times that Ricky used strategies that we had talked about and practiced on earlier occasions that he was able to generalize to occasions that we had not discussed or practiced. I truly believe that kindness is a skill that can be taught, because ultimately kindness is a way of interacting with others. When you think about it, children aren't born with the ability to understand how their actions might affect others. That is a skill developed over time and is also a skill that can be taught. Social and emotional development affects just about every aspect of a child's life and their ability to learn. The thing is, we often neglect this area of development and then get frustrated when children don't have the skills that we expect them to have. We need to treat social-emotional skills just like anything else that we hope that children will learn through our guidance—with intentionality.

These practices benefit children with and without disabilities and can be adapted for use across a wide variety of settings. As parents, we can make a huge difference by teaching our child skills in three distinct areas of social-emotional competence: the ability to understand and regulate emotions, the ability to make friends, and the ability to solve problems.

Research has found that children who have social and emotional competence:

- tolerate frustration better,
- engage in less destructive behavior,
- are healthier,
- are less lonely,
- are less impulsive,
- are more focused, and
- have greater academic achievement (Denham et al., 2003; Leerkes et al., 2008; Nelson, Kendall, and Shields, 2013; Shonkoff and Phillips, 2000).

UNDERSTANDING AND REGULATING EMOTIONS

Have you ever heard the expression that you have to name it to tame it? This is the concept behind emotional literacy as a first step to helping your child to learn how to manage and regulate their emotions. Children, just like adults, have big feelings. Unlike adults, however, children don't have the communication skills or years of experience to know how to cope with those big feelings. This is easy to see when you think about emotions in infants and toddlers. Six-month-old Marie doesn't know why she is sad, but she definitely feels it, and her mother can feel it too when she cries.

Learning how to manage our emotions begins very early. Infants begin to learn about self-regulation by first experiencing it through a caring adult in a process called *coregulation.* Our calm demeanor teaches the infant about how it feels to be calm and eventually how to calm herself. Marie is able to calm herself when her mother holds her close and makes sure that all her needs are met. Coregulation happens when you as the adult provide support to your child in a nurturing relationship. Even adults sometimes need support from others to regulate ourselves. Think about the times that you meet a friend for lunch or call your favorite aunt at the end of a tough day. That's coregulation at work.

Preschool-aged children are typically ready to learn more strategies for how to regulate their emotions on their own. But the time to teach emotional regulation is *not* during the middle of an outburst. The most effective strategies start with prevention. Your child will be more likely to learn emotional regulation skills when you approach the subject during a time when they are calm, relaxed, and ready to understand new information.

The National Center on Pyramid Model Innovations (NCPMI) is a treasure trove of resources on supporting children's social-emotional development. The Pyramid Model includes a set of practices that research has shown to be effective in reducing challenging behavior in young children with and without disabilities. The website offers hundreds of resources including tip sheets, handouts to share with families, visuals, scripted stories, and more. Many of the materials have been translated into Spanish. (See appendix C for a list of resources for this chapter.)

The Pyramid Model offers a range of strategies that families and educators can use to prevent challenging behaviors and promote positive social-emotional development. The NCPMI site describes the model as "a promotion, prevention, and intervention framework early childhood educators can use to support young children's social emotional competence and prevent or reduce challenging behaviors." In addition, research from Hemmeter and colleagues (2016) has found that the practices are effective at supporting social and emotional skills for children with, at risk for, and without disabilities. Many states have adopted the Pyramid Model as their accepted social-emotional framework, and many of the practices are widely used across the country.

THE TIERS OF THE PYRAMID MODEL

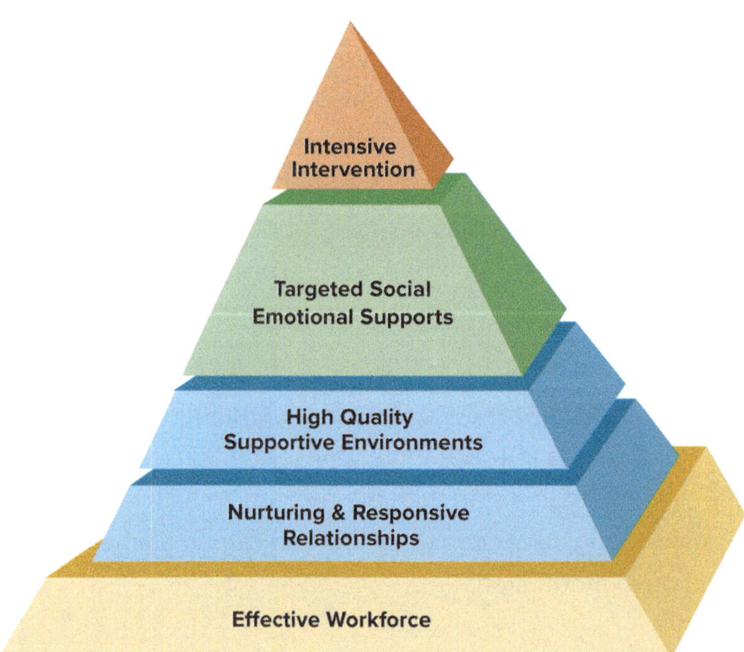

Source: Created by and available from the National Center for Pyramid Model Innovations (NCPMI) at ChallengingBehavior.org

This image details the Pyramid Model framework that is organized in this way:

- Yellow: The yellow tier, effective workforce, is the foundation of the model. It represents national, regional, state, and program systems and policies that support quality practices for children, families, and all those who support them.
- Blue: The blue tiers describe key elements that are essential for all children. Nurturing and responsive relationships and high-quality engaging environments are instrumental for a child's well-being. When these elements are in place, typically the social and emotional development needs of 80 percent of children can be met (Hemmeter, Snyder, Fox, and Algina, 2016).
- Green: For children who are at risk of challenging behavior, targeted social-emotional supports are added. Intentional instruction around the social skills and emotional literacy is particularly important for children who may exhibit challenging behavior that might interfere with their development in many areas, but all children benefit from additional instruction around social and emotional skills. Children need to be taught throughout the day rather than in response to challenging behavior. This level of intentional support can mean a significant shift in practices for some teachers and programs.
- Orange: For children with persistent challenges, intensive, individualized interventions are added to the other tiers. This means individualized intervention of the right intensity, with the right focus, and with the right consistency to address the needs of a child whose challenging behavior is beginning to, or already is, interfering with her development.

The Pyramid Model: Steps for Teaching Social Skills

- Describe the skill.
- Demonstrate the skill the "right way" with an adult.
- Demonstrate the skill the "wrong way" with an adult.
- Have a child practice the skill with an adult.
- Have a child practice the skill with another child.
- Provide positive feedback and support for children attempting and successfully using the skill. (Fox and Lentini, 2006)

The evidence-based practices within the Pyramid Model are profoundly useful for educators in high-quality inclusive programs. The practices benefit children with and without disabilities and can be adapted for use across a wide variety of settings. As parents, we can make a huge difference by teaching children skills in three distinct areas of social-emotional competence: the ability to understand and regulate emotions, the ability to make friends, and the ability to solve problems.

When you give your child the words to describe what they are feeling, you help to strengthen their emotional literacy. Emotional literacy includes the ability to read facial expressions, nonverbal cues, language, and body cues in yourself and in other people. Emotional literacy is a foundation for your child's ability to control their emotions, develop relationships, interact with others, and become an effective problem solver. It is one of the most important areas of development during your child's early years (Hemmeter, Ostrosky, and Fox, 2021). When your child learns how to understand and use these cues, over time they will be on the path to being able to understand the difference between feelings and thoughts, and then will be able to make decisions about how they want to respond to a situation rather than just reacting based on their emotions.

TEACHING EMOTIONAL LITERACY

You can start by teaching your child the words for different emotions and then teach them to use these words to label their own feelings and the feelings of others. You also can teach your child to understand that their feelings can change. I may wake up grumpy, but I don't have to stay grumpy all day. Feelings come and feelings go, and it's important for young children to know that feelings don't last forever. In addition, you can teach your child that they can have more than one feeling at a time about something. They can feel differently about something than someone else feels. And all feelings are valid. As your child's emotional vocabulary grows, their ability to accurately read their own and other's emotions grows, too. Here are some strategies for teaching emotional literacy in early childhood.

Talk about Emotions

Talk about emotions in everyday life. Label your own emotions and the child's emotions as they happen throughout the day. You might say, "Wow! You look surprised! Do you know how I can tell? Your mouth is open, and your eyes are wide." Or "I feel sad. Yesterday, I was happy that Aunt Ellen came to visit, but now I feel sad that it is time for her to go." Start with a few simple emotions such as happy and sad, then move to the more complex emotions such as calm and anxious. Make sure to talk with your child about a range of emotions, including those that feel comfortable and those that feel uncomfortable to you as a parent.

Talk about Facial Expressions

Explain to your child that most people can tell how you are feeling by looking at the expression on your face. Use a mirror so your child can practice making faces that go with the different feeling words. What does your face look like when you are feeling frustrated? excited? worried? calm? elated? embarrassed? scared? hopeful?

Cut out from magazines pictures of faces showing different feelings, and then talk with your child about how they think that the person in the picture feels. NCPMI offers Feeling Faces cards, which are free to download and print (https://challengingbehavior.org). You can use them to talk about the different emotions that we all feel. You can also use them as a way to check in with your child at the start of the day or during a quiet moment together. Your child can also use the feeling faces cards to let you know how they are feeling throughout the day. (See also appendix C.)

Talk about Sensations in the Body

Talk with your child about the fact that sometimes we can feel our feelings in our bodies, even before we know what we are feeling. Together with your child, practice closing your eyes and noticing sensations in the body. Ask your child where they feel big feelings: "What does angry feel like in your tummy?"

> I try to always speak to him and repeat the same feelings or ideas in the same way. He gets it, and eventually he will let you know exactly how he's feeling. We repeat things, and we listen, and then at some point we figure it out. It's such a wonderful moment. We're finally able to address whatever it is that is bothering him or making him happy, or whatever it is that that he needs. Once you figure that out, it is "Yes! Communication!" When it goes well with anyone, it always feels so good.
>
> **—HILDA BERNIER, PARENT**

Practice Describing Feelings

Ask your child to describe their feelings often. Use questions such as, "What happened that surprised you?" "Did that make you feel angry?" "Why do you think Grandma was happy when she saw you? How can you tell that she was happy?"

Children should know that it's okay to have strong feelings such as anger or frustration, but that we all should manage those feelings in a positive way. For example, "I know it made you mad when George took the shovel from you. Next time, you can ask an adult to help you."

Practice Identifying Feelings Clues

Reflect on the fact that some emotions look the same but feel different. For example, we might cry out of happiness or out of sadness. How confusing! Talk with your child about how we get clues about emotions from lots of different forms of information. In this child-care classroom, the educator posted a feelings poster with a mirror beside it. This way, children can practice making the feeling faces to better understand the way they look to others.

Children's Books with a Focus on Feelings

Here is a list of children's books to consider reading with your child:

Bang, Molly. 1999. *When Sophie Gets Angry—Really, Really Angry . . .* New York: Scholastic.

Emberley, Ed, and Anne Miranda. 1997. *Glad Monster, Sad Monster: A Book about Feelings.* New York: LB Kids.

Kachenmeister, Cherryl. 2001. *On Monday When It Rained.* New York: HMH Books for Young Readers.

You can find more wonderful children's books at The Book Vine (https://www.bookvine.com/cat-18-1-472/5-feelings-books.htm). NCPMI also offers a comprehensive list of children's books with social-emotional themes (see appendix C).

Read Books about Emotions

Use children's books that focus on building emotional literacy, either as material for circle-time reading or for small-group book sharing. When reading a story, ask children to imagine what the different characters are feeling. Ask questions such as, "Why do you think she feels that way?"

HELPING CHILDREN MANAGE THEIR EMOTIONS

As your child becomes more and more competent with learning to recognize and name their own emotions and feelings, they can begin to learn how to control their emotions. We have to know what angry feels like before we are able to control our anger. We need to understand what calm looks like and feels like before we are able to calm down. Once your child has the words to use, they can verbalize their feeling rather than having to act it out. We all feel strong emotions in different ways, and as adults, we have likely learned ways to manage these strong emotions. If so, you are already on your way to helping your child to manage their emotions, because serving as a calm role model is the most important practice of all. Even at a very young age, children learn by watching adults. When we respond calmly to situations or show kindness to others, we are teaching our children how to behave through our actions. We truly invite calm into our space by being calm. Your sense of calm creates a safe harbor for your child. Here are a few suggestions to create your own sense of calm:

- Invite calm by being calm.
- Pay attention to your own body language. Are your posture, tone, and pace communicating a sense of calm?
- Slow down and allow your child time to process their own thoughts and feelings.
- Limit your words, especially when your child is upset. They can't process what you are saying until they feel calmer.
- Take deep breaths and remember to consider your child's perspective.

Most of us as adults know how to calm ourselves down, use our words carefully, get help when we need it, and choose to walk away as needed. At least we try to do these things, most of the time. Young children haven't learned these skills yet and need support to learn important strategies and time to practice the new skills. Successful parents are intentional about teaching their children how to express the emotions they are feeling. When we don't teach children how to express emotions in a positive way, they might get carried away with the feeling and express the emotions in inappropriate ways, such as hitting or grabbing a toy, crying and rolling around on the floor, or just plain not following directions. When your child learns ways to communicate emotions appropriately, they are less likely to resort to behaviors that are challenging to adults.

The following are some strategies for teaching your child about how to express and regulate their emotions.

- **Practice using emotional vocabulary:** Use the new emotional vocabulary that children have acquired to help them manage difficult situations. For example, Cody's teacher noticed that another child was rough with him on the playground. His teacher said, "Are you sad because Derrick pushed you? Do you feel frustrated? angry? embarrassed? gloomy? Should we go and tell him how that made you feel?" She told him the story about what was upsetting him and gave him the words for how to describe his feelings. His teacher also served as a role model for self-regulation. This type of calm response can turn down the intensity of the situation, help the child feel understood, and provide a chance to teach the child a helpful next step for dealing with the emotion.
- **Talk about ways to manage emotions:** Use a quiet time at bedtime or during a car ride to talk with your child about how to manage their emotions. You can read books about difficult situations and talk about how your child might respond, use puppets to act out the sequence of events, or engage your child in a role-play activity. Ask your child to close their eyes and imagine they are in a place of calm: Are you in a garden surrounded by flowers? Are you in a fort that you made with blankets and pillows? Are you snuggled in Grandpa's arms? Practice what it feels like to "go" to a calm place. Later, during a stressful time, that can be a place that you suggest to your child as a way to center themselves.
- **Practice paying attention to body sensations:** Try using the NCPMI Relaxation Thermometer visual so that your child can see how their bodies change when they feel strong emotions and when they are relaxed. When your child is feeling calm, practice using it as a way for them to describe how they are feeling. You might model this practice yourself to explain to your child how you are feeling, too. Once they know how to use it, the thermometer can be a great tool for your child to use to let other adults in their life know how they are feeling when they are upset. (See appendix C for a list of resources for this chapter.)
- **Use a Big Feelings Box:** Fill a box with materials, such as the following, that can help your child regulate their emotions. When you introduce the Big Feelings Box to your child, let them know how you use these supplies to help yourself calm down. Many of these items are helpful for

adults to use as stress relievers, too. If your child is old enough, you could place the box within their reach so they can access the supplies independently.

- ➢ Bubbles to blow—a great distraction and calming activity
- ➢ A jump rope—exercise can be an effective stress-management practice
- ➢ Scented hand lotion—if allergies are not an issue, it can be soothing to have someone rub your hands with lotion; this is also a good self-soothing technique
- ➢ Bubble packing material—popping the bubbles is soothing, or your child can stomp on the bubble wrap as a safe way to express strong feelings
- ➢ Art supplies—suggest that your child draw a picture of what happened to make them upset. What happened before you were sad? Then what happened? Ask them to describe the episode by telling you about their picture and what they were thinking and feeling along the way.
- ➢ Musical instrument—shaking a tambourine can distract your child and serve as a stress reducer
- ➢ Paper—ripping it into tiny pieces is a great stress reliever
- ➢ Beads and string—make a necklace or garland as a way to calm and distract the mind
- ➢ Fidget toys—there are lots of options to choose from. Fidget spinners, stress balls, sensory rings, and other squishy toys can be great for relieving anxiety
- ➢ Playdough—squish it out and flatten it like a pancake to express strong feelings

- **Deep breathing and other calming techniques:** Deep breathing stimulates the vagus nerve, which is located on both sides of the voice box. This practice can interrupt the fight, flight, or freeze response that we all go into during a stressful event. In addition, when we're anxious, we tend to take rapid, shallow breaths; deeper breaths from the tummy trigger the relaxation response. Ask the child, "Would it help to take some deep breaths together?" Show them how to rest their hand on their stomach to watch and count their breaths. Or encourage the child to lie down on their back on the carpet, put a stuffed animal on their belly, and practice belly breathing. You know that it's working when the stuffed animal goes up and down on their belly as they breathe. Other breathing strategies include blowing bubbles; blowing into a pinwheel; visualizing smelling flowers and blowing out candles; breathing in through the nose and out through the mouth; and breathing in for a count of three, holding it for a count of three, and letting out the breath slowly, slowly, slowly.

  In addition to deep-breathing exercises, try some of the following calming techniques. And remember, this takes practice. Your child will need time to practice these skills over and over again. If they don't work the first time (or sometimes the twentieth time), don't give up. Keep practicing and keep believing that your child will learn the skills needed to manage their own anxiety and calm the chaos.

- Listen to music.
- Go for a walk.
- Count to ten.
- Get a drink of water.
- Read a story together.
- Take a break in a cozy spot.
- Draw a picture.
- Play with playdough.
- Swing.
- Rock back and forth.
- Hug a favorite toy.
- Do a puzzle together.

Add to the list! You'll find additional calming strategies that work for you. If a stressful event is coming up and you are able to prepare your child for it, you can help to create a calming ritual. Just like athletes who engage in a set of activities that are centering to them before a big game, rituals can work for young children as well. Rituals can provide a sense of stability, something familiar that is within your child's control that can ease anxiety and give them more confidence as the event approaches. For example, Matthew reads a comic book before he goes in for his doctor's appointment. Crystal does ten jumping jacks before her basketball game.

Activating muscles and joints can also bring on a sense of calm in young children. My son really benefitted from this approach with increased focus and attention. His therapist taught me the term *heavy work,* which basically involves pushing around heavy things, such as a vacuum cleaner, pulling a wagon around, or even picking up and moving a piece of furniture from one place to another. It sounds kind of strange, but it's effective.

When your child is in full-on cry mode, it can help to distract them with silliness or humor. My mother used to tell me, "Don't smile or your face will crack!" which of course made me smile or laugh. Laughter really does relieve anxiety by releasing endorphins, which are known to combat stress. Keep a silly joke at the ready for these occasions or cue up a comical video on your smartphone.

Tucker Turtle Takes Time to Tuck and Think is a story that helps children understand how to calm down. Download and print the scripted story for free. There is even a version adapted for home use titled *Tucker Turtle Takes Time to Tuck and Think at Home.* NCPMI also offers a printable visual of the Turtle Technique. (See appendix C for a list of resources for this chapter.)

Pay attention to the environment. Sometimes, the environment itself causes stress for young children, so take a look at your home with this in mind. Do you need to create a quiet space where your child can retreat? As much as you can, remove distracting or disturbing items in the home, such as flickering fluorescent lights.

Each child is unique—one child may want to have a conversation to help her calm down; another may need a hug or deep breaths.

Keep in mind that managing emotions is a skill that takes many years to practice. Even adults often have to work hard to self-regulate. Hopefully, we are able to manage our emotions most of the time, but it is not easy. For some children, the expectations that adults have are just too difficult to manage. We need to be patient while children navigate these waters. Reflect on the child's perspective, and try to be "gentle, gentle" as much as possible.

MAKING FRIENDS

Developing close relationships is the best part of the human experience, and when relationships develop with people outside of the family, children truly flourish. It's one thing to be loved by a parent, grandparent, or sibling, but when a child is loved by a peer, the feeling is truly remarkable. The benefits of friendship in young children are the same that we feel as adults. The research backs this up as well and shows how important friendships are for young children. Friends look out for each

> I've never been sad about June's disability. I'm sad when I think about her not belonging. Or not being appreciated for who she is. I'm sad about the world around her, not about her.
>
> **—JACKIE JOSEPH, PARENT**

other. Friends encourage each other to explore the world and learn new things. Friendships give us a sense of security and belonging and can even be great stress reducers (Geisthardt, Brotherson, and Cook, 2002). In fact, having a friend in preschool correlates with important factors in later life and is an important developmental goal (Rubin, Bukowski, and Parker, 1998). Catherine Bagwell and Michelle Schmidt (2011) write that friendships provide emotional support, practice with compromise, and opportunities to take someone else's perspective. According to Hartup (1992), "the single best childhood predictor of adult adaptation is not school grades and not classroom behavior, but rather the adequacy with which the child gets along with other children."

Friendships are important for all of us, and they are especially important for children with disabilities or suspected delays. Children with certain types of disability, such as vision, hearing, and/or motor impairment, are more likely to have feelings of social isolation that can be harmful to their mental health (Harper and McCluskey, 2002.) It is up to the adults in their lives to do what they can to help them make necessary connections that will lead to friendship and a sense of belonging. For many children, learning how to make friends and get along with

The worries change with the age. When she was younger we were worried about physical things. Can she do it? Is she gonna get hurt? Now we worry about social things. She doesn't understand social cues and doesn't realize when kids are being horrible. And I don't want someone to be able to take advantage of her. But it's that balance of how do I teach you so someone doesn't take advantage of you, but not teach you too much where you're scared. How to strike a balance between what's enough information and what's gonna freak you out?

—PATRICIA REEDY, PARENT

Mazie is still very young now, but I worry that as she gets older she'll start to become more aware. I worry about it all the time. Right now, she's in child care and the kids in her classroom all know her and love her. But I was making Valentine's Day cards for her class this year and it hit me that one day the kids will do it themselves and they get to pick and choose who receives them . . . Mazie may not get any. We just pray that those personality traits that she has—loving and sweet and social—will help in those kinds of situations.

—AMANDA LOVETTE, PARENT

others comes naturally. Friendships just happen. For some kids, making friends is easy, while for other children, the ability to make friends is not so easy and can really be a struggle.

> We realized the kids at school were starting to baby Wren, so I did a slide presentation about Down syndrome for the class and for Down Syndrome Day. It showed the things that she does: like she's an amazing cook, she has knives that are safe for her. I showed all of those things she's so good at. And then to show why Wren practices speech just like other kids practice. When it was over Wren went for a walk with her aide, and I let the kids and ask any question, everything was on the table. It worked really well.
>
> **—KRISTEN JONES, PARENT**

Guralnick and colleagues (2007) found that children with disabilities in inclusive classrooms who have opportunities to interact with typically developing peers demonstrate higher levels of social competence. Yet friendships do not always come naturally, and research by Geisthardt, Brotherson, and Cook (2002) found that it can be especially difficult for children with disabilities. Guralnick and colleagues (2007) found that children with developmental disabilities are often the least preferred play partners of typically developing children. As we learned earlier, play is the way that young children learn, and when children have delayed social skills, their ability to engage in play activities with their peers is affected (Nelson et al., 2007).

Making friends is a tricky business. It involves complex verbal and nonverbal social interactions that can sometimes be elusive for certain children.

Fortunately, friendship skills can be learned. With encouragement and coaching from family members and educators, your child can develop skills that will help them form strong, mutual friendships.

TEACHING FRIENDSHIP SKILLS

I remember one summer day at the playground when Ricky was around four years old. A group of children were playing an elaborate game of pirate ship, and Ricky was interested in all the activity. He walked over to the group and watched for a while. They continued to play and barely noticed that he was standing there. After about ten minutes or so, Ricky came back over to me and sat down. He seemed to be considering his options. Finally, he looked up at me and said, "Mommy, can you introduce me to them?" This was a good first step! He definitely knew that introductions should be made. I think that I did take him over that time and said something along the lines of, "Hi guys! This is Ricky. Can he play with you all?" Then, Ricky would run up to the group and playtime would get rolling. Was that a long-term strategy though? Over time, I learned that it worked best when I would talk with Ricky about the situation ahead of time and make a plan for how he would introduce himself. We practiced saying, "Hi! I'm Ricky. Can I play with you guys?" Or we practiced going over to a child, tapping them on the shoulder and asking if they wanted to play. We talked about offering a specific game to play, like, "Do you want to build a construction site together in the sand box?" This type of role-playing and practice can work wonders.

These types of experiences and practice with social relationships are a huge benefit that parents can intentionally create for their child. Just as you teach your child self-care skills, you can also teach your child important friendship skills, including:

- How to share toys and other materials
- How to take turns
- How to suggest ideas for what to play
- How to work together as a team
- How to give compliments
- How and when to say, "I'm sorry"
- How to understand what a friend is feeling

> The truth is that Emilio deserves to be put on his trajectory, the same as any other child, which is to be included.
>
> **—OLIVIER BERNIER, PARENT**

Additionally, through positive peer influences, your child can learn how to initiate social interactions, respond to social cues, practice giving compliments to peers, and find out how to engage in group-play activities.

SUPPORTING PEER RELATIONSHIPS IN INCLUSIVE SETTINGS

Children with disabilities might be perceived as behaving differently than other children, and as a result they might experience difficult social situations. This is one of the most difficult parts of the parenting journey to navigate, because we hate to see our children excluded or struggle to make friends. We want to protect them from pain. All families do. This inclination to protect our children can even turn into a desire to ask that our children receive services at home, in a special school, or in a separate classroom, rather than in an inclusive classroom. This might seem like a form of protection, and it might be protective in the short term. However, when children learn in a program or classroom

When he was little, I was really worried that he would always feel left out, or that he would get bullied, or that he wouldn't have any friends. It was my dream that he would have a buddy that he could hang out with. Now in secondary school, he does have friends. The kids at his school have been absolutely fantastic. They're so supportive; they're not patronizing.

—LEAH MULLEN, PARENT

that is separate from their peers, they miss the opportunity to build the strengths they will need to thrive in an inclusive world. Children most benefit when they have opportunities to learn friendship skills, as well as opportunities to practice those skills.

When children with and without disabilities are in the same inclusive classroom, peer relationships thrive. Children learn to understand differences and how they are our greatest assets. This learning happens in high-quality, inclusive classrooms, not just by the fact that children are learning and growing side by side, but also due to the actions of the educators and their parent partners. For example, Stanton-Chapman and Snell (2011) used an intervention of shared storybook reading along with pretend-play activities that encouraged children with disabilities to interact with their peers. These were children with language or developmental delays or behavior concerns. This simple intervention led to an increase in children with and without disabilities playing together—even on the playground.

The following are some examples of effective ways to foster friendships between your child and their peers.

- Teach your child prosocial skills: You can teach skills such as sharing toys and even set up situations where there are not enough of a desired toy, so that your child can practice asking for a turn. For example, Murray and Jacquetta are playing with playdough at Murray's house, but there is only one rolling pin on the table. Murray's grandmother notices that Murray really wants the rolling pin, so she suggests, "Let's tap Jacquetta on the shoulder and ask, 'May I have a turn?'" Teaching your child how to ask for a turn, giving them the exact words to use, and then providing opportunities to practice the skill are all important steps.

- Suggest activities that are most fun when played with a friend: Suggest games that take two people, such as rolling a ball back and forth. Peers can help each other and learn from each other through play. And this learning is a two-way street! If your child is nonverbal, a peer can help her to respond to comments from other children. A peer might show your child how to play with a new toy or give suggestions for a play activity. She can give a compliment for a job well done or marvel over a beautiful art project. In return, your child's friend is learning important skills for helping others, building a sense of empathy, and learning how to thrive in a world where we all have diverse abilities.
- Use puppets or stuffed animals to teach and practice social skills: Puppets are great for this. Pretend with your child that two puppets are just getting to know each other. Ask your child what one puppet should say to the other one. How might this puppet ask his friend to play? What should he do? What should she say?
- Use role play to practice these skills: It can start by having your child role-play with you or another family member, but your child can role-play together with their friends as well. This is a great way to work through common situations such as asking to use a toy or inviting a friend to play. The role play is a safe zone in which to practice, and neither friend has to worry about being excluded or having hurt feelings, because the "asking to play" is the whole point of the game.
- Create social stories: As you collect information about the behaviors you'd like to see develop and grow for your child, you can then write social stories to use as a way of teaching the new skills. For example, you can write social stories about such friendship skills as taking turns, giving compliments, and so on. In each story, describe a situation that your child may encounter and the behaviors they should use in that situation. When your child has information that helps them understand the expectations of a situation, they are less likely to act out due to frustration. Social stories can be illustrated with photographs of your child or with graphics you can find online. Often, social stories are written to highlight "challenging" behaviors that adults want to modify. For example, a child who tends to hit other children when frustrated might benefit from reading a story about herself:

> ***Last November, Gabby was angry because Gabriel didn't want to play with her on the playground. Gabriel told Gabby that he was too tired to play, and then Gabby hit Gabriel on his shoulder. That hurt him and wasn't a good solution to the problem. Gabby learned that hitting hurts her friend and makes him want to stay away from her. Now Gabby knows to ask a different friend to play when someone tells her they are too tired to play.***

- You can enhance any story with details about your daily routine, your child's friends, and so on and illustrate it with images of your child as the lead character.
- Observe other children to find common interests: You can also foster friendships just by pointing out shared interests that you see between your child and other children. "Look, Emily! Rodrigo is wearing a shirt with a bulldozer on it. You like bulldozers, too! Maybe you could play together in the sandbox today."
- Give feedback and celebrate effort: Give your child feedback and celebrate their efforts when they initiate interactions with peers. "Jorge, I just overheard you when you asked Margo to play with you. That was really being a good friend." All the children involved in the interaction will learn from this feedback that they are on the right track.

SOLVING PROBLEMS

The ability for your child to persist when faced with obstacles will grow over time. The areas of the brain that help children to persist and regulate themselves is still growing during the early years. Most children under the age of five will likely give up on a problem if their first opportunities to solve it aren't successful. But Webster-Stratton and Hammond (1997) found that preschool-age children can effectively be taught problem-solving skills. As parents, we can support our children as they are learning to persist by giving them tools to come up with a solution when faced with a challenge. Developing their own problem-solving skills can be empowering for children.

With younger children, you can start by working alongside them and showing enthusiasm for their efforts. When they have difficulties, you can convey your confidence that they'll be able to figure this out eventually. You can also let them know that some problems take time to solve and that, when you're stuck, it's okay to come back later and try again. Preschool-aged children benefit when adults help out by putting feelings of frustration into words, understanding that the feeling shouldn't be a barrier to continuing to try or to come back and try later.

You can teach problem solving step by step. The Pyramid Model suggests four essential problem-solving steps for young children to learn and act on. Every conflict becomes a problem to solve. Here are the steps:

1. Name the problem: "We have four kids in the sandbox and only one shovel."
2. Brainstorm solutions: Children can think of solutions in the moment, or they could consult a solution kit or problem-solving solution cards. The strategies might include, "Take Turns," "Use a Timer," "Get a Teacher for Help," "Say, 'Please Stop,'" "Use Kind Words," and others.
3. Consider each solution: Ask, "What would happen if we tried it?" "Would it be safe?" "Would it be fair?" "How would it make everyone feel?"

4. Try one! Try out a solution that everyone thinks will work.

When you first share these steps with your child, you can try using puppets, stuffed animals, books, or other strategies to model the practices. Then, use the pictures to spark conversation about typical problems that your child might encounter. For example, when your child is struggling with waiting and taking turns, a suggested strategy is the use of a timer. You would first introduce the timer to your child, explain how it works and how it can be helpful to know how long the wait will be. Your child might want to discuss the specifics for using the timer, such as where it will be stored, how many minutes to set, and so on. Teaching your child a collaborative approach to problem solving is a way to address an issue up front, *before* any sort of conflict has occurred. Your child will feel a sense of ownership over the solution.

NCPMI offers families an online "Solution Kit" as a way to teach children problem-solving strategies. The kit includes visuals that children can use as they consider how they might resolve a tricky situation such as sharing toys or taking turns. It begins with reading a story with your child called "We Can Be Problem Solvers at Home!" that teaches the problem-solving steps. Then, you can print and cut the Solution Kit pictures into cards. The cards are printed with problem-solving ideas such as, "Take a Break," "Ask for a Hug," or "Get a Timer." To keep them sturdy and together, you can laminate the cards and put them on an O-ring for your child to consult when a conflict arises. Another strategy is to save them to your smartphone or tablet and look at the options together when a problem arises. Give your child lots of encouragement when they use the Solution Kit pictures to solve problems—they really do work. The Solution Kits are available in numerous languages, including Spanish, Hmong, and Somali, on NCPMI's website (https://challengingbehavior.org/). (See appendix C for a list of resources for this chapter.)

This strategy is also helpful to use with siblings, because it encourages children to explore the problem together, rather than always having a parent stepping in to solve it. The siblings or peers find the answer on their own, and they both develop skills that can applied to other areas of life even into adulthood. The approach encourages teamwork, independent thinking, and curiosity. It also builds in the practice of giving your child choices, which can give them a sense of autonomy and control over the situation. Your child will be more likely to buy in to the solution when they can choose which solution to try. You can ask questions to stimulate thinking, such as, "What do you think might work?" or "Is this a big problem or a little problem?" or "Should we find out what or who can help us?" This is also a way to engage your child in problem solving about their behaviors that you find challenging. Rather than getting angry or punishing your child for inappropriate behaviors, you can use the opportunity to think about how their behavior affects others and consider alternatives together.

Once your child is in the habit of using this strategy, you might strengthen their problem-solving skills by considering problems that occur in children's stories. Children's books have lots of examples of how people get along, or don't get along, with each other. When you read to your child, you can choose books that relate to the social skills that you are trying to teach. Give your child the opportunity to ask questions and pose some of your own. For example, you can point out that the children in the story are helping each other, taking turns, or sharing toys. After you read the book, give your child a chance to practice the skill using puppets or role play. Your child will benefit from talking about the social skill and practicing multiple times throughout the day. It helps them process the information and get feedback on their own behavior. Our son used to love the role-playing activities, and we still use the strategy to work through challenges in young adulthood. For example, just recently we role-played a job interview—and Ricky got the job!

MANAGING BEHAVIORS THAT CHALLENGE US

In addition to the planning matrix you completed at the end of chapter 7, you might also find it helpful to create a behavior support plan for your child if they are working on tricky social skills or problem-solving skills. As you figure out strategies to address your child's behaviors that are challenging for you, it's helpful to start with observation, just as you did when you first noticed a concern. Educators do this through a more formalized process, but as parents, we can learn a lot from using a similar approach to observe and analyze a specific behavior that we hope to understand and modify. The word *understand* is key here. This is all about understanding the function of the behavior. Why does it occur? Is there a specific place or time that it occurs? What happens before the behavior occurs? What does your child gain by behaving this way?

FUNCTIONAL BEHAVIOR ASSESSMENT

A functional behavior assessment breaks down the situation in which the behavior happened, considering events before and after the behavior occurs. The assessment considers the environment, people, interactions, materials, and demands that may have something to do with why your child uses that behavior to communicate. You would work with your child's team to collect information about the following:

- Specific details about the challenging behavior
- Events or conditions that increase the likelihood of challenging behavior (called *setting events*)
- What happens before the behavior occurs (called *triggers* or *antecedents*)
- How often, how long, and how intense the behavior is
- Times when the behavior does *not* occur

- Conditions that make the behavior worse or more likely to occur
- Events that typically follow the behavior (called *consequences*)
- Child preferences and strategies tried in the past

A shorthand for this approach is called the ABC Observation. This stands for:

A: Antecedent

B: Behavior

C: Consequence

Collecting this information provides clues about all of the factors frequently related to the occurrence of the challenging behavior. Your child is observed in routines, activities, or situations when the behavior is most likely to occur. You and the team try to think like detectives about your child's behavior, and usually you will find that the behavior occurs at specific times, with certain people, or in particular environments. Sometimes there are signs that your child is becoming more tense, anxious, or frustrated, and usually the challenging behavior will follow. Of course, every child is different, so these warning signs are individual, can be influenced by your child's culture, and can be subtle, such as a foot tapping or heavy breathing or even rosy cheeks or red ears. You and the team will also uncover if there are events or activities that make the behavior more likely to occur, such as when your child is hungry or tired. This process can help you to recognize these early signs and actually prevent the behavior from occurring.

> Emilio has been signing since very young age. To this day he still signs a lot of things when he can't find the word for it. That's been really helpful for his frustration as well.
>
> **—OLIVIER BERNIER, PARENT**

You and the team will complete this process by developing a *hypothesis statement,* a description of everything that is known about the behavior, triggers, and warning signs learned through your observations and assessment. It also includes an informed guess about the purpose or function of the challenging behavior. Sometimes, behaviors serve more than one function. In this case, you and the team will need to sort out all of the circumstances that might lead to the challenging behavior.

BEHAVIOR SUPPORT PLAN

You and the team then will use the hypothesis statement to develop a behavior support plan. This serves as the action plan for the team and will define the strategies to be used, skills to teach, and new ways to respond to the behavior. You'll find lots of resources on the NCPMI site (https://challengingbehavior.org/pyramid-model/behavior-intervention/resources/)

NCPMI suggests that behavior support plans contain the following components:

- Behavior hypothesis statements: A hypothesis statement is your best guess for why the behavior is occurring, so that you can then test it to find out which strategies might help to change the behavior. Behavior hypothesis statements include a description of the behavior, setting events, triggers or antecedents for the behavior, maintaining consequences, and the purpose of the problem behavior.
- Prevention strategies: Strategies that may be used to reduce the likelihood that your child will have problem behavior. These may include environmental arrangements, personal support, changes in activities, new ways to prompt your child, changes in expectations, and more. This part of the plan may include positive reinforcement strategies for promoting your child's use of new skills or appropriate behavior, which may also be included in consequence strategies.
- Replacement skills: Skills to teach that will replace the problem behavior.
- Consequence strategies: Guidelines for how you and other members of the team will respond to problem behaviors in ways that will not maintain the behavior. This part of the plan may include positive reinforcement strategies for promoting your child's use of new skills or appropriate behavior, which may also be included in prevention strategies.
- Long-term strategies: This section of the plan may include long-term goals that will assist your child and family in reaching for your vision for your child: for example, your child will develop friendships or attend a pre-K program.

For the behavior support plan to be most effective, you and the team should monitor it regularly. What is working well? What challenges have arisen? Which strategies should be adjusted or modified? Are we all using the strategies consistently? What are we learning about your child, the learning environments, and the adults in your child's life through this process?

Let's try it out! The activity for this chapter includes some questions for reflection and a sample planning tool that you can use for challenges that arise at home or in the early childhood program.

ACTIVITY: REFLECTING ON YOUR CHILD'S SOCIAL SKILLS

DIRECTIONS

Use this planning tool as a family or together with your child's team. Think about one of your child's behaviors that you find challenging. In the "behavior hypothesis statement" section below, write down a description of the behavior and why you think it is occurring.

Next, describe a short-term goal for a change you hope to see through the prevention strategies. Then, describe a longer-term goal of the social-emotional skills your child will learn as a result of the change.

Consider these questions as you choose the target behavior for this activity:

- What are the social and emotional learning opportunities for my child?
- Who might be potential friends for my child? How can I set up an introduction?
- Where are the places in my community where I can connect with other families and children, with and without disabilities?
- What are my hopes and dreams for my child related to social relationships? What are my fears?

Behavior Hypothesis Statement:

____

Short-Term Goal:

____

Longer-Term Goal:

____

Daily routine event when behavior occurs (getting dressed, dinnertime, bedtime, and so on)	**A: ANTECEDENT** What happens just before the behavior?	**B: BEHAVIOR** Description of the behavior	**C: CONSEQUENCE** What do adults/peers do when the behavior occurs?	**STRATEGY TO TRY** (prevention strategy, replacement skill, alternative consequences)

CHAPTER 9

Taking Care of Yourself and Your Family

We have learned how to take one day at a time, enjoy as much as we can, and just move on from that. That's such a valuable lesson that our kids have taught us.

—PAULINA VARGAS, PARENT

We can't drink from an empty cup, so we need to find ways to fill up our own cups so we can give our best to the children we care about. In this chapter, we'll explore ways to strengthen our own resources and integrate self-care into our daily routines through wellness strategies, such as mindfulness and grounding techniques, and the use of professional-learning communities.

One thing I have learned over the years is that the mental state that I bring to my relationships and everyday life in general is basically a similar or the same mental state that gets reflected back to me by the people I encounter. It's almost creepy. It's generally true that when we put positivity, strength, and happiness into the world, we typically get those "vibes" back in return. Sometimes, I wake up in the morning, and it's like I'm Cinderella on the day the shoe fits. I feel like Snow White with all of the woodland animals gathering around and the birds chirping sweetly as I yawn and stretch. Those days go really well. And then there are other days. I wake up with a headache. My sweet husband was snoring loudly all night long, and I couldn't really sleep. Instead of waking up to chirping birds, I wake up to the sound of the cat vomiting on the floor beside my bed. Ick. Or even better, I *don't* hear the cat vomiting, and I step in it as I climb out of bed. Those are the days that make parenting a major challenge.

Parenting and caregiving in general is such an important role, but it can be very stressful. Supporting young children's social and emotional development depends largely on our ability to build connections, nurture others, and manage our own emotions. Our ability to do all of this is related to our own physical and emotional well-being, and it's not always easy. What is the solution?

WELLNESS AND SELF-CARE

Do you know that phrase, "If mama ain't happy, ain't nobody happy"? It's true for any family member who is shouldering responsibilities. Strategies for stress management, self-care, and physical health are keys to our effectiveness. Good nutrition, exercise, and adequate sleep are foundational to combating the effects of physical, emotional, and mental stress. When we engage in healthy behaviors, we're able to cope more effectively and experience less stress. What can we do to promote wellness and self-care in our busy lives?

Wellness is not simply the absence of illness. Researcher Bill Hettler (1976) defined *wellness* as "an active process of becoming aware of and learning to make choices that lead toward a longer and more successful existence." The National Wellness Institute website suggests that we consider wellness in a holistic way and think about how we are doing in the various dimensions of our lives, including physical, social, intellectual, occupational, emotional, and spiritual wellness. What strategies can we use to promote wellness across these key areas of our lives? Let's explore some that might work for you.

SOCIAL WELLNESS

Friendship and belonging are important for children, but they are also incredibly important for adults. We need people in our lives who care about us, can listen to us, and accept all of who we are. We need people who remind us that we are not alone. Relationships outside of your immediate family can help to offer perspective. Social support is key for our well-being, and having these supports can increase positive feelings such as connectedness and community.

It was a very dark moment for me, and it took me a long time to get out of that feeling of being upset. Because during my pregnancy I did everything right. But then the diagnosis is delivered, and everything is like a doom-and-gloom kind of scenario. Right off the bat you're being bombarded with all this information about things that you are going to have to do that you were not expecting to do. For a long time I was feeling like I was drowning, and I was just trying to stay afloat. But we did have a good support system with our families. And I had a very, very nice group of mom friends that really took me out of that funk. It's good. It was nice to have that support when we needed it the most.

—HILDA BERNIER, PARENT

Had I stayed in the depression and not accepted, not embraced the situation, or allowed my mind to take me to a deeper, darker place, then I wouldn't be an advocate. I wouldn't be present with my son. Now, I love every moment of it.

—LATISHA R. STUCKEY, PARENT

It's been a very long road. I suffered from depression, because it took us so long to have a child. I didn't understand why my only child was special, and that I was going to miss out on so much from not having a typical child. My husband and I have our faith, and we've come back to being strong Christian parents; I leaned on that for understanding. I accepted the fact that my life was going to be different, but it didn't mean that it would be any less.

—AMANDA LOVETTE, PARENT

Friendships keep us from feeling alone in the world. Consider the following strategies for social wellness.

- Build a supportive community of parents or family members to learn and share ideas with each other. The community you build can be a formal community with regular meeting times, or just a group of friends that gets together informally on a regular basis. Organize a regular gathering, such as a book club or monthly potluck, with a group of friends who make you laugh and give you support. Whatever you decide to do as an activity, the main thing is that you have each other to lean on. When parenting gets stressful, it is truly helpful to have a network of people who have been or are going through a similar experience. Many of the parent centers you can connect with through the parentcenterhub.org offer these types of communities or other opportunities to connect with other families.

- Reach out to others through online communities hosted by Facebook or other platforms. Meetup.com is another online source for finding friends in your area or around the world. You can search events in your area or start your own group.
- Find a mentor through your local parent center. A mentor can help you work through issues in your family and provide the support you need when you might question yourself. They may have thought of something you haven't tried before or have resources to share that could be helpful. Most importantly, a mentor is able to listen to you and give you encouragement.
- Ask for help when you need it. This can be difficult, especially at first. It takes bravery to say, "I really need a friend right now." But think about it: how would you react if someone said those words to you? When you ask for help directly, most people feel warmth and care toward you and appreciate the vulnerability that it takes to put yourself out there in that way. Be ready to offer specifics about what others might do to help. Do you need a moment alone? Would it be a lifesaver to have someone care for your children on a Saturday afternoon? Ask! Would a home-cooked meal for your family give you a much-needed break? Ask! Would it be a relief to have someone pick up a few things at the grocery store for you? Ask! They can always say no. Reach out for help—and then be prepared to give help yourself when your friend reaches out.

EMOTIONAL WELLNESS

When I was a child, I learned a trick from a nun who visited patients in the hospital where I was recovering from surgery. She happened to be in my hospital room when the phlebotomist came in to take a sample of blood. You may know how it is in a hospital—people are poking and prodding you all the time. This nun could tell that I was a little bit anxious about the whole thing. This is the strategy she taught me: When you start to feel anxious or stressed, take a moment for some deep breathing. When you breathe in, think, "I am," and when you breathe out, think, "at peace." Try it! I use this trick all the time, and it does help to bring down the temperature on my stress levels.

As adults, we spend time teaching children skills to manage their emotions. These strategies can be useful for our own emotional wellness as well. As adults, we're able to understand our emotions in an intellectual way that children aren't quite ready to grasp. We can learn the relationships among our thoughts, our emotions, and our behavior. For example, we might feel a certain way, which leads us to think about the situation a certain way, which leads us to behave a certain way. We don't have to be yanked around by our emotions if we change the way that we think about them. Changing the way we think changes the way we act. Stress comes from our perception of the situation, because technically, the actual situation is not stressful. Our thoughts about it *make it* stressful, so if we just change our thoughts . . . Easier said than done, right? Try these emotional wellness strategies in addition to your efforts to weed out those pesky unhelpful thoughts.

- Start by asking yourself, "Is this thought true? Is it helpful?" Sometimes, our thoughts are based on an accurate perception of the situation, and sometimes they are just plain wrong. For example, a coworker and I were having a discussion, and she suddenly put her head in her hands and began rubbing her eyes. My immediate reaction was panic and stress. Oh no! What did I say? Did I offend her? Have I hurt her feelings? I could feel the stress build as I started to ramble on and backtrack from whatever I had been saying. She suddenly looked up and said, "Jani, I am so sorry. Did I tell you that my uncle passed away last week? Please forgive me, but I didn't hear what you were just saying because I started thinking about him and felt sad." Boom! This new information showed me that my perception of the situation was entirely wrong. The stress I had been feeling a moment before just evaporated, and my emotions turned to care for my colleague. This kind of thing happens in all kinds of situations, within relationships at work and in everyday life. Taking a moment to pause and question your thoughts in this way can break the spell that the emotion is creating and make space for your reaction to be based on what is really going on.
- Try using grounding strategies when difficult emotions arise. Grounding, or centering, refers to a set of simple strategies that can help you detach from emotional pain, such as anxiety, anger, sadness, or frustration. You consciously distract yourself temporarily from the emotions. This approach won't solve the problem, but it will give you temporary control over your feelings and provide a bit of space between your emotions, thoughts, and how you choose to act on those thoughts.

There are two types of grounding strategies—mental and physical. Mental grounding involves focusing your mind elsewhere. For example, you might focus on your environment and, in your mind, describe to yourself everything you see or hear in great detail. Or you might count down from ten to one or think about a pleasant or comforting place or meal or person. You can also try to focus your mind on soothing things or soothing words. For example, you might say to yourself, "You are a good person and you're trying really hard. This is just a difficult day." Say kind words to yourself as if you were talking to a friend or small child. Picture a favorite person in your mind and imagine that person smiling at you or giving you a caring hug. Think of things you are looking forward to in the next week, or think about a saying or quotation that brings you peace, such as, "This, too, shall pass," or the serenity prayer. I like this quotation by Eleanor Roosevelt: "No one can make you feel inferior without your consent." I think about it sometimes as a way to ground myself and to serve as a reminder that I am in control of my own feelings, especially those feelings about my own self-worth.

Physical grounding involves focusing on your senses. For example, you might grab tightly to the arms of the chair you're sitting in and really focus on that sensation. Or you might go to the bathroom and run cool water over your hands. You might touch various objects around you and pay close attention to the texture, temperature, or weight of each object. You might wiggle your toes and focus on that sensation, or breathe deeply and pay attention to each inhale and exhale (just as my friendly nun taught me to do).

When I attend a long meeting, I often put a familiar object, such as a seashell or a smooth stone, in my pocket to help me center if necessary. Have you heard of emotional eating? It isn't necessarily a bad thing if you understand the reason behind it. We do this as a form of physical grounding because emotional eating distracts us from the stressful emotion we are experiencing. It's the unconscious way our body is trying to help us distract and remove ourselves from the situation. This is a good reminder that *you* are in control of how you choose to respond to the emotions that you feel.

Which grounding method do you like best? Choose one or a few and practice using them. Like any other skill, grounding takes practice, and it's helpful to practice during nonstressful situations so you can become comfortable with the process. Then, when you need to use the skill, you'll be ready with it in your coping strategies toolbox.

Unhelpful thoughts can sap the energy we need. We need to spend our energy on choices and activities that will help and are within our control. Another strategy to provide space before unhelpful thoughts take over is called *thought stopping*. The idea is to notice your own unhelpful thoughts and practice using a trigger word to stop the thoughts. For example, if you start to think, "What's the point in even trying?" interrupt the thought by telling yourself, "Stop!" or "Hold on now!" This gives you a moment to get back on track and replace the unhelpful thought with one that is supportive and helpful, such as "You are smart! You've got this!" You might even visualize the unhelpful thought in a hot air balloon floating away.

Hopefully, some of these strategies will resonate with you, and you will add some coping skills to your emotional wellness toolkit. Keep in mind that sometimes it is best to seek support from a mental-health provider. There's help out there, and it's okay to ask for it. This in itself is a form of self-care. You are not alone. Many people are in similar situations, so there are national hotlines available to help.

- **Alcoholics Anonymous:** (https://www.aa.org/) Online information on help and resources, including local AA resources, for alcohol addiction and abuse.
- **Childhelp Hotline:** Live, toll-free hotline with resources to aid in every child abuse and neglect situation. Text and live chat are also available: 800-4-ACHILD (800-422-4453)
- **Disaster Distress Helpline:** Live, toll-free crisis counseling and referral support for people experiencing emotional distress related to natural or human-caused disasters: (800-985-5990)
- **FindTreatment.gov:** SAMHSA online resource for learning about and finding treatment for substance use disorders
- **National Association for Children of Addiction (NACoA):** (https://nacoa.org/) Online information, help, and resources for children, teens, and adults: 888-554-COAS (888-554-2627) (toll-free)
- **National Domestic Violence Hotline:** Free, confidential, 24/7 help for those experiencing domestic violence: 800-799-SAFE (800-799-7233) (toll-free)

- **Parent Helpline:** Trained parent advocates provide support to empower parents: 855-4A PARENT (855-427-2736) (toll-free)
- **SAMHSA National Helpline:** Substance Abuse and Mental Health Services Administration (SAMHSA) offers this free, confidential helpline that is available 24/7, 365 days a year. Find treatment referral and information for individuals and families facing mental or substance use disorders: https://www.samhsa.gov/
- **StrongHearts Native Helpline:** Safe, confidential, and anonymous help for American Indians and Alaska Natives experiencing domestic, dating, or sexual violence. Culturally appropriate support: 844-7NATIVE (844-762-8483) (toll-free)
- **Suicide Prevention Lifeline:** The Lifeline provides 24/7, free, and confidential support for people in distress. Find prevention and crisis resources for you or your loved ones, and best practices for professionals: 800-273-TALK (800-273-8255) (toll-free)

> I can accept the grief. It's okay to be upset. It's okay to be disappointed. You have to figure it out. Grief is gonna hit you at different times. It's okay to feel that—you just can't live there. You feel it. You acknowledge it. You move on.
>
> **—PATRICIA REEDY, PARENT**

INTELLECTUAL WELLNESS

In 1988, Carol Dweck and Ellen Leggett introduced the notion that the way people think about the limitations of their own intelligence affects their ability to learn and reach goals. They found that students either maintain a fixed mindset or a growth mindset about their own intelligence. The students with a fixed mindset believed that their intelligence was something already set and predetermined and that, no matter how hard they tried or how much they studied, they would only get so far because of the limitations on their own intelligence. The students with a growth mindset, on the other hand, believed that their intelligence was changeable and could grow with hard work and persistence. As you might imagine, Dweck and Leggett found that students with a growth mindset tended to be more successful in their ability to reach learning goals and embrace challenges (Dweck and Leggett, 1988).

This research can tell us a great deal about our own mindsets and how we tend to view our own competence, intelligence, and capacity for overcoming challenges. Parents who maintain a growth mindset will be more likely to seek strategies that foster intellectual wellness and, as a result, will be able to learn from the mistakes we make and persist in the face of challenges. They will take pleasure in learning new information and will strive to grow and learn throughout their parenting journey. Consider the following strategies we can use to foster intellectual wellness.

- **Joining family learning communities:** Learning communities (or communities of practice) are not just a strategy to support social wellness. They also promote intellectual wellness by providing opportunities to share experiences, exchange perspectives on common problems, and learn from other families in a supportive environment. By being involved with a community of learners, we have a chance to reflect on their own parenting practices. As a result, we discover new information and new insights. Virtual learning communities are becoming increasingly popular because they are easy to access and can connect families with others without regard to distance. Not sure about how to approach a situation with your child? There may be a parent across the country who has figured out some solutions.

June was born December 26, and I think in February I could remember life again. I remember my mom saying a couple weeks after we got her diagnosis, "Are you realizing, though, that you're crying less every day?" I'm not proud of that. But I say it because it's honest. It's real. I felt so much shame because I thought I would not have responded like that. But then, every day I got out of bed a little bit more. My mom would come to check on my mental health. She would bring me food. I was really kind of going through the motions, but after about six weeks, we got early intervention therapies. At that point, we had already told all of our friends and family about June, and so we started working toward what our new life would be. That it is different than what we had expected it would be. Every day it got a little bit more like our life again. Those moments are where you wish you could go back and tell yourself that you're going to love her so much for exactly who she is. Stop wasting your time wishing her away, because you're never going to want her to be different as soon as you just get to know her a little bit. I think that's part of the process.

—JACKIE JOSEPH, PARENT

- **Connecting with another parent:** Many Parent Training and Information Centers offer mentoring opportunities for families who are looking to build their advocacy skills, learn strategies for supporting their child, and share and receive feedback from another parent or family member. Early childhood educators benefit from a similar approach when they engage with a peer mentor or coach. The concept is that we all benefit from a collaborative partnership built on rapport, trust, and a shared understanding of the goals of the relationship. Typically, a mentor or parent partner will provide a safe space for you to ask questions, discuss problems, get support, gather feedback, reflect on parenting practices, and brainstorm new ideas. Sometimes, the mentor is an experienced parent who has supported other families in the past and can step into a sort of "expert" role, while other times the other parent is a peer who is navigating similar issues as yours. The conversations you have can take place virtually by using technology or face to face. Together, you can work on shared goals and put the goals in writing into an action plan, if that would be helpful. As you navigate your parenting journey, a mentor can help with feedback that is shared in a supportive way to help you gain confidence and competence. When new skills are honed, the two partners can celebrate that success together.
- **Reflecting on your own parenting journey:** Whether it is with a mentor or on your own, it's always helpful to reflect on your own experiences as a parent. By reflecting on your parenting, you can identify any barriers to learning that might exist and problem solve strategies for providing the best supports for your child. The reflection process will also help you to understand yourself better. Keep the growth mindset in mind. Instead of thinking, "I just can't do this," think, "Up until now, I haven't learned how to do this." Instead of thinking, "This isn't working," think, "What am I missing?" or "What else can I try?" Asking yourself questions will help you understand what your strengths are and recognize any areas where you might benefit from supports or new ideas.
- **Writing in a journal:** In her book *Writing as a Way of Healing,* Louise DeSalvo (2000) shares that writing our deepest thoughts and feelings in a personal journal is linked with "improved immune function, improved emotional and physical health, and positive behavioral changes." Some families find that a journal is helpful to keep track of the caregiving practices that have been most successful, as well as progress they or their child are making. Your journal might include notes about what is and what isn't working in your family. It can also be a place where you reflect on your life outside your role as parent or caregiver, and the personal growth you are making over time.

SPIRITUAL WELLNESS

Spirituality is a personal thing. Spiritual wellness, however, isn't necessarily about religion. The National Wellness Institute (n.d.) suggests that spiritual wellness is about forming a positive perception of meaning and purpose in life. This can arise just from being open to different cultures and religions or from giving your time to volunteer or participate in community-service activities.

Spiritual wellness can also be built through spending time alone in personal reflection, as you think about your own values and how you might make decisions that are complementary to your values. A key strategy that I use to promote spiritual wellness is through the practice of mindfulness.

What Is Mindfulness?

Mindfulness has been growing in popularity. Researcher Jon Kabat-Zinn (2003) defines this practice as "the awareness that emerges through paying attention on purpose, in the present moment, and non-judgmentally to the unfolding of experience moment by moment." Through nonjudgmental awareness of the present moment, we are able to recognize our own thoughts, feelings, and behaviors as they arise, without getting stuck in our usual, automatic responses. And there are many benefits. First of all, it's free. You don't need any books or gadgets to practice mindfulness, and through the practice we are able to "wake up" to what we are really experiencing in the moment. Most importantly, it is backed by science. Kabat-Zinn (2003) found that mindfulness helps us to:

- experience life clearly, as it happens, without an emotional charge;
- discover what is the wisest and kindest way to respond in the moment;
- connect with ourselves and with the children in our lives;
- slow down when we need to; and
- become more aware of our choices in a situation and reduce impulsive reactions.

If you aren't already convinced, you will be when you learn that mindfulness has been shown to be an effective intervention for symptoms related to illness and mental health problems (Davis and Hayes, 2012). It is scientifically proven to improve mental and physical health. Research has found that mindfulness can reduce blood pressure, help us manage pain, decrease stress and anxiety, treat clinical depression, and increase our ability to manage our emotions and impulses (Davidson et al., 2003; Grossman, Niemann, Schmidt, and Walach, 2004).

Mindfulness requires us to be fully present and focused. The practice involves bringing awareness to something specific, such as your breath. The focused attention brings our thoughts into view, but the practice requires that we simply notice our thoughts and keep from analyzing them or trying to think about what they mean. We pay attention to thoughts and feelings without trying to distinguish whether they are right or wrong. Over time, you start to recognize unhealthy patterns of thinking. There is mindful sitting, mindful standing, mindful journaling, mindful breathing, mindful walking, and even mindful eating.

Now, you might be thinking, "Jani, you're getting too 'woo-woo' for me." I'm telling you, though, it works! Let's think about a typical day that has built-in time for mindfulness.

Mindfulness throughout the Day

First, start off your day right. Researchers have found that we release the most stress hormones within minutes after waking (Hirotsu, Tufik, and Andersen, 2015). Why? Because thinking of the day ahead triggers our fight-or-flight instinct and releases the stress hormone cortisol into our blood. Instead, try this: When you wake up, spend two minutes in your bed simply noticing your breath. As thoughts about the day pop into your mind, let them go and return to your breath.

Later, when you get to your first event of the day, take ten minutes to boost your brain with a short mindfulness practice before you dive into activity. Close your eyes, relax, and sit upright. Place your full focus on your breath. Simply maintain an ongoing flow of attention on the experience of your breathing: inhale, exhale, inhale, exhale. To maintain your focus, count silently at each exhalation. Any time you find your mind distracted, simply release the distraction by returning your focus to your breath. Most important, allow yourself to enjoy these minutes. Throughout the rest of the day, other people and competing urgencies will fight for your attention, but for these ten minutes, your attention is all your own.

Try mindful eating during lunch with all or some of your food. Pay attention to the colors, smells, textures, flavors, temperatures, and even the sounds of your food. What are you feeling in your body? Where in the body do you feel hunger? Where do you feel satisfaction? What does half- or three-quarters-full feel like? Watch the impulses that arise in your mind after taking a few sips or bites. Your mind might suggest that you grab a book, call someone on your cell phone, or get some additional work done. Simply notice the impulse and return your awareness to the act of eating. When you are finished eating, explore your thoughts and sensations. Is there a lingering taste from lunch? How do you feel physically and emotionally? Take a little while to consider the experience. There are no rights or wrongs, just individual experiences. This may be your first experience of eating lunch without that feeling of being on autopilot. Research by Killingsworth and Gilbert (2010) showed that people spend almost 47 percent of their waking hours thinking about something other than what they're doing. Break the spell and enjoy the feeling of being present while eating lunch.

As the day progresses and your brain starts to tire, mindfulness can help you stay sharp and avoid poor decisions. After lunch, set a timer on your phone to ring every hour. When the timer rings, stop what you're doing and engage in one minute of mindfulness practice. Another option is to use the regular transitions that are built into your typical routine as mindfulness-break reminders. When you do the activity in your routine, focus completely on what you are doing: the body movements, the tastes, the touch, the smells, the sights, the sounds, and so on. When thoughts arise, acknowledge them, let them be, and bring your attention back to the activity. You'll find that, again and again, your attention will wander. As soon as you realize this has happened, gently acknowledge it, note what distracted you, and bring your attention back to your senses.

Free mindfulness and meditation apps are available to help with guided meditations, relaxing music, and featured talks with experts in the field. You can listen through your computer or download an app to your smartphone. A few of my favorites include the following:

- Insight Timer
- UCLA Mindful
- 10 Percent Happier
- Calm

Finally, as the day comes to an end and you start to wind down, apply mindfulness. For at least ten minutes at the end of your day, turn off your phone, shut off the radio, and simply be. Let go of any thoughts that arise. Attend to your breath. Pay attention to how you are feeling internally; doing this will allow you to let go of the stresses of the day so you can be fully present with your family.

REFLECTING ON YOUR OWN WELLNESS

We all have areas where we can grow and develop. Your ability to stay well is one of those areas. It really depends on your own life and the stressors you encounter. For our last activity in the book, we will do some reflection on the key areas of wellness in your own life, so that you can reflect on areas to build in self-care strategies for yourself. These strategies will ultimately benefit you, your child, and family. Take a look at the wellness wheel activity at the end of this chapter, and do some reflecting when you are ready.

YOUR FEELINGS, REVISITED

In general, the feelings you have as a parent are all over the map. This is true for all parents, and when you add a disability or suspected delay to the equation, you can be sure that the full spectrum of emotions will be felt. Guilt, joy, fear, sadness, happiness, uncertainty, elation, despair, confusion, anxiety, encouragement, anguish, hopefulness—just "all the feels" as they say. It might even feel like the stages of grief. The families I interviewed reflected on this time and again. The way they felt sad or scared in the beginning, and worried that they would never adjust to their "new normal":

You will worry. We all worry. It is normal to worry and that is okay. I first want to make sure you take that in and realize that you are *so* not alone in this. At this point, I'm going to have to confess that this section is somewhat of a "do as I say, not as I did," kind of thing. I was a serious worrier all through Ricky's childhood. You probably guessed that, given my previously confessed Mama Bear tendencies. Worrying seems to be in my nature, but it really is not helpful. In *Born Extraordinary: Empowering Children with Difference and Disabilities,* Meg Zucker (2023) writes that parents of children with disabilities in particular "can't make decisions on their behalf based on fear. You need to resist the urge to overprotect, while finding the courage to follow their lead. You'll need to preserve their pride as they yearn to be independent, despite a world that perceives them as helpless. You'll discover the benefits of family support that flows both ways; and you'll need to help your children discern between cruelty and curiosity while preparing them for anything." Isn't that the most beautiful advice you've ever heard?

> I joke with my husband that I worry about the boys, and he worries about money, and then we have all the worry covered.
>
> **—ANDIE AMOSSON, PARENT**

I love the truth she writes about family support flowing both ways, because I have learned just as much or more from Ricky than I ever was able to teach him. He taught me to trust his abilities, and that reminded me to trust my own abilities. He showed me that he could grow into self-assurance and confidence, and that helped me to be more confident as well. He reacted to hurtful things without letting them get him down, and, well, let's just say that I'm still a work in progress in that regard.

> Phillip was first diagnosed in February, and it took me pretty much the rest of the year to fully grasp it. It was just heavy, overwhelming. My system automatically got depressed. I was sleeping more. I would only do what I had to do. That was a moment where sadness took over, mostly because I was just so uncertain. I didn't know what services were needed or necessary or how to access them. I didn't know which way to go. I worried if I would have support from my family. Will they be accepting? How will they feel? But over time I began to embrace it. Seeing his first step, seeing what he was capable of doing, seeing that he picked up signing. It opened a new world of possibilities.
>
> **—LATISHA R. STUCKEY, PARENT**

During my interviews with families, I noticed another interesting trend. Every family I spoke with shared a bit about the sadness, fear, and sometimes guilt, but they also shared that in retrospect, they wouldn't have it any other way. They all adore their children exactly as they are.

It's not always easy, for sure. Parents do not want their child to have to feel the pain of disability, physical or social pain, but they love and appreciate their child for everything they are—including the disability. Would Ricky be the same Ricky without ADHD? No way on Earth!

He's energetic and exuberant, and I love that about him. He still has trouble getting "from point A to point B," just as Miss Amy described him in preschool. But he has a sense of humor about it and can laugh about the distractibility. He makes these self-deprecating jokes that are so charming. You would love him. My son is beyond adorable and my heart overflows with love to even write these words about him.

> My life is much better with my kids. Even with all of the bad things and sad things that have happened, there are so many good things and things that other people take for granted. The little things are like the biggest achievements. So you enjoy it more. When people say, "Oh, I was blessed with typical kids," it's like no, you don't know what you're missing. I'm a better person because of them.
>
> **—ANDIE AMOSSON, PARENT**

Would I be the same Jani without SMD? Not a chance! My life experiences have given me endless stories to share, and my disability helps me connect with other people. People remember me. I stand out in the crowd. There are many, many advantages to standing out in the crowd. The features of our disabilities are not the whole picture of who we are, but they are part of the picture. Disability has shaped each of us in different ways, but ultimately for the better. SMD has made me better. This is the honest truth, and I hope it brings you a little bit of peace.

WHAT WILL YOU DO NEXT?

As we near the end of this journey, I am hopeful that you have learned a lot. I hope you have gained knowledge about the early intervention (EI) and early childhood special education (ECSE) systems, your child, and yourself. In chapter 2, we focused on your role as an advocate for your child, and I hope that you will wear that title proudly and also think about your role as an advocate for children with disabilities in general.

> You don't expect for your child to have these types of problems. Am I capable of giving him what he needs, meeting those needs without having support and people coaching me through? Gradually, through a lot of grief, I think it made me who I am today, the advocate I am today.
>
> **—ARIELLE BRANCH, PARENT**

Throughout this book, I have woven data, information, and stories about inclusion in early childhood. I hope you will reflect on the experiences that make up the stories from your own life and will examine your own attitudes and beliefs about the inclusion of children with disabilities in our schools and in our communities. It is an important vision, and we are not there yet as a society. Will you help us to get there? Will you be an advocate for inclusion?

This quote from an old Breton fisherman's prayer really speaks to my heart: "The sea is so wide, and my boat is so small" (National Archives, n.d.). It does seem as though the sea is wide, and that we have a long way to go to make early childhood inclusion the norm rather than the exception. My boat is small, but I also know that my boat is not the only boat. I have many partners in this work, including you. Together, we make a mighty fleet. It is going to take each of us to build a system of inclusion for each and every child. We can do it, though!

> My boat is small, but I also know that my boat is not the only boat. I have many partners in this work, including you. Together, we make a mighty fleet moving toward this vision of inclusion.

Consider the following strategies for next steps in your journey to advocate for inclusion in early childhood education.

First, we advocate for inclusion by expecting our early childhood programs to be inclusive. Think about the early childhood program your child attends or is planning to attend, whether it is a parent play group, child care, Head Start, pre-K, library story hour, or another type of program. How can you create an expectation that these programs are as inclusive as possible? Do you need to talk with other families about this goal? program leaders? school administrators? funders? Be prepared to share concrete examples of what you hope to achieve as you advocate for inclusion within the program. Use the data and research I shared in the introduction of this book. Try to have an impact on the things that you can control in the little part of the world where your child is growing up and where you live and work. If we all did this, we would be a powerful parent force.

Reflect on your current parenting approaches and think about areas that you might work on. Are you using inclusive language? Are there things that you do as a parent that you hope to fine-tune? Do you believe that *each and every child belongs* in all early childhood programs? (P.S. The answer is yes!)

> I remember in the beginning we were wondering if we were ever going to genuinely laugh again without concern. You know? But June just makes us laugh every single day.
>
> **—JACKIE JOSEPH, PARENT**

Advocacy itself can take many forms. Some advocates donate money. Others show up at protests or set up meetings with elected officials. Still others advocate for inclusion on social media or within their own child's program, or they take time to educate friends and family members. We all can share stories and engage others in conversation. All of these efforts matter.

Remember that you are now part of that mighty fleet. You are not the only one thinking about inclusion, and when you talk with others and share your stories, you are creating a ripple in the water that will become a wave. Find other families who share your values and passion. Join a parent group; lean on each other and build each other up. They are the best people in the world, and together you can create a supportive community. You will need those members of your fleet, because there are plenty of people out there who do not yet understand. Together, we are strong. We have resilience and energy and grit that is matched only by those qualities in the children we love.

*****

Dandelions are definitely my favorite weed. Doesn't this image just sing childhood to you? Such a lovely experience, to teach your child about the fun of blowing dandelion seeds for the first time. I think that I love dandelions because they remind me of us, this mighty force of families, early intervention specialists, therapists, and early childhood educators. Like a child blowing the seeds from a dandelion, we too provide the same little push, the lightest puff of air, that can make all of the difference in the world for a child. Our empathy, understanding, and care can mean the difference between shame and pride for a child with a disability. Inclusion versus exclusion. Thank you for joining in this work with me. The children we love are worth the fight, and if we work together, every child can fly.

ACTIVITY: REFLECTION WITH A WELLNESS WHEEL

DIRECTIONS

The six sections in the wheel below represent your life. Rank your level of satisfaction with each area on a scale of 1 to 5.

1 means you are struggling and feel unfulfilled in that area.

5 means you're satisfied with that area and don't think it needs much improvement.

Go with your gut on this one. Color the number of spaces on the wheel that match your ranking, starting from the inside and working out. Once you're finished, ask yourself:

- Which section of my wheel has the most color?
- Which section of my wheel has the least color?
- If this isn't the first time you've completed this activity, how has your wheel changed? What might have caused those changes?

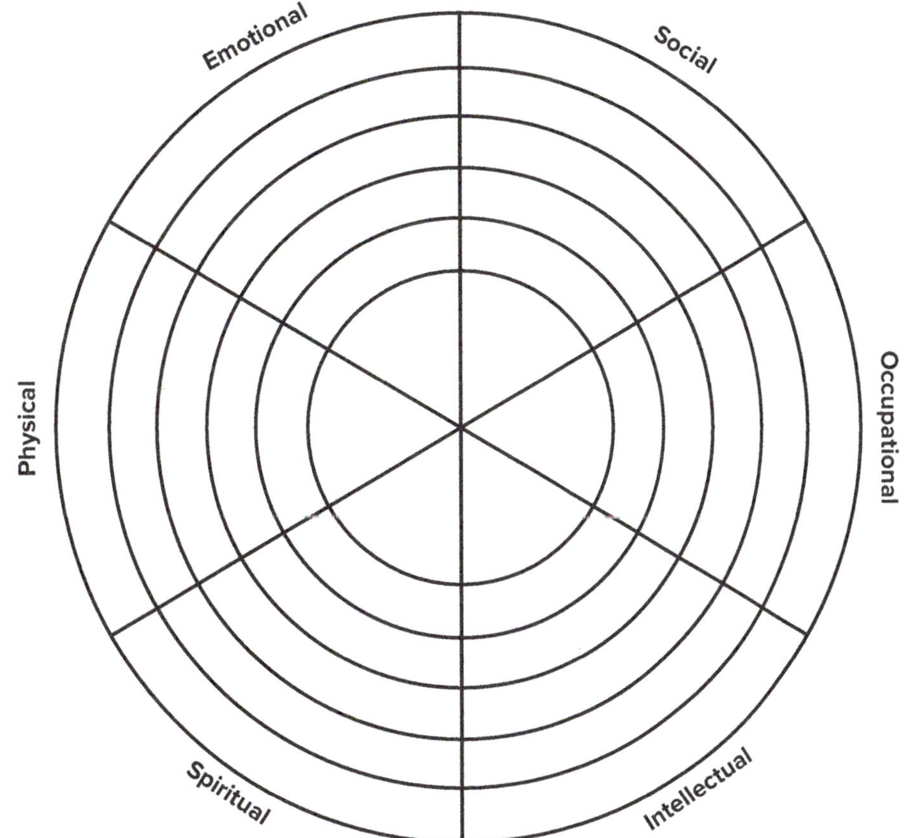

APPENDIX A: GLOSSARY OF TERMS

504 Plan: "a plan that specifies the accommodations and modifications necessary for a student with a disability to attend school with her or his peers; named for Section 504 of the federal Rehabilitation Act of 1973, which prohibits discrimination against individuals with disabilities, ensuring that children with disabilities have equal access to public education; students with 504 plans do not meet the eligibility requirements for special education under IDEA" (IRIS Center, 2021)

Ableism: "a set of beliefs or practices at the individual, community, or systemic level that devalues and discriminates against people with physical, intellectual, or psychiatric disabilities and often rests on the assumption that disabled people need to be 'fixed' in one form or the other" (Smith, n.d.)

Access: "providing a wide range of activities and environments for every child by removing physical barriers and offering multiple ways to promote learning and development" (DEC and NAEYC, 2009)

Accessibility: "the extent to which a facility is readily approachable and usable by individuals with disabilities, particularly such areas as the personnel office, worksite, and public areas" (University of Massachusetts Lowell, 2019)

Accommodation: "an adaptation or change to educational environments and practices designed to help students overcome the challenges presented by their disabilities and to allow them to access the same instructional opportunities as students without disabilities. An accommodation does change the expectations for learning or reduce the requirements of the task" (IRIS Center, 2021)

Acquisition: the stage of the learning cycle when the child has begun to learn how to complete the target skill correctly but is not yet accurate or fluent in the skill. The goal in this phase is to improve accuracy (Haring, Lovitt, Eaton, and Hansen, 1978)

Activity Planning Matrix: a chart that lists the daily schedule of activities down the lefthand column and the child's current objectives or target behaviors across the top. Within the boxes is a description of how the objective or target behavior would be embedded into each of the activities (NCPMI, n.d.)

Adaptation: a "term used to describe allowable changes in educational environments or practices (i.e., supports or services) that help a student overcome the barriers imposed by a disability and provide them with opportunities to achieve the same outcomes and obtain the same benefits as students without disabilities" (IRIS Center, 2021)

Adverse Childhood Experiences (ACEs): "preventable, potentially traumatic events that occur in childhood (0–17 years), such as neglect, experiencing or witnessing violence, and having a family member attempt or die by suicide. Also included are aspects of a child's environment that can undermine their sense of safety, stability, and bonding, such as growing up in a household with substance use; mental health problems; or instability due to parental separation or incarceration of a parent, sibling, or other member of the household" (CDC, 2019)

Antecedents (or Triggers): the "events that happen right before a behavior occurs" (FPG, UNC, n.d.)

Assessment: the process of gathering information to make decisions. Assessment informs intervention, and as a result, is a critical component of services for children who have or are at risk for delays/disabilities and their families. In early intervention and early childhood special education, assessment is conducted for the purposes of screening, determining eligibility for services, individualized planning, monitoring child progress, and measuring child outcomes (DEC, 2014)

Assistive Technology: "any item, piece of equipment, or product system, whether acquired commercially off the shelf, modified, or customized, that is used to increase, maintain, or improve functional capabilities" (Sandall et al., 2005)

At-Risk: "a term used to describe students whose condition or situation makes it probable for them to develop disabilities" (IRIS Center, 2021)

Attention Deficit Hyperactivity Disorder (ADHD): one of the most common mental disorders affecting children. Symptoms of ADHD include inattention (not being able to keep focus), hyperactivity (excess movement that is not fitting to the setting), and impulsivity (hasty acts that occur in the moment without thought) (American Psychiatric Association, 2021)

Augmentative and Alternative Communication (AAC): the supplementation or replacement of natural speech and/or writing using aided and/or unaided symbols. The use of aided symbols requires a transmission device (Lloyd, Fuller, and Arvidson, 1997)

Authentic Assessment: practices include methods and strategies for identifying the contextual and adult behavior that promote a child's participation and learning in everyday activities. The assessment practices involve observing children's engagement in everyday activities, the learning opportunities that occur in the activities, child strengths and abilities displayed in the activities, and the adult behavior that can support child participation and learning in the activities (ECTA, 2020a)

Autism Spectrum Disorder (ASD): a "developmental disability that can result in significant delays and developmental differences in a number of areas, including communication, social interaction, and behavior" (IRIS Center, 2021)

Behavior Hypothesis Statements: include a description of the behavior, triggers or antecedents for the behavior, maintaining consequences, and the purpose of the problem behavior (NCPMI, n.d.)

Behavior Support Plan: a team's action plan outlining the specific steps to be used to promote a child's success and participation in daily activities and routines. Essential components of the behavior support plan are prevention strategies, the instruction of replacement skills, new ways to respond to problem behavior, and lifestyle outcome goals (NCPMI, n.d.)

Cerebral Palsy: "a nonprogressive, neuromotor impairment that affects body movements and muscle coordination" (IRIS Center, 2021)

Child Find: "this law requires all school districts to identify and evaluate all children ages birth through 21 who have or are suspected of having a disability, regardless of severity, to determine if they need special education services" (IRIS Center, 2021)

Collaboration: "any collective action in which two or more individuals work together toward a common goal of planning, implementing, or evaluating a specific aspect of an educational program for a student or group of students" (IRIS Center, 2021)

Communication Board: "a form of assistive technology consisting of photographs, symbols, words/phrases, or any combination of these designed to make language visible and accessible for individuals with speech impairments" (IRIS Center, 2021)

Consent: within "IDEA has a very specific meaning that rises out of, and is closely tied to, its provisions regarding prior written notice. *Consent,* in IDEA, means informed written consent . . . intended to inform parents fully about a specific issue. Only by building that foundation of understanding can informed consent be given" (Küpper and Rebhorn, 2007)

Consequence Strategies: guidelines for how the adults will respond to problem behaviors in ways that will not maintain the behavior; may include positive reinforcement strategies for promoting the child's use of new skills or appropriate behavior (this may also be included in prevention strategies) (NCPMI, n.d.)

Coregulation: "reciprocal process between child and caregiver characterized by warm, responsive interactions . . . the process by which children develop social and emotional capacities via the caregiving relationship. Close physical contact, calming touch, supportive vocalizations and modeling are primary modes of coregulation. Over time and with support, a child internalizes the caregiver's regulatory capacities through practice and reinforcement" (Gehl and Hackbert, 2019)

Cross-Sector: includes the major organizations, agencies, and institutions in a state that provide services and support the development and learning of young children, their families, and the practitioners who serve them (ECTA, 2015)

Cultural Responsiveness: an awareness of the various cultures represented by a program's population and effort to align practices with the values and beliefs of these cultures. Practices and products that are culturally responsive are communicated in a way that is both understandable and relevant to constituent groups (NCPMI, n.d.)

Culture: the languages, customs, beliefs, rules, arts, knowledge, and collective identities and memories developed by members of all social groups that make their social environments meaningful (American Sociological Association, n.d.)

Curriculum: the plans for the learning experiences through which children acquire knowledge, skills, abilities, and understanding (NAEYC, 2020a)

Curriculum Modification: "a change to the ongoing classroom activity or materials in order to facilitate or maximize a child's participation in planned activities and routines" (Sandall and Schwartz, 2008)

Developmental Milestones: the behaviors that mark stages of typical growth . . . most children pass through specific changes at approximately the same time as they get older (Cleveland Clinic, 2021)

Developmental Screening: "a process involving partnerships with parents to identify concerns about a child's development" (CDC, 2019)

Differentiated Instruction: "an instructional approach that accommodates the diversity of students by coping with student diversity, adopting specific teaching strategies, invoking a variety in learning activity, monitoring individual student needs, and pursuing optimal learning outcomes" (Suprayogi and Valcke, 2016)

Down Syndrome: "a disorder arising from chromosome defect (i.e., an extra chromosome on the twenty-first pair) that often results in identifiable physical characteristics (e.g., short stature, broad facial profile) and that usually causes delays in physical and intellectual development" (IRIS Center, 2021)

Early Intervention Services: "specialized services provided to very young children at risk for or showing signs of developmental delay" (IRIS Center, 2021)

Embedded Instruction or Embedded Learning: multiple, brief teaching interactions between a teacher and child during everyday activities. By identifying functional behavior targets, selecting classroom activities best suited for embedded learning opportunities, and using planned and intentional instructional strategies, teachers can help children learn new behavior for participating in classroom activities throughout the day (ECTA Center, 2017)

Emotional Literacy: the ability to give word meaning, such as *angry, frustrated, happy,* and *proud,* to one's emotions. Children who have larger emotional vocabularies tend to exhibit less problem behavior (NCPMI, n.d.)

Emotional Regulation: "the ability to control one's state or behavior in order to achieve individual goals, handle everyday stress, and deal with various social situations appropriately" (IRIS Center, 2021)

Equality: "in the context of instructional supports and accommodations, term used to describe a state in which each student is given precisely the same tools to complete a learning task or assignment, even at the expense of their ability to do so" (IRIS Center, 2021)

Equitable Learning Opportunities: "learning opportunities that not only help each child thrive by building on each one's unique set of individual and family strengths—including cultural background, language(s), abilities and disabilities, and experiences—but also are designed to eliminate differences in outcomes that are a result of past and present inequities in society" (NAEYC, n.d.)

Equity: "in the context of instructional supports and accommodations, term used to describe a state in which each student is given what he or she needs to successfully complete a learning task or assignment" (IRIS Center, 2021)

Ethnicity: groups that share a common identity-based ancestry, language, or culture; often based on religion, beliefs, and customs as well as memories of migration or colonization (Stanford University, n.d.)

Evaluation: the procedures used by appropriate qualified personnel to determine a child's initial and continuing eligibility for services and supports (American Speech-Language-Hearing Association, 2021)

Evidence-Based Practices: interventions or supports that have published research documenting their effectiveness. Practices that are considered evidence based are ones that have been demonstrated as effective within multiple research studies that document similar positive outcomes. In this guide, the term "evidence-based practices" is used interchangeably with "recommended practices" and in some cases "targeted practices" when describing statewide initiatives to improve child outcomes (NCPMI, n.d.)

Executive Functions: "the mental processes that control and coordinate activities related to learning, including processing information, retaining and recalling information, organizing materials and time, and using effective learning and study strategies" (IRIS Center, 2021)

Fading: strategy of "gradually reducing the prompt by reducing the intensity, increasing the response interval, or [changing] the location of the prompt" (FPG, UNC, n.d.)

Fidelity: the degree to which an intervention or practice is delivered as intended by the developers and achieves expected results. Fidelity implies strict and continuing faithfulness to the original innovation or practice and can be measured and compared to previous or future efforts to deliver the intervention or practice (NCPMI, n.d.)

Flow: a highly focused mental state conducive to productivity (Csikszentmihalyi, 1990)

Fluency: the stage of the learning cycle when a child is able to complete a target skill accurately but works slowly. The goal of this phase is to increase the child's speed of responding (Haring et al., 1978)

Free Appropriate Public Education (FAPE): ensures that "each eligible student with a disability receives an individualized education that meets his or her unique needs and is provided in conformity with the student's IEP at no cost to the child or family" (IRIS Center, 2021)

Functional Behavior Assessment (FBA): "a process used to develop an understanding of a child's challenging behavior. The goal of functional behavioral assessment is to identify the function of the child's behavior—the reason or purpose why a child behaves as he/she does in specific situations" (NCPMI, n.d.)

Functional Outcomes: a collection of behaviors across many aspects of development that a child needs to know or do to be successful in everyday life (ECTA, n.d.)

Generalization: the stage of the learning cycle when a child is accurate and fluent in using the skill; the child is not yet able to modify or adapt the skill to fit novel task demands or situations. Here the goal is for the child to be able to identify elements of previously learned skills that they can adapt to the new demands or situation (Haring et al., 1978)

Heavy Work: any type of activity that pushes or pulls against the body, such as swimming or vacuuming; the resistance creates the push or pull (Morin, n.d.)

Historical Trauma: "the cumulative emotional and psychological wounding over the lifespan and across generations, emanating from massive group trauma experiences. Examples of historical trauma include the multigenerational effects of white supremacy reflected in colonization, genocide, slavery, sexual exploitation, forced relocation, and incarceration based on race or ethnicity" (NAEYC, n.d.)

Home visit: "term used to describe instruction delivered primarily in a student's home rather than in a school or center" (IRIS Center, 2021)

Hypothesis Statement: within the context of a behavior support plan, a description of everything that is known about the behavior, triggers, and warning signs learned through a functional behavioral assessment process; also includes an informed guess about the purpose or function of the challenging behavior (NCPMI, n.d.)

Implicit Bias: "the automatic and unconscious stereotypes that drive people to behave and make decisions in certain ways" (Staats et al., 2015)

Inclusion: "embodies the values, policies, and practices that support the right of every infant and young child and his or her family, regardless of ability, to participate in a broad range of activities and contexts as full members of families, communities, and society. The desired results of inclusive experiences for children with and without disabilities and their families include a sense of belonging and membership, positive social relationships and friendships, and development and learning to reach their full potential. The defining features of inclusion that can be used to identify high quality early childhood programs and services are access, participation, and supports" (DEC and NAEYC, 2009)

Individualized Education Program (IEP): "a written education plan for a child with disabilities (ages 3–21) developed by a team of professionals (e.g., teachers, therapists) and the child's parents; it is reviewed and updated yearly and describes how the child is presently doing, what the child's learning needs are, and what services the child will need" (CONNECT and DEC, n.d.)

Individualized Family Service Plan (IFSP): "a written plan for an infant or toddler with disabilities (birth–3) developed by a team of professionals (e.g., teachers, therapists) and the child's family; it is reviewed and updated yearly and describes how the child is presently doing, what the child's learning needs are, and what services the child will need" (CONNECT and DEC, n.d.)

Individualized Instruction: the idea that each student learns differently and thus in order to accommodate these differences, instruction should be personalized, matched, or adapted to the experiences, aptitudes, and interests of each student (Waxman, Alford, and Brown, 2013)

Infant and Early Childhood Mental Health: "the developing capacity of the child from birth to 5 years of age to form close and secure adult and peer relationships; experience, manage, and express a full range of emotions; and explore the environment and learn—all in the context of family, community, and culture" (Zero to Three, 2016)

Internalized Ableism: "the way that an individual absorbs and applies the beliefs and moral judgments of the dominant ableist culture, at a subconscious level" (Neurodiverging.com, 2023)

Interdisciplinary Team: "group of professionals from different disciplines who work together to plan and manage a student's IEP" (IRIS Center, 2021)

Intersectionality: the "overlapping and interdependent systems of oppression across, for example, race, gender, ability, and social status. Intersectionality encourages us to embrace and celebrate individuals' multiple social identities . . . [and] highlights the complex and cumulative effects of different forms of structural inequity that can arise for members of multiple marginalized groups" (NAEYC, n.d.)

Itinerant Teacher: an educator who teaches students or who consults with others in more than one setting (IRIS Center, 2021)

Learning Cycle: a sequential process for both learning and instruction. It places focus on a series of steps that encourage a more thorough understanding and a deeper application of content. The learning cycle has four stages: acquisition, fluency, maintenance, and generalization (Haring et al., 1978)

Least Restrictive Environment (LRE): "requires that students with disabilities be educated with their non-disabled peers to the greatest appropriate extent" (IRIS Center, 2021)

Least-to-Most Prompts (also called "the system of least prompts"): "a hierarchy of prompts that are ordered from the least to the most assistance needed for the child to perform a behavior. For each trial, the adult initially gives the child an opportunity to perform the behavior without prompts; if the child does not respond correctly, the adult delivers the least controlling prompt and gives the child another opportunity to respond. Again, if the child does not respond or starts to respond incorrectly, the adult delivers the next more controlling prompt. This continues on each trial until the child responds correctly or the most controlling level of prompt is provided" (NCPMI, n.d.)

Maintenance: stage of the learning cycle when the child is accurate and fluent in using the target skill but does not typically use it in different situations or settings (Haring et al., 1978)

Mediation: "process through which a neutral party facilitates a meeting between parents and school officials to resolve disagreements about a student's individualized education program and questions about his or her placement and services" (IRIS Center, 2021)

Medically Fragile: "term used to describe children whose medical conditions are subject to sudden change or that place them at risk for developmental delays" (IRIS Center, 2021)

Mentoring: "a method of ongoing support in which a more-experienced or more-knowledgeable person helps a less-experienced or less-knowledgeable person to learn or refine skills" (IRIS Center, 2021)

Modeling: "an instructional strategy in which an adult demonstrates a response. There are two types of modeling: verbal and nonverbal. In verbal modeling, an adult uses language to demonstrate how to say or do something. . . . In nonverbal modeling, an adult uses physical movements, signs, or gestures to demonstrate how to say or do something" (CONNECT and DEC, n.d.)

Modifications: "any of a number of services or supports that allow a student to access the general education curriculum but in a way that fundamentally alters the content or curricular expectations in question" (IRIS Center, 2021)

Most to Least Prompts: "a series of two or more prompts that provide progressively decreasing amounts of assistance. This strategy always begins with the most help a child needs in order to be able to do something with few or no errors. Over time, as the child learns the skill, the amount of support the adult provides decreases until the child is able to do the skill independently" (NCPMI, n.d.)

Multidisciplinary Team: "a team of teachers, educational professionals (e.g., related services personnel, school psychologist), administrators, specialists, and parents or guardians who assess the individual needs of students to determine eligibility for special education and develop individualized education programs (IEP); often called IEP teams" (IRIS Center, 2021)

Multitiered Systems of Support (MTSS): "data-driven, problem-solving framework to improve outcomes for all students. MTSS relies on a continuum of evidence-based practices matched to student needs." PBIS and the Pyramid Model are examples of MTSS centered on social behavior. RTI is another example of a MTSS. A MTSS typically includes three tiers: tier 1, Universal Prevention (All); tier 2, Targeted Prevention (Some); and tier 3, Intensive, Individualized Prevention (Few) (Center on PBIS, 2021)

Observation: "the act of careful watching and listening; the activity of paying close attention to someone or something in order to get information" (Merriam-Webster, 2021)

Participation: using a range of instructional approaches to promote engagement in play and learning activities and a sense of belonging for every child (DEC and NAEYC, 2009)

Peer-Mediated Intervention: a systematic teaching strategy in which typically developing children are taught to deliver specific social and communicative behavior to children with social-skill deficits (NCPMI, n.d.)

People-First Language: "a preferred method for referring to individuals with disabilities that emphasizes a word order placing mention of the individual before her or his disability (e.g., 'a person who is blind' rather than 'a blind person'), current terminology, and positive or neutral descriptions" (IRIS Center, 2021)

Physical Environment: "the overall design and layout of a classroom, including its learning centers, materials, and furnishings" (IRIS Center, 2021)

Picture Exchange Communication System (PECS): behavior-based intervention that teaches the learner to use visual-graphic symbols to communicate with others. Learners with ASD are taught to give a picture or graphic symbol of a desired item to a communicative partner in exchange for the actual item through a six-phase process (National Professional Development Center on ASD, 2019)

Placement: "term used to specify the educational setting in which special education services will be provided" (IRIS Center, 2021)

Positive Behavioral Interventions and Supports (PBIS): an individualized process for understanding and resolving the problem behavior of children, based on values and empirical research. It offers an approach for developing an understanding of why the child engages in problem behavior and strategies for preventing the occurrence of problem behavior while teaching the child new skills. Positive behavior support offers a holistic approach that considers all factors that impact on a child and the child's behavior. It can be used to address problem behaviors that range from aggression, tantrums, and property destruction to social withdrawal (NCPMI, n.d.)

Practice-Based Coaching (PBC): focuses on the implementation of specified practices; occurs in the context of a collaborative partnership and uses a cyclical process of action planning, observation, reflection, and feedback for supporting practitioners' use of recommended practices (NCPMI, n.d.)

Practices: "what professionals do with, and for, children and their families to support optimal development in young children and family capacity to support their children" (ECTA, 2020b)

Prior Written Notice: "the public agency's obligation to inform parents a reasonable time before it proposes to take specific actions or refuses to take specific actions" (Küpper and Rebhorn, 2007)

Procedural Safeguards Notice: "the comprehensive written explanation that public agencies must provide parents on specific occasions to, among other things, fully inform them of IDEA's procedural safeguards. 'Upon initial referral or parent request for evaluation' are two occasions that trigger the provision of the procedural safeguards notice" (Küpper and Rebhorn, 2007)

Prompts: "instructions, gestures, demonstrations, touches, or other things we can do to increase the likelihood that children will respond how we want them to. Prompting helps children complete tasks that might otherwise be too difficult or contain multiple or complex steps. Supporting children using prompts (and providing positive descriptive feedback) helps them learn to complete tasks independently" (Barton Lab, n.d.)

Pull-Out Program: an "educational program in which instruction and related services are delivered to students with disabilities outside the general education classroom" (IRIS Center, 2021)

Pyramid Model for Supporting Social Emotional Competence in Infants and Young Children ("Pyramid Model"): "a promotion, prevention, and intervention framework early childhood educators can use to support young children's social emotional competence and prevent or reduce challenging behaviors" (NCPMI, n.d.)

Race: a social and political construction—with no inherent genetic or biological basis—used by social institutions to arbitrarily categorize and divide groups of individuals based on physical appearance (particularly skin color), ancestry, cultural history, and ethnic classification (Wijeysinghe, Griffin, and Love, 1997)

Racial Disparity: an unequal outcome one racial group experiences as compared to the outcome for another racial group (Fong, McCoy, and Detlaff, 2014)

Referral: "process through which a student is sent to another professional for services to support his or her academic, social, or behavioral needs" (IRIS Center, 2021)

Reliability: scores on a developmental screening tool will be stable regardless of when the tool is administered, where it is administered, and who is administering it. Reliability answers the question: Is the tool producing consistent information across different circumstances? Reliability provides assurance that comparable information will be obtained from the tool across different situations (U. S. Department of Health and Human Services, 2014)

Related Services: "part of special education that includes services from professionals (e.g., occupational therapist [OT], physical therapist [PT], Speech-Language Pathologist [SLP]) from a wide range of disciplines typically outside of education, all designed to meet the learning needs of individual children with disabilities" (IRIS Center, 2021)

Replacement Skills: the skills to teach that will replace a problem behavior (NCPMI, n.d.)

Response Prompt: "teacher/parent behavior targeted at eliciting a child to present correct responding in a method appropriate to that child's communication capabilities. Response prompts are used to increase the probability of correct responding from the child" (Wolery, Ault, and Doyle, 1992)

Response to Intervention (RTI): "a multi-tier approach to the early identification and support of students with learning and behavior needs." For RTI implementation to work well, the following essential components must be implemented with fidelity and in a rigorous manner: high-quality, scientifically based classroom instruction, ongoing student assessment, universal screening and progress monitoring, tiered instruction, and parent involvement (RTI Action Network, n.d.)

Routines to the Third Power (Routines^3): a way to maximize learning opportunities by breaking the daily schedule into smaller and smaller increments; also known as "a routine within a routine within a routine" (Dunlap et al., 2017)

Scaffolding: the practice of having an adult "provide the encouragement and the guidance to enable a child to reach beyond their current capacity. The model must be competent in order for the child to develop the skill" (Gehl and Hackbert, 2019)

Screen Reader Software: "any of a variety of computer programs or applications that enable a computer to convey information through non-visual means (e.g., text-to-speech, braille); a type of assistive technology commonly used by individuals who are blind, but also by those with low vision and learning disabilities" (IRIS Center, 2021)

Self-Contained Class: "a special classroom, usually located within a regular public school building, that exists only for students with disabilities" (IRIS Center, 2021)

Self-Regulation: the "capacity to be aware of and manage emotions to maintain a state and sense of calm . . . includes a wide range of internal processing such as inhibiting, initiating, and modulating of emotions and then choosing behaviors that make sense for the given situation" (Gehl and Hackbert, 2019)

Sensory Processing Disorder (also called Sensory Integration Disorder): "difficulty processing information from the senses . . . and responding appropriately to that information. These children typically have one or more senses that either over- or underreact to stimulation. Sensory processing disorder can cause problems with a child's development and behavior." (University of Michigan Health, 2021)

Sensory Reinforcers (or Sensory Supports): "activities or sensations the child enjoys experiencing, such as sitting in a rocking chair, getting lotion applied to hands, or playing with a favorite spinning top" (FPG, UNC, n.d.)

Service Coordination: "the process of facilitating students' access to services, and coordinating the services, supports, and resources as identified on the IFSP or IEP; assures that services will be provided in an integrated way and that they will not be needlessly duplicated" (IRIS Center, 2021)

Setting Events: the ecological events or conditions that increase the likelihood of challenging behavior (NCPMI, n.d.)

Social Environment: the "way that a classroom environment influences or supports the interactions that occur among young children, teachers, and family members" (IRIS Center, 2021)

Social Stories (also called Scripted Stories): "help children understand social interactions, situations, expectations, social cues, the script of unfamiliar activities, and/or social rules"; "brief descriptive stories that provide information regarding a social situation" (Broek et al., 1994; NCPMI, n.d.)

Special Health-Care Needs: physical, intellectual, and developmental disabilities, as well as long-standing medical conditions, such as asthma, diabetes, a blood disorder, or muscular dystrophy (CDC, 2021)

Specialized Services: “those services delivered to some children in a program, but not all, including early intervention, special education, related services and others” (ECTA, 2020a)

Specially Designed Instruction (SDI): “adapting, as appropriate to the needs of an eligible child . . . content, methodology, or delivery of instruction—[t]o address the unique needs of the child that result from the child’s disability and [t]o ensure access of the child to the general curriculum” (Council for Exceptional Children, 2021)

Strength-Based Approach: an assumption that all children and families have resources, personal characteristics, and relationships that can be mobilized to enhance their learning, development, and well-being, no matter how many risk factors or challenges they face (Center for the Study of Social Policy, 2021)

Supports: “broader aspects of the system such as professional development, incentives for inclusion, and opportunities for communication and collaboration among families and professionals to assure high quality inclusion” (DEC and NAEYC, 2009)

Temporal Environment: “the timing, sequence, and length of routines and activities that take place in a classroom throughout the day” (IRIS Center, 2021)

Toxic Stress: “excessive or prolonged activation of stress response systems in the body and brain. Toxic stress response can occur when a child experiences strong, frequent, and/or prolonged adversity—such as physical or emotional abuse, chronic neglect, caregiver substance abuse or mental illness, exposure to violence, and/or the accumulated burdens of family economic hardship—without adequate adult support . . . [P]rolonged activation of the stress response systems can disrupt the development of brain architecture and other organ systems and increase the risk for stress-related disease and cognitive impairment well into the adult years” (Center on the Developing Child, 2021b)

Trauma: “an experience of serious adversity or terror—or the emotional or psychological response to that experience” (Center on the Developing Child, 2021a)

Trauma-Informed Care: an approach that focuses on prevention to help children manage symptoms and triggers that cause challenge and stress; an approach that “realizes the widespread impact of trauma and understands potential paths for recovery; recognizes the signs and symptoms of trauma in clients, families, staff, and others involved with the system; and responds by fully integrating knowledge about trauma into policies, procedures, and practices, and seeks to actively resist re-traumatization” (SAMHSA, 2014)

Universal Design: the philosophy of developing and designing physical environments to be accessible, to the greatest extent possible, to the people who use them, without the need for adaptation (Center for Applied Special Technology, 2008)

Universal Design for Learning: an educational framework based on the learning sciences, which informs the design and development of flexible instructional practices, materials, and tools that address the variability of all learners. This framework is essential to allow children with disabilities ways to engage with learning and to develop knowledge and skills in early childhood programs (Center for Applied Special Technology, 2008)

Validity: the scores on a screening tool accurately capture what the tool is meant to capture in terms of content. Validity answers the question: Is the tool assessing what it is supposed to assess? (U. S. Department of Health and Human Services, 2014)

Vicarious Trauma: type of trauma that results when caregiving professionals are repeatedly exposed to the traumatic experiences or trauma stories of the clients they care for. Characterized by extreme symptoms with persistent heightened arousal at one end and emotional numbing and withdrawal at the other (Gehl and Hackbert, 2019)

Visual Supports (also called Visual Cues): concrete cues that are paired with, or used in place of, a verbal cue to provide the learner with information about a routine, activity, behavioral expectation, or skill demonstration (Sam et al., 2019)

Work Samples: collections of children's drawings, paintings, writing samples, or photographs that represent the best examples of what a child knows and is able to do at a given point in time

Zone of Proximal Development: the space between what a learner can do without assistance and what a learner can do with adult guidance or in collaboration with more capable peers (Vygotsky, 1978)

APPENDIX B: DISABILITY LAWS

FEDERAL LEGISLATION RELATED TO YOUNG CHILDREN WITH DISABILITIES

This is a brief overview of some of the key legislation related to infants, toddlers, and preschoolers with disabilities or suspected delays. If you're interested in learning more, the resources section at the end of this book includes links to information with detailed guidance for interpreting the legislation, and the glossary can also help if any words seem strange or new. For now, this is the view from 30,000 feet above.

INDIVIDUALS WITH DISABILITIES EDUCATION ACT (IDEA)

The Individuals with Disabilities Education Act of 1973 was reauthorized in 2004 and is the key federal law that governs how states, territories, jurisdictions, and public agencies (referred to throughout this book simply as *states*) provide services for infants, toddlers, preschoolers, and school-aged children with disabilities. IDEA supports providing early intervention services to eligible infants, toddlers, and their families and providing a free appropriate public education through special-education services to eligible children ages three through twenty-one. The federal Office of Special Education Programs (OSEP) administers funding to states to enact the legislative intentions of IDEA. States then share a portion of the funding with local agencies. Programs serving infants and toddlers, birth through age two, fall under Part C. Programs serving children ages three through five fall under Part B, Section 619.

Where can I learn more about IDEA? A good place to start is the website developed and maintained by the U. S. Department of Education: https://sites.ed.gov/idea/

Part C—Programs for Infants and Toddlers with Disabilities

States receive Part C grants to provide comprehensive early intervention services for children birth through age two who have disabilities or developmental delays and their families. State legislators determine which agency—such as a health, human services, or education agency—will receive and administer Part C funds. The services must be provided in the child's "natural environment," which means the environment where the child spends the majority of time, such as the child's home, child-care program, Early Head Start program, or grandparent's house.

Where Do I Find Out about Part C Eligibility Guidelines in My State?

The Part C eligibility criteria for each state are listed on the ECTA Center's Part C eligibility page. To connect families with resources in your state, it is important that you know the specifics related to eligibility. A good place to find that information is through your state Parent Training and Information Center (PTI). There are nearly 100 PTIs and Community Parent Resource Centers (CPRCs) in the United States and its territories. You can find your parent center online. (See appendix C for a list of resources.)

The services a child receives are determined by the Individualized Family Service Plan (IFSP) team. The IFSP team includes the child's parent or guardian, early intervention service providers, and other team members. Infants and toddlers are eligible if they are experiencing a developmental delay and/or have a diagnosed medical condition. There is state discretion in defining these criteria, which may include infants or toddlers who are at risk for a delay or disability. It is important that you know how your state defines eligibility, and you can find that information on your state's Part C website.

Part B, Section 619—Preschool Grants Programs

Part B, Section 619 of IDEA authorizes grants to states to provide special education and related services to children with disabilities ages three through five. Just as in Part C, some eligibility and service components are left up to the states to determine, including the ability to serve two-year-old children with disabilities who will turn three during the upcoming school year. States must make a free and appropriate public education (FAPE) available to all eligible children with disabilities ages three through five. These early childhood special education and related services must be provided, to the maximum extent appropriate, in the "least restrictive environment" (LRE) based on the child's unique strengths and needs. This means that when a decision is made about where IDEA services are to be provided to the child, the first option should be the place where the child would typically be if she did not have a disability at all. For preschoolers, this would likely be in a child-care program, Head Start or public prekindergarten program, or other regular early childhood education setting.

Children are deemed eligible for early childhood special-education services through what is called a *multidisciplinary evaluation.* A team of qualified professionals and the parent or guardian of the child jointly make the determination of eligibility based on the child's educational needs. Special education and related services are then outlined in the child's Individualized Education Program (IEP).

Both Parts C and B, Section 619 require multidisciplinary teams to evaluate and develop service plans for eligible children using different eligibility criteria, evaluation procedures, types of services, service settings, and systems of payment. It is important to know about the distinctions between Parts C and B, Section 619, eligibility and services, including how they are defined and carried out in your state.

AMERICANS WITH DISABILITIES ACT (ADA)

The ADA is a civil-rights law that addresses equal opportunity and reasonable accommodations for people of all ages with disabilities. Enacted in 1990 and amended in 2008, the law prohibits discrimination against people with disabilities in schools, employment, transportation services, and other public services. Head Start, public prekindergarten, child care, and other early childhood programs must comply with ADA; however, religious organizations are exempt and do not have to comply. Under ADA, programs must implement policies, practices, and procedures so that everyone, including children with disabilities, can fully participate in the programs. ADA also includes requirements intended to ensure that new public facilities are accessible for everyone and that owners of older facilities remove barriers when this can be done without undue expense.

Where can I learn more about ADA? A good place to start is the website developed and maintained by the U. S. Department of Justice: https://www.ada.gov/index.html

In addition, programs cannot use eligibility criteria that explicitly exclude children with disabilities. For example, a child-care program cannot require that all children be toilet trained, because this may result in discrimination against children with disabilities. Programs cannot exclude children unless they pose a “direct threat” to the health or safety of others or unless their participation would require “fundamental alteration” of the program. Finally, programs cannot charge higher fees for children with disabilities or refuse a child admission because of concern about increases to insurance costs.

SECTION 504 OF THE REHABILITATION ACT OF 1973 (“SECTION 504”)

Section 504 is also civil rights legislation and applies to any entity that receives federal funds through a grant, loan, or contract. In early childhood programs, this might include funding for Head Start, child-care subsidy, public prekindergarten services, and/or the federal food and nutrition program. Generally speaking, Section 504 states that individuals with disabilities cannot be discriminated against or excluded from participation in any program or activity receiving federal funds. In addition, accommodations may be required to ensure that individuals are not excluded. The federal statute for Section 504 is brief and powerful:

> ***No otherwise qualified individual with a disability in the United States . . . shall, solely by reason of her or his disability, be excluded from the participation in, be denied the benefits of, or be subjected to discrimination under any program or activity receiving Federal financial assistance (Pub. L. 93–112, 1973).***

Where can I learn more about Section 504? A good place to start is the website developed and maintained by the Federal Department of Education: https://www2.ed.gov/about/offices/list/ocr/504faq.html

What does it mean to have a disability under Section 504? The criteria are much broader than the criteria for IDEA and ADA. There are three possible ways to be considered eligible under Section 504:

- An individual can have either a physical or mental impairment that substantially limits one or more major life activities;
- or has a record of such an impairment;
- or is being regarded as having such an impairment.

There is no religious exemption under Section 504 as there is within ADA. If an early childhood program is run by a religious entity and the program receives federal funds, the provisions of Section 504 still apply.

APPENDIX C: ONLINE RESOURCES TO SUPPORT FAMILIES OF CHILDREN WITH DISABILITIES

CHAPTER 1: I HAVE A CONCERN ABOUT MY CHILD'S DEVELOPMENT. NOW WHAT?

Ages and Stages Questionnaires, 3rd edition (ASQ-3): https://www.easterseals.com/mtffc/asq

Birth to 5: Watch Me Thrive! https://www2.ed.gov/about/inits/list/watch-me-thrive/index.html

Centers for Disease Control Developmental Milestone Resources and Tools: www.cdc.gov/Milestones

Early Childhood Technical Assistance Center: https://ectacenter.org

- DEC Recommended Practices, Guides for Families: http://ectacenter.org/decrp/type-pgfamily.asp
- ECTA Practice Guides for Families—Assessment: https://ectacenter.org/decrp/type-pgfamily.asp#pgfamily-assessment

Head Start:

- Head Start Early Childhood Learning and Knowledge Center: https://eclkc.ohs.acf.hhs.gov
- Head Start Child Screening and Assessment Topic Page: https://eclkc.ohs.acf.hhs.gov/child-screening-assessment

National Association for the Education of Young Children: https://www.naeyc.org

PACER Center (Parent Special Education Information): https://www.pacer.org/parent

Parent Training and Information Center: https://www.parentcenterhub.org/find-your-center

Start Early: https://www.startearly.org

Exploring Your Own Feelings

The Envelope: https://theenvelope.commons.gc.cuny.edu/thought-provocations/

Forget Me Not: Inclusion in the Classroom: https://www.forgetmenotdocumentary.com/

Including Samuel, 2007 documentary film about inclusion: https://includingsamuel.com/

National Father's Network: https://fathersnetwork.org

The Unplanned Journey: https://www.parentcenterhub.org/journey

"Welcome to Holland" by Emily Perl Kingsley: https://www.dsasc.ca/uploads/8/5/3/9/8539131/welcome_to_holland.pdf

You Are Not Alone: https://www.parentcenterhub.org/notalone/

CHAPTER 2: ADVOCATE—YOUR MOST IMPORTANT ROLE

Disability Laws and Federal Guidance

The Americans with Disabilities Act (ADA) and Child Care, Frequently Asked Questions: https://www.pacer.org/parent/php/php-c51a.pdf

Differences between IDEA Part C and IDEA Part B: http://www.infanthearing.org/earlyintervention/docs/aspect-idea-part-c-and-idea-part-b.pdf

Division for Early Childhood (DEC) of the Council for Exceptional Children and NAEYC Joint Position Statement on Inclusion: https://www.naeyc.org/sites/default/files/globally-shared/downloads/PDFs/resources/position-statements/ps_inclusion_dec_naeyc_ec.pdf

Policy Statement on Inclusion of Children with Disabilities in Early Childhood Programs: https://sites.ed.gov/idea/idea-files/policy-statement-inclusion-of-children-with-disabilities-in-early-childhood-programs/

U. S. Department of Justice, Civil Rights Division, Disability Rights Section. 2020. "A Guide to Disability Rights Laws." https://www.ada.gov/cguide.htm

Research Compilations on Inclusion

ECTA Compilation of Research and Studies on Inclusion: https://ectacenter.org/topics/inclusion/research.asp

Fact Sheet of Research on Preschool Inclusion: https://ectacenter.org/~pdfs/topics/inclusion/research/Research_Supporting_Preschool_Inclusion_R.pdf

Preschool Inclusion: Key Findings from Research and Implications for Policy: http://www.nccp.org/wp-content/uploads/2020/05/text_1154.pdf

OSEP-Funded National Technical Assistance Centers

Center for IDEA Early Childhood Data Systems (DASY Center): https://dasycenter.org/

The Early Childhood Personnel Center: https://ecpcta.org/

Early Childhood Technical Assistance (ECTA) Center: http://ectacenter.org

- ECTA Inclusion Resources: https://ectacenter.org/topics/inclusion/research.asp
- Indicators of High-Quality Inclusion: https://ectacenter.org/topics/inclusion/indicators.asp

IRIS Center: https://iris.peabody.vanderbilt.edu/

Office of Special Education Programs Technical Assistance Network: https://osepideasthatwork.org/sites/default/files/OSEPplacemat-508_updated%2004.01.20.pdf

Other Related National Centers

Beach Center on Disability: https://beachcenter.lsi.ku.edu/

Caring for Our Children: http://nrckids.org/CFOC

Division for Early Childhood (DEC) of the Council for Exceptional Children: http://www.dec-sped.org

DEC Recommended Practices: https://www.dec-sped.org/dec-recommended-practices

Head Start Center for Inclusion: http://headstartinclusion.org/

Head Start Early Childhood Learning and Knowledge Center (ECLKC): https://eclkc.ohs.acf.hhs.gov

National Resource Center for Health and Safety in Child Care and Early Education: https://nrckids.org/

Information about Specific Conditions

Fact Sheets About Specific Disabilities: https://www.parentcenterhub.org/specific-disabilities/

American Speech-Language-Hearing Association (ASHA): https://www.asha.org/

American Association on Intellectual and Developmental Disabilities: https://www.vmrc.net/national-resources/

Attention Deficit Hyperactivity Disorder (ADHD): https://www.psychiatry.org/patients-families/adhd/what-is-adhd and https://www.additudemag.com/

The Autism Society: https://www.autismsociety.org/

Children and Families Affected by Parental Substance Use Disorders (SUDs): https://ncsacw.samhsa.gov/topics/parental-substance-use-disorder.aspx

ECTA Compilation of Information, Specific Disability Populations: https://ectacenter.org/topics/earlyid/idspecpops.asp

Easter Seals: https://www.easterseals.com/

Fetal Alcohol Syndrome: https://www.cdc.gov/ncbddd/fasd/index.html

Fragile X Syndrome: https://medlineplus.gov/genetics/condition/fragile-x-syndrome/

Head Start Disability Guides: https://headstartinclusion.org/tip-sheets/disability-guides/

Learning Disabilities: https://www.nichd.nih.gov/health/topics/learningdisabilities

Little People of America (information about dwarfism): https://www.lpaonline.org/

Muscular Dystrophy Association: https://www.mda.org/

National Association of Councils on Developmental Disabilities: https://www.nacdd.org/

National Center on Birth Defects and Developmental Disabilities (NCBDDD): https://www.cdc.gov/ncbddd/

National Center on Deaf-Blindness: https://www.nationaldb.org/

National Down Syndrome Society: https://www.ndss.org/

National Institute on Deafness and Other Communication Disorders: https://www.nidcd.nih.gov/

Prevent Blindness: https://preventblindness.org/your-babys-developing-sight/

Spina Bifida Association: https://www.spinabifidaassociation.org/

United Cerebral Palsy: https://ucp.org/

Creating a Vision for Your Child

49 Phrases to Calm an Anxious Child: https://psychcentral.com/blog/stress-better/2016/03/49-phrases-to-calm-an-anxious-child#1

Affirmations: https://powerofmisfits.com/mind/affirmations-for-confidence-self-esteem/

Family Stories, Tips from Dads: https://www.pacer.org/ec/stories-advice/advice-to-parents.asp

NCPMI, My Teacher Wants to Know: https://challengingbehavior.cbcs.usf.edu/docs/ttyc/TTYC_MyTeacherWantstoKnow.pdf and https://challengingbehavior.org/docs/My-teacher-wants-to-know.pdf

PACER Center, Advocating for your child: https://www.pacer.org/ec/

CHAPTER 3: UNDERSTANDING EARLY INTERVENTION: SERVICES FOR INFANTS AND TODDLERS

ECTA Early Intervention: https://ectacenter.org/topics/eiservices/eiservices.asp

Interagency Coordinating Councils: https://ectacenter.org/topics/intercoord/intercoord.asp

ECTA information on Part C eligibility: https://ectacenter.org/topics/earlyid/partcelig.asp

IFSP Process: Planning and Implementing Family-Centered Services in Natural Environments: http://ectacenter.org/topics/ifsp/ifspprocess.asp

List of State Part C Coordinators: http://ectacenter.org/contact/ptccoord.asp

Parent Training and Information Center, Building the Legacy for Our Youngest Children with Disabilities: https://www.parentcenterhub.org/legacy-partc/

Parent Training and Information Center, Training Curriculum on Part B of IDEA 2004: https://www.parentcenterhub.org/legacy/

Part C of IDEA: https://ectacenter.org/partc/partc.asp

CHAPTER 4: UNDERSTANDING EARLY CHILDHOOD SPECIAL EDUCATION: SERVICES FOR PRESCHOOLERS

Eligibility and Service Delivery Policies: Differences between IDEA Part C and IDEA Part B: http://www.infanthearing.org/earlyintervention/docs/aspect-idea-part-c-and-idea-part-b.pdf

Individualized Education Program (IEP) Basics: https://eclkc.ohs.acf.hhs.gov/children-disabilities/article/individualized-education-program-iep-basics

List of State Section 619 Coordinators: http://ectacenter.org/contact/619coord.asp

Office of Head Start fact sheet, ideas for children who do not qualify for IDEA: https://eclkc.ohs.acf.hhs.gov/publication/services-children-who-do-not-qualify-idea-fact-sheet

A Parent's Guide to A Successful Kindergarten Transition: https://www.eparent.com/education/a-parents-guide

Team Decisions for Preschool Special Education Services: Guiding Questions: https://ectacenter.org/~pdfs/topics/inclusion/team-decisions-guiding-questions.pdf

Parent Rights and Dispute Resolution

Center for Appropriate Dispute Resolution in Special Education (CADRE): https://www.cadreworks.org/

ECTA Family Rights and Dispute Resolution: https://ectacenter.org/topics/procsafe/procsafe.asp

IDEA Dispute Resolution Parent Guides and Companion Videos: https://www.cadreworks.org/resources/cadre-materials/idea-dispute-resolution-parent-guides

Parental Rights under IDEA: https://www.parentcenterhub.org/parental-rights/?cid=6cd3ef53c5c965f0991afb8822d6db84

CHAPTER 5: WORKING AS A TEAM WITH YOUR CHILD'S TEACHERS AND OTHER PROFESSIONALS

CADRE Working Together Series: https://www.cadreworks.org/resources/cadre-materials/working-together-series

ECTA Practice Guides for Families, Teaming and Collaboration:
https://ectacenter.org/decrp/type-pgfamily.asp#pgfamily-teaming
https://ectacenter.org/decrp/type-pgfamily.asp#pgfamily-environment

Letter to a Teacher's Aide: https://loveinadifferentlanguage.com/blog/2016/2/7/to-the-teachers-aide-in-my-sons-special-eduaction-classroom-i-see-what-you-are-doing

Practice Improvement Tools: Teaming and Collaboration (ECTA): https://ectacenter.org/decrp/topic-teaming.asp

CHAPTER 6: INCLUSIVE SPACES FOR LEARNING AT HOME, SCHOOL, AND IN THE COMMUNITY

AbleNet: https://www.ablenetinc.com/

Cadan Assistive Technologies: http://tfeinc.com/

Creating Inclusive Environments and Learning Experiences for Infants and Toddlers: https://childcareta.acf.hhs.gov/infant-toddler-resource-guide/

ECTA:

- Assistive Technology Checklist from ECTA: https://ectacenter.org/~pdfs/decrp/ENV-5_Assistive_Tech_2018.pdf
- ECTA Assistive Technology Resources: https://ectacenter.org/topics/atech/atech.asp
- ECTA Practice Guides for Families, Learning Environments: https://ectacenter.org/decrp/type-pgfamily.asp#pgfamily-environment
- Practice Improvement Tools: Environment (ECTA): https://ectacenter.org/decrp/topic-environment.asp

Head Start Resources on Culture and Language: https://eclkc.ohs.acf.hhs.gov/culture-language

International Children's Digital Library: http://www.childrenslibrary.org/

The PACER Simon Technology Center: https://www.pacer.org/stc/

STEM Innovation for Inclusion in Early Education ("STEMIE") Center:

- Resources: https://stemie.fpg.unc.edu/resources
- STEMIE Guide to Adaptations: https://stemie.fpg.unc.edu/guide-adaptations

Transition visuals: https://challengingbehavior.cbcs.usf.edu/docs/Transition-visual_cards.pdf

CHAPTER 7: WORKING ON IFSP OR IEP GOALS AT HOME AND IN SCHOOL

How to Support Your Child with Embedded Learning Opportunities at Home

Activity Matrix: Organizing Learning throughout the Day: https://eclkc.ohs.acf.hhs.gov/video/activity-matrix-organizing-learning-throughout-day

Highly Individualized Teaching and Learning: https://eclkc.ohs.acf.hhs.gov/children-disabilities/article/highly-individualized-teaching-learning

Home Activity Matrix: https://ceecs.education.ufl.edu/wp-content/uploads/2021/06/Home-Activity-Matrix-Fillable.pdf

Positive Solutions for Families: Family Routine Guide: https://challengingbehavior.org/docs/Positive-Solutions_Family-Routine_Guide.pdf

How to Support Children with Embedded Learning Opportunities in School

Autism Focused Resources and Modules (AFIRM):

- AFIRM Resources and Modules: https://afirm.fpg.unc.edu/afirm-modules
- Using Visual Supports: https://afirm.fpg.unc.edu/visual-cues-introduction-practice

"Break It Down: Turning Goals into Everyday Teaching Opportunities": https://eclkc.ohs.acf.hhs.gov/video/break-it-down-turning-goals-everyday-teaching-opportunities

CONNECT Modules: http://community.fpg.unc.edu/connect-modules/learners

ECTA Center:

- Division for Early Childhood (DEC) Recommended Practices Performance Checklists: http://ectacenter.org/decrp/type-checklists.asp
- ECTA Center child outcomes infographic: https://ectacenter.org/~pdfs/eco/three-child-outcomes-breadth.pdf
- Practice Guides for Practitioners: http://ectacenter.org/decrp/type-pgpractitioner.asp
- Practice Improvement Tools—Instruction (ECTA): https://ectacenter.org/decrp/topic-instruction.asp
- Preschool During the Pandemic: Early Childhood Education in Extraordinary Times: https://ectacenter.org/topics/disaster/preschoolpandemic.asp

Effective Instruction: Embedding IEP Goals: https://eclkc.ohs.acf.hhs.gov/video/effective-instruction-embedding-iep-goals

Head Start:

- Embedded Learning for Infants and Toddlers: https://headstartinclusion.org/tip-sheets/infant-and-toddlers/
- Head Start Center on Inclusion: https://headstartinclusion.org/

Responsive Routines Planning Form: https://challengingbehavior.org/docs/Caregiver-Responsive-Routines-Planning_Form.pdf

Snack Talk Tip Sheet: https://haringcenter.org/wp-content/uploads/2020/12/Snack-Talk-Tip-Sheet.pdf

SpecialQuest Multimedia Training Library: https://eclkc.ohs.acf.hhs.gov/children-disabilities/specialquest-multimedia-training-library/specialquest-multimedia-training-library

CHAPTER 8: HELPING YOUR CHILD MAKE FRIENDS, DEAL WITH BIG EMOTIONS, AND GET ALONG WITH OTHERS

Teaching Social-Emotional Skills

Book list: https://www.thinkinclusive.us/post/10-childrens-books-with-disabled-characters

Center of Excellence for Infant and Early Childhood Mental Health Consultation: https://www.ecmhc.org/index.html

Children's Books with a Social-Emotional Theme: https://challengingbehavior.cbcs.usf.edu/docs/booknook/ChildrensBookList.pdf

DEC Position Statement on Challenging Behavior and Young Children: https://challengingbehavior.cbcs.usf.edu/docs/DEC_PositionStatement_ChallengingBehavior.pdf

ECTA Practice Guides for Families, Interactions: https://ectacenter.org/decrp/type-pgfamily.asp#pgfamily-interaction

Facilitating Individualized Interventions to Address Challenging Behavior: https://www.ecmhc.org/documents/CECMHC_FacilitatingToolkit.pdf

National Center for Pyramid Model Innovations (NCPMI): http://challengingbehavior.cbcs.usf.edu

National Child Traumatic Stress Network: https://www.nctsn.org/

Pyramid practices that can be used during virtual learning: https://challengingbehavior.cbcs.usf.edu/docs/Pyramid-Virtual-Learning-Checklist.pdf

Social stories: https://headstartinclusion.org/tools-and-supports/social-stories/

Visual Supports from the Head Start Center on Inclusion: https://headstartinclusion.org/tools-and-supports/classroom-visuals-and-supports/

Understanding and Regulating Emotions

Feeling Faces Cards: https://challengingbehavior.cbcs.usf.edu/docs/FeelingFaces_cards_EN-Blank.pdf

NCPMI Relaxation Thermometer: https://challengingbehavior.cbcs.usf.edu/docs/Relaxation-Thermometer.pdf

Tucker Turtle Takes Time to Tuck and Think at Home: https://challengingbehavior.cbcs.usf.edu/docs/TuckerTurtle_Story_Home.pdf

Turtle Technique: https://challengingbehavior.cbcs.usf.edu/docs/TurtleTechnique_steps.pdf

Making Friends

Peer-Mediated Skills: https://challengingbehavior.cbcs.usf.edu/docs/Peer-Mediated-Skills.pdf

Peer Support for Children with Special Needs: https://childcare.extension.org/peer-support-for-children-with-special-needs/

Teaching Friendship Skills (visual supports): https://challengingbehavior.cbcs.usf.edu/docs/Peer-Mediated-Skills.pdf

Managing Behaviors That Challenge Us

Challenging Behavior Tips: https://headstartinclusion.org/tip-sheets/challenging-behavior-tips/

Head Start Resources on Effectively Addressing Behaviors: https://eclkc.ohs.acf.hhs.gov/mental-health/article/effectively-addressing-behaviors

Home rules poster: https://challengingbehavior.org/docs/Rules_poster_home_sample.pdf

NCPMI Behavioral Intervention Process: https://challengingbehavior.cbcs.usf.edu/Pyramid/pbs/process.html

NCPMI Problem-Solving Solution Kits, home edition: https://challengingbehavior.cbcs.usf.edu/docs/Solution_kit_cards_home.pdf

CHAPTER 9: TAKING CARE OF YOURSELF AND YOUR FAMILY

10 Percent Happier: https://www.tenpercent.com/

Calm: https://www.calm.com

Child Care Aware of America State-by-State Resources: https://www.childcareaware.org/resources/map/

Early Childhood Workforce Index 2020: https://cscce.berkeley.edu/workforce-index-2020/

Getting Started with Mindfulness: A Toolkit for Early Childhood Organizations: https://www.zerotothree.org/resources/2896-getting-started-with-mindfulness-a-toolkit-for-early-childhood-organizations

Head Start Resources on Staff Well-Being: https://eclkc.ohs.acf.hhs.gov/mental-health/article/promoting-staff-well-being

I Deserve Self Care Worksheet: https://www.childwelfare.gov/pubPDFs/parental_resilience_conversation_guide_2021.pdf

Insight Timer: https://insighttimer.com/

National Wellness Institute Six Dimensions of Wellness: https://nationalwellness.org/resources/six-dimensions-of-wellness/

Taking Care of Ourselves: https://www.ecmhc.org/materials_families.html

REFERENCES AND RECOMMENDED READING

20 USC 1400. 2004. *Individuals with Disabilities Education Improvement Act of 2004.*

42 USC 9801 et seq. 2007. *Head Start Act*. https://eclkc.ohs.acf.hhs.gov/sites/default/files/pdf/HS_Act_2007.pdf

Adams, Ansel, and Mary Street Alinder. 1996. *Ansel Adams: An Autobiography*. Boston, MA: Little, Brown.

Adichie, Chimamanda. 2016. "The Danger of a Single Story." Facing History and Ourselves. https://www.facinghistory.org/resource-library/danger-single-story

American Psychiatric Association. 2021. "What Is ADHD?" American Psychiatric Association. https://www.psychiatry.org/patients-families/adhd/what-is-adhd

American Sociological Association. n.d. "Culture." American Sociological Association. https://www.asanet.org/topics/culture

American Speech-Language-Hearing Association. 2021. "IDEA Part C: Evaluation and Assessment Definitions." ASHA. https://www.asha.org/advocacy/federal/idea/idea-part-c-evaluation-and-assessment-definitions/#:~:text=Evaluation%20means%20%22the%20procedures%20used,%C2%A7303.321(b)

Annamma, Subini A., Amy L. Boelé, Brooke A. Moore, and Janette Klingner. 2013. "Challenging the Ideology of Normal in Schools." *International Journal of Inclusive Education* 17(12): 1278–1294.

Avramidis, Elias, Phil Bayliss, and Robert Burden. 2000. "A Survey into Mainstream Teachers' Attitudes Towards the Inclusion of Children with Special Educational Needs in the Ordinary School in One Local Education Authority." *Educational Psychology* 20(2): 191–211.

Avramidis, Elias, and Brahm Norwich. 2002. Teachers' Attitudes Towards Integration/Inclusion: A Review of the Literature." *European Journal of Special Needs Education* 17(2): 129–147.

Bagwell, Catherine L., and Michelle E. Schmidt. 2011. *Friendships in Childhood and Adolescence.* New York: Guilford.

Barreto Florencia B., et al. 2017. "Family Context and Cognitive Development in Early Childhood: A Longitudinal Study." *Intelligence* 65: 11–22.

Barth, Richard P., et al. 2007. *Developmental Status and Early Intervention Service Needs of Maltreated Children*. Washington, DC: U. S. Department of Health and Human Services, Office of the Assistant Secretary for Planning and Evaluation.

Barton, Erin E. n.d. "Dignity and Disability: Treating Children with Disabilities with Dignity and Respect." Barton Lab, Vanderbilt University. https://cdn.vanderbilt.edu/vu-web/lab-wpcontent/sites/96/2020/06/30142553/Dignity-Disability-Intro.pdf

Barton, Erin E., and Barbara J. Smith. 2014. "Fact Sheet of Research on Preschool Inclusion." Denver, CO: Pyramid Plus: The Colorado Center for Social Emotional Competence and Inclusion.

Barton, Erin E., and Barbara J. Smith. 2015a. "Advancing High Quality Preschool Inclusion: A Discussion and Recommendations for the Field." *Topics in Early Childhood Special Education* 35(2): 69–78.

Barton, Erin E., and Barbara J. Smith. 2015b. *The Preschool Inclusion Toolbox: How to Build and Lead a High-Quality Program*. Baltimore, MD: Paul H. Brookes Publishing.

Barton Lab. n.d. "What Is a Prompt?" Barton Lab, Vanderbilt University. https://cdn.vanderbilt.edu/vu-web/lab-wpcontent/sites/96/2020/02/12211548/Prompting-Procedures.pdf

Bernier, Olivier, dir. 2022. *Forget Me Not: Inclusion in the Classroom*. 1 hour, 43 minutes. https://www.forgetmenotdocumentary.com

Boyle, Coleen A., et al. 2011. "Trends in the Prevalence of Developmental Disabilities in U. S. Children, 1997-2008." *Pediatrics* 127(6): 1034–1042.

Broek, E., et al. 1994. *The Original Social Story Book*. Arlington, TX: Future Education. https://carolgraysocialstories.com

Bronfenbrenner, Urie. 1986. "Ecology of the Family as a Context for Human Development: Research Perspectives." *Developmental Psychology* 22(6): 723–742.

Burke, Jenene. 2012. "'Some Kids Climb Up; Some Kids Climb Down': Culturally Constructed Play-Worlds of Children with Impairments." *Disability and Society* 27(7): 965–981.

Campbell, Frances, et al. 2014. "Early Childhood Investments Substantially Boost Adult Health." *Science* 343(6178): 1478–1485.

Center for Applied Special Technology. 2008. Universal Design for Learning Guidelines: Version 1.0. Wakefield, MA: CAST. https://udlguidelines.cast.org/more/downloads

Center for Parent Information and Resources. 2017. "Parental Rights under IDEA." Center for Parent Information and Resources. https://www.parentcenterhub.org/parental-rights/

Center for Parent Information and Resources. 2019. "Five Options, 1-2-3." Center for Parent Information and Resources. https://www.parentcenterhub.org/disputes-overview/

Center for the Study of Social Policy. 2021. "Strengthening Families." Center for the Study of Social Policy. https://cssp.org/our-work/project/strengthening-families/

Center on Positive Behavioral Interventions and Supports. 2021. "Tiered Framework." Center on PBIS. https://www.pbis.org/pbis/tiered-framework

Center on the Developing Child. 2021a. "ACEs and Toxic Stress: Frequently Asked Questions." Center on the Developing Child, Harvard University. https://developingchild.harvard.edu/resources/aces-and-toxic-stress-frequently-asked-questions/

Center on the Developing Child. 2021b. "Toxic Stress." Center on the Developing Child, Harvard University. https://developingchild.harvard.edu/science/key-concepts/toxic-stress/

Centers for Disease Control and Prevention. n.d. *Watch Me! Celebrating Milestones and Sharing Concerns.* Centers for Disease Control and Prevention. https://www.cdc.gov/ncbddd/watchmetraining/docs/Watch-Me-Training-PDF-7.12.22-508.pdf

Centers for Disease Control and Prevention. 2019. *Preventing Adverse Childhood Experiences: Leveraging the Best Available Evidence.* Atlanta, GA: National Center for Injury Prevention and Control, Centers for Disease Control and Prevention.

Centers for Disease Control and Prevention. 2021. "Children and Youth with Special Healthcare Needs in Emergencies." CDC. https://www.cdc.gov/childrenindisasters/children-with-special-healthcare-needs.html

Chacon, Jenifer, and Kathy L. Reschke. 2021. "Safeguarding the Well-Being of Babies in the Midst of Unprecedented Turmoil." *Zero to Three* 41(3): 51.

Cleveland Clinic. 2021. "Child Development." Cleveland Clinic. https://my.clevelandclinic.org/health/articles/21559-child-development

Cole, Patricia, Kaitlin Trexberg, and Mollyrose Schaffner. 2023. *State of Babies Yearbook 2023.* Washington, DC: Zero to Three.

Committee on Practice and Ambulatory Medicine et al. 2019. "Recommendations for Preventive Pediatric Health Care." *Pediatrics* 143(3): e20183971.

CONNECT Modules and Division for Early Childhood. n.d. "Glossary." Connect: The Center to Mobilize Early Childhood Knowledge. https://connectmodules.dec-sped.org/glossary/

Council for Exceptional Children. 2021. "Specially Designed Instruction." Council for Exceptional Children. https://exceptionalchildren.org/topics/specially-designed-instruction

Crain, William. 2010. *Theories of Development: Concepts and Applications.* 6th edition. Upper Saddle River, NJ: Prentice Hall.

Csikszentmihalyi, Mihaly. 1990. *Flow: The Psychology of Optimal Experience.* New York: Harper and Row.

Davidson, Richard J., et al. 2003. "Alterations in Brain and Immune Function Produced by Mindfulness Meditation." *Psychosomatic Medicine* 65(4): 564–570.

Davis, Daphne M., and Jeffrey Hayes. 2012. "What Are the Benefits of Mindfulness?" *American Psychological Association* 43(7): 64.

Denham, Susanne A., et al. 2003. "Preschool Emotional Competence: Pathway to Social Competence?" *Child Development* 74(1): 238–256.

DeSalvo, Louise. 2000. *Writing as a Way of Healing: How Telling Our Stories Transforms Our Lives.* Boston, MA: Beacon.

Division for Early Childhood of the Council for Exceptional Children. 2014. "DEC Recommended Practices." https://divisionearlychildhood.egnyte.com/dl/7urLPWCt5U/?

Division for Early Childhood and the National Association for the Education of Young Children. 2009. "Early Childhood Inclusion: A Joint Position Statement of the Division for Early Childhood and the National Association for the Education of Young Children." Chapel Hill, NC: FPG Child Development Institute, the University of North Carolina at Chapel Hill.

Dunlap, Glen, et al. 2017. *Prevent, Teach, Reinforce for Families: A Model of Individualized Positive Behavior Support for Home and Community*. Baltimore, MD: Paul H. Brookes Publishing.

Dweck, Carol S., and Ellen L. Leggett. 1988. "A Social-Cognitive Approach to Motivation and Personality." *Psychological Review* 95(2): 256–273.

Early Childhood Technical Assistance Center. n.d. "Team Decisions for Preschool Special Education Services: Guiding Questions." https://ectacenter.org/~pdfs/topics/inclusion/team-decisions-guiding-questions.pdf

Early Childhood Technical Assistance Center. 2015. *A System Framework for Building High-Quality Early Intervention and Preschool Special Education Programs.* Chapel Hill, NC: Frank Porter Graham Child Development Institute, University of North Carolina at Chapel Hill.

Early Childhood Technical Assistance Center. 2017. "Embedded Instruction Practices." https://ectacenter.org/~pdfs/decrp/PG_Ins_EmbeddedInstr_prac_print_2017.pdf

Early Childhood Technical Assistance Center. 2020a. "Indicators of High-Quality Inclusion: Glossary." ECTA. https://ectacenter.org/topics/inclusion/indicators-glossary.asp

Early Childhood Technical Assistance Center. 2020b. "Practices." https://ectacenter.org/practices.asp#:~:text=Practices%20are%20what%20professionals%20do,outcomes%20for%20children%20and%20families

The Education Trust, National Center for Learning Disabilities, and Zero to Three. 2021. *Our Youngest Learners: Increasing Equity in Early Intervention.* https://edtrust.org/wp-content/uploads/2014/09/Increasing-Equity-in-Early-Intervention-May-2021.pdf

Feinberg, Emily, Michael Silverstein, Sara Donahue, and Robin Bliss. 2011. "The Impact of Race on Participation in Part C Early Intervention Services." *Journal of Developmental and Behavioral Pediatrics* 32(4): 284–291.

Feldman, Ruth, and Arthur I. Eidelman. 2009. "Biological and Environmental Initial Conditions Shape the Trajectories of Cognitive and Social-Emotional Development Across the First Years of Life." *Developmental Science* 12(1): 194–200.

Fong, Rowena, Ruth McRoy, and Alan Detlaff. 2014. "Disproportionality and Disparities." Encyclopedia of Social Work. http://oxfordre.com/socialwork/view/10.1093/acrefore/9780199975839.001.0001/acrefore-9780199975839-e-899

Fox, Lise, and Rochelle Lentini. 2006. "You Got It! Teaching Social and Emotional Skills." *Young Children* 61(6): 36–42.

Frank Porter Graham Child Development Institute (FPG) at the University of North Carolina at Chapel Hill (UNC). n.d. "Glossary." ASD Toddler Initiative. https://asdtoddler.fpg.unc.edu/glossary.html

Gauvreau, Ariane N. 2017. "Using 'Snack Talk' to Promote Social Communication in Inclusive Preschool Classrooms." *Young Exceptional Children* 20(4): 187–197.

Gehl, Maria, and Lucianne Hackbert. 2019. "Getting Started with Mindfulness: A Toolkit for Early Childhood Organizations." Zero to Three. https://www.zerotothree.org/resources/2896-getting-started-with-mindfulness-a-toolkit-for-early-childhood-organizations#chapter-1833

Geisthardt, Cheryl L., Mary Jane Brotherson, and Christine C. Cook. 2002. "Friendships of Children with Disabilities in the Home Environment." *Education and Training in Mental Retardation and Developmental Disabilities* 37(3): 235–252.

Gilliam, Walter S., and Golan Shahar. 2006. "Preschool and Child Care Expulsion and Suspension: Rates and Predictors in One State." *Infants and Young Children* 19(3): 228–245.

Gilliam, Walter S., et al. 2016. *Do Early Educators' Implicit Biases Regarding Sex and Race Relate to Behavior Expectations and Recommendations of Preschool Expulsions and Suspensions?* New Haven, CT: Child Study Center, Yale School of Medicine.

Glascoe, Frances P. 2000. "Early Detection of Developmental and Behavioral Problems." *Pediatrics in Review* 21(8): 272–280.

Grossman Paul, Ludger Niemann, Stefan Schmidt, and Harald Walach. 2004. "Mindfulness-Based Stress Reduction and Health Benefits: A Meta-Analysis." *Journal of Psychosomatic Research* 57(1): 35–43.

Guralnick, Michael J. 2001. "A Developmental Systems Model for Early Intervention." *Infants and Young Children* 14(2): 1–18.

Guralnick, Michael J., Brian Neville, Mary A. Hammond, and Robert T. Connor. 2007. "The Friendships of Young Children with Developmental Delays: A Longitudinal Analysis." *Journal of Applied Developmental Psychology* 28(1): 64–79.

Hampshire, Patricia K., and Patrick Mallory. 2021. "A Tiered Approach to Implementing Universal Symbols for Entering Inclusive Early Childhood Playgroups." *Teaching Exceptional Children* 53(6): 414–423. https://doi.org/10.1177/0040059920970989

Haring, Norris G., Thomas Lovitt, Marie Eaton, and Cheryl Hansen. 1978. *The Fourth R: Research in the Classroom.* Columbus, OH: Charles E. Merrill.

Harper, Lawrence V., and Karen S. McCluskey. 2002. "Caregiver and Peer Responses to Children with Language and Motor Disabilities in Inclusive Preschool Programs." *Early Childhood Research Quarterly* 17(2): 148–166.

Hartup, Willard W. 1992. "Having Friends, Making Friends, and Keeping Friends: Relationships as Educational Contexts." ERIC Digest. https://files.eric.ed.gov/fulltext/ED345854.pdf

Hauser-Cram, Penny, Marji E. Warfield, Jack P. Shonkoff, and Marty W. Krauss. 2001. "Children with Disabilities: A Longitudinal Study of Child Development and Parental Well-Being." *Monographs of the Society for Research in Child Development* 66(3): 1–131.

Hemmeter, Mary Louise, Patricia A. Snyder, Lise Fox, and James Algina. 2016. "Evaluating the Implementation of the *Pyramid Model for Promoting Social Emotional Competence* in Early Childhood Classrooms." *Topics in Early Childhood Special Education* 36(3): 133–146.

Hemmeter, Mary Louise, Michaelene Ostrosky, and Lise Fox. 2021. *Unpacking the Pyramid Model: A Practical Guide for Preschool Teachers*. Baltimore, MD: Paul H. Brookes Publishing.

Hettler, Bill. 1976. "Six Dimensions of Wellness." National Wellness Institute. https://nationalwellness.org/resources/six-dimensions-of-wellness/

Hirotsu, Camila, Sergio Tufik, and Monica L. Andersen. 2015. "Interactions Between Sleep, Stress, and Metabolism: From Physiological to Pathological Conditions." *Sleep Science* 8(3): 143–152.

IRIS Center. 2021. "Glossary." The IRIS Center, Peabody College, Vanderbilt University. https://iris.peabody.vanderbilt.edu/resources/glossary/

Kabat-Zinn, Jon. 2003. "Mindfulness-Based Interventions in Context: Past, Present, and Future." *Clinical Psychology: Science and Practice* 10(2): 144–156.

Killingsworth, Matthew, and Daniel Gilbert. 2010. "A Wandering Mind Is an Unhappy Mind." *Science* 330(6006): 932.

Kingston, Dawn, Suzanne Tough, and Heather Whitfield. 2012. "Prenatal and Postpartum Maternal Psychological Distress and Infant Development: A Systematic Review." *Child Psychiatry Human Development* 43(5): 683–714.

Kozlowski, Jani. 2022. *Every Child Can Fly: An Early Childhood Educator's Guide to Inclusion*. Lewisville, NC: Gryphon House.

Küpper, Lisa, and Theresa Rebhorn. 2007. "Module 10: Initial Evaluation and Reevaluation." *Building the Legacy: Training Curriculum on IDEA*. https://www.parentcenterhub.org/wp-content/uploads/repo_items/legacy/10-trainerguide.pdf

Leerkes, Esther, et al. 2008. "Emotion and Cognition Processes in Preschool Children." *Merrill-Palmer Quarterly* 54(1): 102–124.

Lipkin, Paul H., et al. 2020. "Promoting Optimal Development: Identifying Infants and Young Children With Developmental Disorders Through Developmental Surveillance and Screening." *Pediatrics* 145(1): e20193449.

Lloyd, Lyle L., Donald R. Fuller, and Helen H. Arvidson. 1997. *Augmentative and Alternative Communication: A Handbook of Principles and Practices*. Boston: Allyn and Bacon.

Maushart, Susan. 2000. *The Mask of Motherhood: How Becoming a Mother Changes Our Lives and Why We Never Talk About It*. New York: Penguin.

McWilliam, R. A. 2010. *Routines-Based Early Intervention: Supporting Young Children With Special Needs And Their Families*. Baltimore, MD: Paul H. Brookes Publishing.

Meek, Shantel, et al. 2020. *Start with Equity: From the Early Years to the Early Grades*. Tempe, AZ: Children's Equity Project, Sanford School of Social and Family Dynamics, Arizona State University, and Washington, DC: Bipartisan Policy Center.

Merriam-Webster.com. 2021. "Observation." Merriam-Webster Dictionary. https://www.merriam-webster.com/dictionary/observation

Merriam-Webster.com. 2023. "Hysteria." Merriam-Webster Dictionary. https://www.merriam-webster.com/dictionary/hysteria

Morin, Amanda. n.d. "Heavy Work and Sensory Processing Issues: What You Need to Know." Understood. https://www.understood.org/en/articles/heavy-work-activities

National Archives. n.d. "Breton Fisherman's Prayer Plaque." Artifact MO 63.4861. John F. Kennedy Presidential Library and Museum. https://jfk.archives.gov/objects/14098/breton-fishermans-prayer-plaque

National Association for the Education of Young Children. n.d. "Definitions of Key Terms." NAEYC. https://www.naeyc.org/resources/position-statements/equity/definitions

National Association for the Education of Young Children. 2003. *Early Childhood Curriculum, Assessment, and Program Evaluation*. Position statement. Washington, DC: NAEYC. https://www.naeyc.org/sites/default/files/globally-shared/downloads/PDFs/resources/position-statements/CAPEexpand.pdf

National Association for the Education of Young Children. 2019. "Advancing Equity in Early Childhood Education." Position statement. Washington, DC: NAEYC. https://www.naeyc.org/sites/default/files/globally-shared/downloads/PDFs/resources/position-statements/advancingequitypositionstatement.pdf

National Association for the Education of Young Children. 2020a. "Developmentally Appropriate Practice." Position statement. Washington, DC: NAEYC. https://www.naeyc.org/resources/position-statements/dap

National Association for the Education of Young Children. 2020b. "Professional Standards and Competencies for Early Childhood Educators." Position statement. Washington, DC: NAEYC. https://naeyc.org/resources/positionstatements/professional-standards-competencies

National Association for the Education of Young Children. 2022. *Developmentally Appropriate Practice in Early Childhood Programs Serving Children from Birth Through Age 8*. 4th ed. Washington, DC: NAEYC.

National Center for Pyramid Model Innovations. n.d. "Glossary of Terms." NCPMI. https://challengingbehavior.cbcs.usf.edu/Pyramid/overview/glossary.html

National Professional Development Center on ASD. 2019. "Components of the Autism Focused Intervention Resources and Modules (AFIRM)." Chapel Hill, NC: The University of North Carolina at Chapel Hill, Frank Porter Graham Child Development Institute, National Professional Development Center on Autism Spectrum Disorder.

National Scientific Council on the Developing Child. 2020. *Connecting the Brain to the Rest of the Body: Early Childhood Development and Lifelong Health Are Deeply Intertwined.* Working Paper No. 15. https://harvardcenter.wpenginepowered.com/wp-content/uploads/2020/06/wp15_health_FINALv2.pdf

Nelson, Catherine, et al. 2007. "Keys to Play: A Strategy to Increase the Social Interactions of Young Children with Autism and Their Typically Developing Peers." *Education and Training in Developmental Disabilities* 42(2): 165–181.

Nelson, Helen, Garth Kendall, and Linda Shields. 2013. "Children's Social/Emotional Characteristics at Entry to School Nurses." *The Journal of Child Health Care* 17(3): 317–331.

Neurodiverging.com. 2023. "What Is Internalized Ableism? Neurodivergent People Need to Know." Neurodiverging. https://www.neurodiverging.com/what-is-internalized-ableism-neurodivergent-people-need-to-know/

North Carolina Department of Health and Human Services, Division of Public Health, Women's and Children's Health Section, Early Intervention Branch. 2020. North Carolina Infant-Toddler Program. https://beearly.nc.gov

Office of Head Start, Administration for Children and Families, Department of Health and Human Services. 2016. "Head Start Performance Standards." *Federal Register* 81(172): 61294–61453. https://www.federalregister.gov/documents/2016/09/06/2016-19748/head-start-performance-standards

Office of Special Education Programs (OSEP). n.d.a. *At a Glance: An Introduction to Part C of the Individuals with Disabilities Education Act (IDEA).* https://collab.osepideasthatwork.org/system/files/at_a_glance_an_introduction_to_part_c_1.pdf

Office of Special Education Programs (OSEP). n.d.b. "Let's Get Started: Part B Section 619—At a Glance." OSEP Collaboration Spaces. https://collab.osepideasthatwork.org/welcome-world-part-b-section-619/lets-get-started

Peer, Justin, and Stephen Hillman. 2014. "Stress and Resilience for Parents of Children with Intellectual and Developmental Disabilities: A Review of Key Factors and Recommendations for Practitioners." *Journal of Policy and Practice in Intellectual Disabilities* 11(2): 92–98.

Prellwitz, Maria, and Lisa Skär. 2007. "Usability of Playgrounds for Children with Different Abilities." *Occupational Therapy International* 14(3): 144–155.

Pub. L. 93-112. 1973. *Rehabilitation Act of 1973*, §504.

Prenatal-to-3 Policy Impact Center. 2020. *Prenatal-to-3 State Policy Roadmap 2020: Building a Strong and Equitable Prenatal-to-3 System of Care*. Child and Family Research Partnership. Lyndon B. Johnson School of Public Affairs, University of Texas at Austin. https://pn3policy.org/wp-content/uploads/2020/09/Prenatal-to-3-State-Policy-Roadmap-2020.pdf

Rao, Pratiksha T. 2021. "A Paradigm Shift in the Delivery of Physical Therapy Services for Children with Disabilities in the Time of the COVID-19 Pandemic." *Physical Therapy* 101(1): pzaa192.

Rausch, Alissa, Ellie Bold, and Phillip Strain. 2021. "The More the Merrier: Using Collaborative Transdisciplinary Services to Maximize Inclusion and Child Outcomes." *Young Exceptional Children* 24(2): 59–69.

Rausch, Alissa, Jaclyn Joseph, and Elizabeth Steed. 2019. "Dis/ability Critical Race Studies (DisCrit) for Inclusion in Early Childhood Education: Ethical Considerations of Implicit and Explicit Bias." *Zero to Three* 40(1): 43–51.

Ray, Robin A., and Annette F. Street. 2005. "Ecomapping: An Innovative Research Tool for Nurses." *Journal of Advanced Nursing* 50(5): 545–552.

Rebhorn, Theresa. n.d. "Developing Your Child's IEP." Center for Parent Information and Resources. https://www.parentcenterhub.org/pa12/

Response to Intervention Action Network. n.d. "What Is RTI?" RTI Action Network. http://www.rtinetwork.org/learn/what/whatisrti

Ripat, Jacquie, and Pam Becker. 2012. "Playground Usability: What Do Playground Users Say?" *Occupational Therapy International* 19(3): 144–153.

Rubin, Kenneth H., William Bukowski, and Jeffrey Parker. 1998. "Peer Interactions, Relationships, and Groups." In *Handbook of Child Psychology: Social, Emotional, and Personality Development*. Hoboken, NJ: John Wiley and Sons.

Sam, Ann M., et al. 2019. "Visual Cues: Introduction and Practice." Autism Focused Intervention Resources and Modules. FPG Child Development Institute, University of North Carolina at Chapel Hill. https://afirm.fpg.unc.edu/visual-cues-introduction-practice

Sandall, Susan, and Ilene Schwartz. 2008. *Building Blocks for Teaching Preschoolers with Special Needs.* 2nd edition. Baltimore, MD: Paul H. Brookes.

Sandall, Susan, et al. 2005. *DEC Recommended Practices: A Comprehensive Guide.* Longmont, CO: Sopris West Educational Services.

Sandall, Susan, et al. 2019. *Building Blocks for Teaching Preschoolers with Special Needs*. 3rd edition. Baltimore, MD: Paul H. Brookes Publishing.

Sheldon, M'Lisa L., and Dathan D. Rush. 2013. *The Early Intervention Teaming Handbook: The Primary Service Provider Approach*. Baltimore, MD: Paul H. Brookes Publishing.

Shonkoff, Jack P., and Deborah A. Phillips, eds. 2000. *From Neurons to Neighborhoods: The Science of Early Childhood Development.* National Research Council and Institute of Medicine. Washington DC: National Academies Press.

Siller, Michael, et al. 2021. "Inclusive Early Childhood Education for Children With and Without Autism: Progress, Barriers, and Future Directions." *Frontiers in Psychiatry* 12.

Smith, Leah. n.d. "#Ableism." Center for Disability Rights. http://cdrnys.org/blog/uncategorized/ableism/

Snow, Kathie. 2016. "People First Language." Disability is Natural. https://nebula.wsimg.com/1c1af57f9319dbf909ec52462367fa88?AccessKeyId=9D6F6082FE5EE52C3DC6&disposition=0&alloworigin=1

Spiker, Donna, Glenna C. Boyce, Lisa K. Boyce. 2002. “Parent-Child Interactions when Young Children Have Disabilities.” *International Review of Research in Mental Retardation* 25: 35–70. 10.1016/S0074-7750(02)80005-2

Staats, Cheryl, Kelly Capatosto, Robin A. Wright, and Danya Contractor. 2015. *State of the Science: Implicit Bias Review 2015*. Columbus, OH: Kirwan Institute for the Study of Race and Ethnicity, The Ohio State University.

Stanford University. n.d. “Race and Ethnicity.” Gendered Innovations in Science, Health and Medicine, Engineering, and Environment, Stanford University. https://genderedinnovations.stanford.edu/terms/race.html

Stanton-Chapman, Tina L., and Martha E. Snell. 2011. “Promoting Turn-Taking Skills in Preschool Children with Disabilities: The Effects of a Peer-Based Social Communication Intervention.” *Early Childhood Research Quarterly* 26(3): 303–319.

Steed, Elizabeth A., Rachel Stein, and Renee Charlifue-Smith. 2022. “Initial Evaluation Practices to Identify Young Children with Delays and Disabilities During the COVID-19 Pandemic.” *Journal of Early Intervention* 45(331):105381512211279.

Stegelin, Dolores A. 2018. *Preschool Suspension and Expulsion: Defining the Issues*. Greenville, SC: Institute for Child Success.

Strain, Phillip S., and Edward H. Bovey II. 2008. “LEAP Preschool.” In *Preschool Education Programs for Children with Autism*. Austin, TX: Pro-Ed.

Substance Abuse and Mental Health Services Administration (SAMHSA). 2014. *SAMHSA’s Concept of Trauma and Guidance for a Trauma-Informed Approach*. HHS Publication No. (SMA) 14-4884. Rockville, MD: Substance Abuse and Mental Health Services Administration. https://ncsacw.samhsa.gov/userfiles/files/SAMHSA_Trauma.pdf

Suprayogi, Muhamad N., and Martin Valcke. 2016. “Differentiated Instruction in Primary Schools: Implementation and Challenges in Indonesia.” *International Scientific Research Journal* 72(6): 2–18.

University of Massachusetts Lowell. 2019. “Diversity Peer Educators: Info and Glossary, Fall 2019.” Lowell, MA: University of Massachusetts. https://www.uml.edu/student-services/Multicultural/Resources/Glossary.aspx

University of Michigan Health. 2021. “Sensory Processing Disorder.” University of Michigan Health. https://www.uofmhealth.org/health-library/te7831

U. S. Department of Education. 2022. *44th Annual Report to Congress on the Implementation of the Individuals with Disabilities Education Act, 2022*. Washington, DC: Office of Special Education and Rehabilitative Services, U. S. Department of Education. https://sites.ed.gov/idea/2022-individuals-with-disabilities-education-act-annual-report-to-congress/

U. S. Department of Education, Office for Civil Rights. 2014. *Civil Rights Data Collection, Data Snapshot: Early Childhood Education*. Issue brief no. 2. https://www2.ed.gov/about/offices/list/ocr/docs/crdc-early-learning-snapshot.pdf

U. S. Department of Health and Human Services. 2014. *Birth to 5: Watch Me Thrive! A Compendium of Screening Measures for Young Children*. Washington, DC: U. S. Department of Health and Human Services. https://www.acf.hhs.gov/sites/default/files/documents/ecd/screening_compendium_march2014.pdf

U. S. Government Accountability Office. 2023. "Special Education: Additional Data Could Help Early Intervention Programs Reach More Eligible Infants and Toddlers." GAO. https://www.gao.gov/products/gao-24-106019

Vygotsky, Lev S. 1978. *Mind in Society: The Development of Higher Psychological Processes*. Cambridge, MA: Harvard University Press.

Waxman, Hersh C., Beverly Alford, and Danielle Brown. 2013. "Individualized Instruction." In *International Guide to Student Achievement*. New York: Routledge.

Webster-Stratton, Carolyn, and Mary Hammond. 1997. "Treating Children with Early-Onset Conduct Problems: A Comparison of Child and Parent Training Interventions." *Journal of Consulting and Clinical Psychology* 65(1): 93–109.

Weglarz-Ward, Jenna M., and Rosa M. Santos. 2018. "Parent and Professional Perceptions of Inclusion in Childcare: A Literature Review." *Infants and Young Children* 31(2): 128–143.

Weglarz-Ward, Jenna M., Rosa M. Santos, and Jennifer Timmer. 2019. "Factors that Support and Hinder Including Infants with Disabilities in Child Care." *Early Childhood Education Journal* 47: 163–173.

Whittingham, Koa. 2014. "Parents of Children with Disabilities, Mindfulness and Acceptance: A Review and a Call for Research." *Mindfulness* 5: 704–709.

Wijeyesinghe, Charmaine L., Pat Griffin, and Barbara Love. 1997. "Racism Curriculum Design." In *Teaching for Diversity and Social Justice: A Sourcebook*. New York: Routledge.

Wolery, Mark, Melinda J. Ault, and Patricia M. Doyle. 1992. *Teaching Students with Moderate to Severe Disabilities: Use of Response Prompting Strategies*. New York: Longman.

Zablotsky, Benjamin, et al. 2019. "Prevalence and Trends of Developmental Disabilities among Children in the US: 2009–2017." *Pediatrics* 144(4): e20190811.

Zeanah, Paula D., Brian Stafford, Geoffrey Nagle, and Thomas Rice. 2005. "Addressing Social-Emotional Development and Infant Mental Health in Early Childhood Systems." Building State Early Childhood Comprehensive Systems Series, No. 12. Los Angeles, CA: National Center for Infant and Early Childhood Health Policy.

Zero to Three. 2016. "Infant–Early Childhood Mental Health." Zero to Three. https://www.zerotothree.org/resources/110-infant-early-childhood-mental-health

Zero to Three. 2023. *State of Babies Yearbook 2023*. Washington, DC: Zero to Three.

Zucker, Meg. 2023. *Born Extraordinary: Empowering Children with Differences and Disabilities*. New York: TarcherPerigee.

INDEX

C

D